D0872275

LINKING DISORDERS TO DELINQUENCY

Linking Disorders to Delinquency

To Delinquency

Treating High-Risk Youth
in the Juvenile Justice System

Christopher A. Mallett

FIRST**FORUM**PRESS

A DIVISION OF LYNNE RIENNER PUBLISHERS, INC. • BOULDER & LONDON

Published in the United States of America in 2013 by
FirstForumPress
A division of Lynne Rienner Publishers, Inc.
1800 30th Street, Boulder, Colorado 80301
www.firstforumpress.com

and in the United Kingdom by
FirstForumPress
A division of Lynne Rienner Publishers, Inc.
3 Henrietta Street, Covent Garden, London WC2E 8LU

Library of Congress Cataloging-in-Publication Data
Mallett, Christopher A.
Linking disorders to delinquency: treating high-risk youth in the
  juvenile justice system / Christopher A. Mallett.
Includes bibliographical references and index.
ISBN 978-1-935049-58-6 (hbk.: alk. paper)
1. Juvenile delinquents—United States. 2. Youth—United States. I. Title.
HV9104.M24 2012
364.36—dc23   2012038649

British Cataloguing in Publication Data
A Cataloguing in Publication record for this book
is available from the British Library.

This book was produced from digital files prepared by the author
using the FirstForumComposer.

Printed and bound in the United States of America

∞   The paper used in this publication meets the requirements
     of the American National Standard for Permanence of
     Paper for Printed Library Materials Z39.48-1992.

5 4 3 2 1

*For my Dad, a lifelong inspiration
to educators, writers, and his sons*

Contents

Tables and Figures

Tables

Figures

Acknowledgments

I would like to acknowledge two former graduate assistants for their contributions: Adrienne Lisan for her editorial gifts and command of the written word, and Marielee Santiago for her database searches and study retrievals. In addition, P. Sanchez provided support throughout this writing process.

1

Children and Youth at Risk

The sheer number of youth who become formally involved with the juvenile courts—over one million each year across the United States—is a sober reminder of the significant social problems posed by juvenile delinquency. Equally concerning, this involvement with the juvenile courts all too frequently forecasts a preciptious pathway to even further difficulties.

Preventing delinquency and ongoing offending behaviors is important so that youth can avoid the harmful effects of detention and incarceration, and the potential involvement with the adult criminal justice system. It is likely that early preventative and interventive efforts with these children and youth will effectively divert many harmful outcomes, alternatively allowing successful young adulthood development. This is possible because the risk factors for delinquency are well known and children and youth with these factors can be identified; once identified, there are many effective diversion pathways. While most children and youth at risk for delinquency never become involved with the juvenile courts because of various protections from these risks and individual resiliency to their effects, the concern here is for those who are not so fortunate.

This book focuses on children and youth who have certain delinquency risk factors, including a number of disabilities and trauma experiences that increase their chances for involvement with the juvenile courts. The issues of concern include mental health disorders, substance use and abuse, certain special education disabilities (primarily learning disabilities and emotional disturbances), and maltreatment victimizations. Such early problems do not inevitably portend delinquency, and the majority of similarly affected youth do not break the law or become involved with the juvenile courts. Nonetheless, youth involved with the juvenile courts have much higher incidences of these disabilities and trauma experiences when compared with youth not involved in the juvenile court system. In other words, strong correlations exist between these incidences and delinquency. A link that becomes stronger the further a youth penetrates the juvenile justice system. It bears reinforcing that this link is strongest for serious, chronic, and violent youthful offenders. A group that is also most likely to be held in detention centers and juvenile incarceration facilities, and to be involved with the adult criminal justice system. Within these facilities a majority of youthful offenders have multiple disabilities and trauma experiences.

Child and youth disabilities and trauma experiences are often interrelated and comorbid, which complicates prevention and/or recovery efforts and interventions for youth-caring system personnel, policy makers, and other stakeholders. Thus, complex and intransigent vulnerabilities, combined with comorbid difficulties and risks, comprise the backgrounds of many children and youth who slip toward some low level offending and, disconcertingly, serious juvenile offending.

This book investigates how these disability and trauma risks impact children and youth, how these risks often comingle throughout childhood and adolescent developmental stages, and how ultimately the comorbidity of these difficulties has a strong impact on delinquent behaviors. Vital to solving the multi-faceted social problem of serious youthful offending is early intervention with risk identification and preventative measures for youthful victims of maltreatment and for youngsters suffering from mental health disorders and school difficulties (often learning disabilities), along with coordination of such efforts across the at-risk child and youth-caring systems.

Some of the key, and, at times, overlooked barriers to decreasing serious youthful offending are: failing to identify these risks during childhood or early adolescence, failing to intervene in timely or appropriate ways, and causing discord and disruption because of separate child and youth service delivery systems. This book ultimately advocates for the coordination of preventative and treatment efforts across child welfare, mental health, substance abuse, school, and juvenile court systems. A recommendation that has been voiced previously by various national stakeholder groups, but, for a variety of reasons, has rarely been actualized.

The case for these recommendations is argued through seven sequential chapters. This first chapter provides an overview of the child and youth risk factors for delinquency and explains why some children are at greater risk than others. This is followed by a review of the disproportionate number of youth with these disabilities and trauma experiences who are formally involved with the juvenile courts, making the subsequent link to detention and incarceration. In Chapter Two the epidemiology of these child and youth disorders and trauma experiences is reviewed, as an explanation of how each of these problems (maltreatment, mental health disorders, substance abuse, and learning disabilities) is linked to juvenile delinquency. In Chapter Three the onset and occurrence of each disability type is reviewed for primary school-aged children; preventative and treatment options are also thoroughly discussed. Similarly, in Chapter Four the onset and occurrence of each disability type is reviewed, though for secondary school-aged youth, including a similarly formatted discussion of treatment and programming options. This is followed by a highlight of what the juvenile justice system and other stakeholders may find as solutions to working more productively with low-level juvenile offenders with these disabilities and trauma experiences (Chapter Five) and serious youthful offenders (Chapter Six). Chapter Seven completes this review by presenting the challenges inherent in moving from a punitive juvenile justice system to one focused on treatment, by discussing the barriers in coordinating between child and youth disability systems, and by highlighting a number of successful system efforts. However, significant change is necessary to turn around the current juvenile justice system, with its deleterious outcomes for some of society's most vulnerable children and youth, to one that provides opportunities for young adulthood success.

Delinquency and Disability Risk Factors

Children and youth typically experience increased risk for involvement with the juvenile courts as a result of a combination of risk factors, rather than any single experience, leading to offending behaviors and delinquency. These risks often include poverty, family dysfunction, violence, trauma, academic and learning problems, mental health difficulties, and unstable and disorganized neighborhoods, among others. Yet, for a variety of reasons, many children and youth are resilient to the effects of these risk factors. Though many individual, family, and community issues are quite common and affect delinquency, the focus here is on four distinct, though often interrelated problems: (1) maltreatment victimization, (2) mental health disorders, (3) substance use and abuse, and (4) special education disabilities, primarily learning disabilities. Not only are these problems disproportionately apparent in juvenile court populations, but also once youth who are afflicted with such issues become involved with the juvenile courts, the likelihood and risk are high for detention, incarceration, and involvement with the adult criminal justice system, at great personal, fiscal, and social cost for the youth, juvenile courts, and communities.

Risk factors are internal or external conditions that make the disability or difficulty more likely an outcome for children and youth when compared to those who do not experience these conditions. The outcomes of interest here include maltreatment victimization, emotional problems (including mental health disorders), substance abuse, learning disabilities, and delinquency. Though separate and distinct at-risk child and youth service delivery systems are designed to address dif ferent risks and problem areas, children and youth who become involved with any one of the systems often share many common risk factors.

Many child and youth disabilities, and related difficulties such as academic problems and mental health disorders, come to the attention of systems designed to identify the problem, intervene, and provide treatment. These at-risk child and youth service delivery systems are primarily focused on four discrete areas: (1) special education, (2) mental health and substance abuse, (3) child welfare, and (4) juvenile justice. The special education system identifies and addresses physical, learning, and developmental disabilities through local public and private school districts. The mental health and substance abuse system includes both public and private agency providers offering treatment services for children, youth, and their families. The public child welfare system is responsible for protecting children and youth from abuse and neglect through investigations and child and family supervision. The juvenile justice system aims to ensure community safety, as well as youth rehabilitation and accountability for those who commit status offenses (for example, truancy, breaking curfews, alcohol possession) and crimes. However, the juvenile justice system also often becomes the system of last resort for many youth affected by the problems on which this tract is focused.

A significant number of risk and predictive models for these child and youth disability and maltreatment outcomes have been developed, including separation into demographic/historical factors (Heilbrun, 1997), criminology and clinical frameworks (Monahan et al., 2001), a psychosocial paradigm (Kashani, Jones, Bumby, and Thomas, 1999), and an ecological model (United States Department of Health and Human Services, 2001). The ecological model is of most use here because of its focus on the etiology and interrelations of the risk factors. This model typology separates these risks as they relate to the individual, family, and community. An organization schema utilized here (DeMatteo and Marczyk, 2005; Hawkins et al., 2000).

Many of these child and youth difficulties are intertwined yet with other problems. In other words, researchers are still working to determine which children and youth are more at risk for which difficulty or disability, and from there are trying to understand how these disabilities affect or cause deleterious societal outcomes, including offending behaviors and delinquency. What follows is a review of what is known to date.

Individual Risk Factors

Factors that increase the likelihood that an individual child or youth will develop a special education disability, in particular learning disabilities, include living in poverty, family dysfunction, being adopted, male gender, and low household educational attainment (Altarac & Saroha, 2007). Special education disabilities, in turn, are a risk factor for delinquent behaviors and juvenile detention (Mallett, 2008; Mears and Aron, 2003. Many mental health problems, including a history of early aggression (ages six to thirteen), hyperactivity, and substance abuse or dependence, are also risk factors for youthful offending behaviors (Chassin, 2008; Grisso, 2008; Hawkins et al., 2000; Loeber and Hay, 1996).

Maltreatment victimization (neglect, physical abuse, and sexual abuse) has a wide range of harmful outcomes and increases risk for further difficulties. Harmful outcomes may include poor cognitive development (Guterman, 2001; Wiggins, Fenichel, and Mann, 2007), mental health problems (Mallett, 2012), and drug use or abuse (Kelley, Thornberry, and Smith, 1997; Wiebush, Freitag, and Baird, 2001). In particular, maltreatment has a profound educational impact on many children and youth, including lower academic performance and grades, falling behind in grade levels, lower standardized testing and proficiency scores, and significantly higher risk for learning disabilities and emotional disturbances (Courtney, Roderick, Smithgall, Gladden, and Nagaoka, 2004; Courtney, Terao, and Bost, 2004; Smithgall et al., 2004). Of particular concern are maltreated children who are placed into foster care. These youngsters are much more likely to be identified with special education disabilities and much less likely than non-disabled peers to complete high school (Children's Law Center, 2003; Smithgall, et al., 2004).

Many of these maltreatment outcomes are also correlated with youthful offending behavior and delinquency. Children and youth who have been maltreated are more likely to engage in offending and delinquent behaviors compared to those without maltreatment histories

(Maxfield, Weiler, and Widom, 2000). The stronger maltreatment links to delinquency are for youth who have been victims of physical abuse and neglect, though researchers are still trying to determine the etiology and differential impact these types of specific maltreatment typologies have on delinquent activities and offending behaviors (Mallett, Stoddard-Dare, and Seck, 2009; Yun, Ball, and Lim, 2011). Repeat maltreatment victimization predicts the earlier initiation and often greater severity of delinquent acts (Stewart, Livingston, and Dennison, 2008). In fact, when other risks are accounted for this link appears to be strongest in predicting serious or chronic youthful offending (Ireland, Smith, and Thornberry, 2002; Lemmon, 2006; Smith, Ireland, and Thornberry, 2005).

Family Risk Factors

One of the family risk factors present across disability and maltreatment outcomes is living in poverty and experiencing the multitude of challenges and difficulties this upbringing imposes. Children who grow up in low-income families are more likely to be retained or held back a grade level in school (Bradley and Corwyn, 2002; Mears and Aron, 2003), to not graduate from high school (Brooks-Gunn and Duncan, 1997; Wald and Martinez, 2003), to have both internalizing (i.e., depression and anxiety) and externalizing (i.e., conduct disorder) behavior problems (Koball, Dion, Gorhro, Bardo, Dworsky, Lansing, et al., 2011; Moore and Redd, 2002), to develop learning disabilities (Mallett, 2011b), and to engage in delinquent activities (Hawkins et al., 2000; Loeber and Farrington, 1998).

Unstable upbringings within families have a significant impact on children. Family dysfunction, when measured in terms of witnessing violent treatment of family members, is a risk for later youth delinquency (Dembo et al., 2000; Felitti et al., 2008). In addition, criminal activity, particularly by parents (Dong et al., 2004), early parental loss (Farrington, 1997), parent/child separation (DeMatteo and Marczyk, 2005; Henry et al., 1996), and residential instability (Felitti et al., 2008; Hawkins et al., 1998) are risk factors for delinquent activities, emotional problems, substance use and abuse, poor academic outcomes, and maltreatment victimization. As can be seen, risk factors for some areas are outcomes for other problems, and vice versa; providing further evidence of the complex interplay of causation and the difficulties in both studying and effectively intervening in these comorbid issues.

Community Risk Factors

The less well organized and cohesive the community the greater the risk is for poor child and youth outcomes. Crime, including drug-selling, and low-income housing in the community are linked to delinquent youth behaviors (Maguin et al., 1995), as is the exposure to violence within the community. Witnessing violence has been associated with aggressive behavior, poor school performance, and increased mental health difficulties, including depression, anxiety, and trauma (Gorman-Smith and Tolan, 1998; Margolin and Gordis, 2000; Miller et al., 1999; Schwartz and Gorman, 2003). These more violent communities are often disproportionately composed of minority populations and poor (Kracke and Hahn, 2008). The inter-relationship of risks across the individual, family, and community is often confounding.

Resilient or Vulnerable Children and Youth

Children and youth will react to these individual, family, and community risk factors in varying ways. Some children and youth are highly resilient to such experiences while others are greatly affected and troubled. The term "resilient" has been operationalized in a number of ways, though considerable debate remains on how best to study this concept (Luthar, 2003; Masten, 2001; Rutter, 2006). Resiliency has, for instance, been defined as the capacity for children and youth to thrive in the face of these risks and difficulties, avoiding many of the deleterious effects. A second definition states that resiliency is the process of, or capacity for, a successful adaption despite the circumstances (Masten, Best, and Garmezy, 1990). However the term is defined, many children and youth are simply able to withstand the challenge of numerous problems and risk factors without sustaining harmful long-term consequences (Fergus and Zimmerman, 2004).

The degree of resilience that an individual has depends on a complex interaction of risks factors, balanced with protective factors (Buffington, Dierkhising, and Marsh, 2010). Protective factors are often considered and measured as the absence of risk factors (Hawkins et al., 2000). However, specific protective factors have been identified that may minimize certain childhood and youth risks. For example, a strong relationship with a positive parent or parental figure may be protection enough for a child to overcome maltreatment experiences and subsequent school and academic difficulties; or, the school that the child attends may provide enough of a support system that the dysfunctional family system does not greatly impact development; or the family environment may provide a stable enough home that even a very low-income and violent neighborhood won't significantly impede the child's development (Fraser, 2004; Richters and Martinez, 1993).

When measuring and identifying childhood resiliency factors that protect from dysfunction, poverty, and related difficulties, there is a significant interplay among heritable factors, individual characteristics, and experiences over time (Collishaw, Pickles, Messer, Rutter, Shearer, and Maughan, 2007). These may include individual cognitive factors such as self-regulation abilities and intelligence, biological factors such as stress and reactivity, inter-personal factors such as peer affiliations, and family-related factors including parenting abilities (Caspi et al., 2002; Masten et al., 1999; Werner and Smith, 2001).

In a number of reviews of children who have experienced trauma or maltreatment some specific protective factors were identified: above-average cognitive abilities and learning styles, an internal locus of control, the presence of spirituality, external attributions of blame from traumatic events, and emotional support (Cicchetti et al., 1993; Heller et al., 1999; McGee, Wolfe, and Olson, 2001). The presence of these protections, or other factors yet to be identified, may be behind the growing evidence that the mental health of a substantial minority of maltreated children is relatively unaffected by their adversity (McGloin and Widom, 2001). Also, children and youth who are not maltreated but who are exposed to other risk factors are still at risk for the development of mental health difficulties, substance abuse problems, learning/academic problems, and possible subsequent delinquency. Nonetheless, many of these children are also resilient and adapt and develop well into adolescence without significant trouble (Luther, 2003; Mears and Aron, 2003; National Center for Children in Poverty, 2000). Thus, in the end, it is still difficult to predict how an individual child or youth will respond to these risk factors and harmful experiences.

From Delinquency and Disability Risks to the Juvenile Courts

While a significant number of children and youth are resilient to the impacts of maltreatment, mental health difficulties, and learning problems, too often these risk factors impact their development and lead to offending, aggressive, and delinquent activities (Mallett, 2011b). The connection with these difficulties and disabilities has been identified by many researchers and stakeholders and termed the pathway from maltreatment to delinquency, the school-to-prison pipeline, and from poverty to prison, among others (Children's Defense Fund, 2009; Mulvey, 2011). Before explicating these "pathways" for youth who become involved with the juvenile courts, it is important to understand the costs of the juvenile justice system. Expenses that rise exponentially the deeper youth are involved with the juvenile justice system.

The number of youth referred annually and nationally to the juvenile courts is substantial. Over 2.0 million arrests of youth under age eighteen (Puzzanchera, 2009), over 900,000 youth formally processed and involved (Knoll and Sickmund, 2010), more than 350,000 youth held in detention centers (Holman and Ziedenberg, 2006; Sickmund, 2009) and more than 90,000 youth held in correctional facilities. That is, incarcerations for more serious and chronic youthful offenders (Davis et al., 2008; Hockenberry, Sickmund, and Sladky, 2010). Calculated as a daily census, over 60,000 youth are being held each day in a detention, incarceration, or residential facility by order of a juvenile court (Sickmund, 2009). Of these youth who are formally involved and adjudicated delinquent (an official court order providing legal control over the youth), over 70 percent are male (though the female proportion has increased over the past two decades), over 64 percent are Caucasian (though a disproportionate number are minority), approximately 50 percent are younger than age 16, and the offenses committed include property (36 percent), public order (28 percent), person-related (25 percent), and drug-related violations (11 percent) (Knoll and Sickmund, 2010).

Since 1990, the number of youth formally involved with the juvenile courts has increased over 30 percent, with only a slight downward trend recently (see Figure 1.1). This most recent decrease is primarily attributable to two factors. First, some jurisdictions and states gave rehought the punishment model within the juvenile courts, with a corresponding move toward rehabilitation, diversion, and treatment when appropriate. Second, the 2008 2009 economic recession has greatly affected state and local budgets, forcing significant expenditure decreases. At the state level this means less funding for state correctional facilities, where youth with more serious offenses are sentenced to serve incarceration time; at the local level, juvenile court and detention center operations have been reduced, because a large majority of these funds are from county budgets.

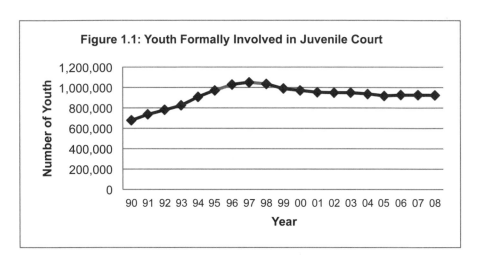

Figure 1.1: Youth Formally Involved in Juvenile Court

Sickmund, M., Sladky, A., and Kang, W. (2010) Easy access to juvenile court statistics: 1985-2008. National Center for Juvenile Justice, Pittsburgh, PA.

Juvenile Detention

Detention center placement is ideally utilized to protect the youth and/or the community, and occurs for either pre-trial holding (adjudication determination) and/or post-trial sentencing purposes for both low-level and more serious offenses. In many jurisdictions, detention centers also serve as the point of intake and initial detention after youth are arrested by law enforcement. While still serving these purposes, detention centers have also shifted over the past decade to holding many more non-violent offenders (Knoll and Sickmund, 2010). Lengths of stay can vary from less than a day for minor offenses to months for complicated and serious offenses. These placements have increased over time and, not surprisingly, mirror the trends of the increased formally juvenile court-involved youth (see Figure 1.2).

Two areas of concern related to race and gender are of significance for youth entering the juvenile courts over the past decade. The first issue, though not fully understood, is that race is a significant predictor of detention placement (and incarceration) outcomes. An African-American youth is six times more likely to be detained, and a Hispanic youth three times more likely, than a Caucasian youth, even when accounting for many of the important legal factors that influence these detention decisions such as number of offenses and offense type (Bishop, 2006; Kempf-Leonard, 2007; Puzzanchera, Adams, and

Snyder, 2008). This phenomenon has lead to what is called a "disproportionate minority confinement" (DMC) problem; and is a major focus of attention for national, state, and local stakeholders who are trying to understand and address this vexing problem (Mauer and King, 2007; National Council on Crime and Delinquency, 2007; Piquero, 2008).

The second issue is the increase in adolescent females' involvement with the juvenile courts over the past two decades (Zahn et al., 2010), which has lead to the increased supervision and detention of female offenders (Tracy, Kempf-Leonard, and Abramoske-James, 2009). Though studies demonstrate that adolescent females today are not more violent than adolescent females in prior decades, this increased involvement with the juvenile courts may reflect differential treatment, mandatory arrest polices for domestic violence (Zahn et al., 2008), other changes in law enforcement policies (e.g., releasing status offenders from detention centers), or a decrease in public tolerance for juvenile crime (Chesney-Lind, 1995; Feld, 2009; Pasko and Chesney-Lind, 2010). Though the reasons for increased female adolescent involvement with the juvenile courts and detention centers is not clear, females still make up only 15 to 20 percent of annual juvenile arrests (Feld, 2009). However, female adolescents' arrest rates have risen slightly over the past twenty years for all four crime categories: violent, property, person, and drug (Puzzanchera and Kang, 2008). Of significant concern, though, is that post-arrest, female youthful offenders are more likely to be detained than male youthful offenders (Chesney-Lind and Irwin, 2008). Consequently, one in five female youthful offenders is placed into a locked detention center, totaling over 70,000 annually (Knoll and Sickmund, 2010; Sickmund, 2008).

A growing consensus has begun to conclude that, notwithstanding continuing concern about reoffending all the youth in question, detention stays do not meet the main functions of the juvenile courts - youth and community safety maintenance - and that the experience of detention itself may be part of the problem (Mallett and Stoddard-Dare, 2010). Indeed, detention placement has increasingly been found to have a causal impact on increased youth re-offending and recidivism (Justice Policy Institute, 2009; Soler, Shoenberg, and Schindler, 2009). In other words, the experience of detention makes it more likely that detained youth, particularly non-violent and status offenders, will continue to engage in delinquent behavior, and it may increase the odds of recidivism (Holman and Ziedenberg, 2006). While the reasons behind this are still being investigated, it is known that detained youth are more likely than non-detained youth to further penetrate the juvenile justice

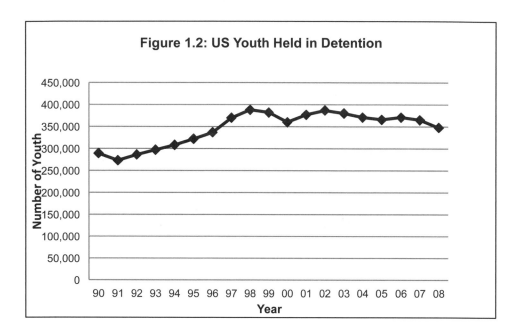

Figure 1.2: US Youth Held in Detention

Sickmund, M., Sladky, A., and Kang, W. (2010) Easy access to juvenile court statistics: 1985-2008. National Center for Juvenile Justice, Pittsburgh, PA.

system, with prior commitment being the most significant predictor of recidivism (Fendrich and Archer, 1998; Sheldon, 1999). Additionally, and of concern, detention placement has been found to cause a muchgreater chance of youth being incarcerated later in a state facility (Office of State Courts Administrator, 2003).

Incarceration: Juvenile Facilities

Juvenile correctional facility placement represents the most restrictive option for the juvenile courts - typically years-long incarceration of youth. Such placements are less frequent for less serious youthful offenders but are used for more serious matters and entail longer sentences than detention (Holman and Ziedenberg, 2006; Mallett, Williams, and Marsh, 2012). For these more serious offenders, incarceration outcomes are not encouraging. Placement into these facilities has either no correlation with youth re-arrest or recidivism rates (Loughran et al., 2009; Winokur et al., 2008) or it is associated with increased risk for youth re-arrest or recidivism (Myner et al., 1998).

As evidenced in many reviews, a large percentage of incarcerated youth reoffended within eighteen to thirty months of their release from these facilities (Petrosino, Turpin-Petrosino, and Guckenburg, 2010). While incarcerated, many of these youth do not receive services that may assist in mitigating the prior offending behavior; in other words, they are not provided with rehabilitative services that may be warranted (Annie E. Casey Foundation, 2009).

Incarceration: Transfers of Youth to the Criminal Courts

The incarceration of youthful offenders is not limited to juvenile detention and state jail facilities; it also includes the adult criminal justice system. This was not always the case. Juvenile courts, and subsequently detention facilities, were established in all states by 1945, with the intention of keeping incarcerated youth separate so that so that youth could be rehabilitated and returned to their communities (Coalition for Juvenile Justice, 1998; Krisberg, 2005). In 1966, though, the United States Supreme Court (in *Kent v. U.S.*) determined that transferring juvenile offenders to adult criminal courts was permissible, although certain procedures and reviews of circumstances were necessary, including the seriousness and type of offense, prosecutorial merit of the complaint, youth maturity, home environment, and previous court history (Mallett, 2007). During the 1970s and 1980s as the movement to be "tough on crime" shifted the juvenile and adult courts away from rehabilitation, state legislatures made automatic (and prosecutorial) youth transfers more common (Feld, 1987; Griffin, 2003; Griffin et al., 2011).

Little is different today in the handling of serious youthful offenders. In 2011, all fifty states had transfer laws that allowed or required the criminal prosecution of some youthful offenders, often mandating the transfer of these youth from the juvenile courts to the adult criminal courts (Griffin et al., 2011). Most states place the responsibility on the prosecution to show that the youthful offender should be transferred and tried in adult criminal court, with many taking into account the nature of the alleged crime and the individual youth's history, age, maturity, and other rehabilitative concerns (Neelum, 2011). In twenty-nine states, however, transfers to criminal court are automatic if the youth commits a certain type of offense and is a certain minimum age (e.g., in New York, a fourteen-year-old may be transferred automatically for certain weapon-possession crimes, while murder is the offense most common for automatic transfer in these twenty-nine states). It is difficult to know how many youth are ultimately transferred to the criminal courts because states do not consistently report this information. Reports from a number of states have found that nine of every 1,000 delinquency cases are transferred automatically, without any judicial or prosecutorial review; this could extrapolate to over 175,000 youth annually across the country, though this cannot be confirmed (Griffin, et al., 2011). It was reported, however, in a 2009 survey of adult jails nationwide, that over 7,000 of the inmates (less than 1 percent) were under the age of eighteen (Minton, 2010).

Transfers of youth to the adult criminal justice system are controversial because they divide the youthful offender population into two categories; those worthy of rehabilitation and those subject to retributive punishment (Fagan, 2008; Singer, 1996). The concern about bifurcating this population is that the latters' rights to due process might be violated, that significant mitigating circumstances around youth development and disabilities may not be reviewed prior to transfer, and that public policy goals of increased public safety and youth accountability are not met (Green, 2005; Mallett, 2007; Marrus and Rosenberg, 2005; Tanenhous and Drizin, 2002). There is little evidence that these state transfer laws have reduced arrest or crime rates (Fagan, 1995; Stolzenberg and D'Alessio, 1997) or recidivism (Bishop, 2000; Howell, 1996; Redding, 2010). In fact, transferred youth appear more likely to reoffend (Lanza-Kaduce et al., 2005; Winner et al., 1997). In addition, many youth sentenced to adult criminal facilities serve no longer than the maximum time they would have served within the juvenile justice system (Bishop, 2000). These detention and incarceration policies absorb a significant portion of local and state juvenile justice dollars, often leaving fewer resources available for diversion, treatment, or other efforts for low-level youthful offenders.

The Costs of Confinement

Policy makers are increasingly concluding that, excepting the smaller number of youth who pose a serious community risk, detaining and incarcerating large numbers of youthful offenders, whether in juvenile or adult facilities, is not sound fiscal public policy. The costs of these placements are substantial, with over $5.0 billion spent annually incarcerating youth in juvenile institutions; youth placement in adult correctional facilities is above and beyond even that figure (Council of Juvenile Correctional Administrators, 2009; Justice Policy Institute, 2009). In comparison, the costs of all other juvenile court administrative, programming, and supervision efforts are estimated to be half as much as these facility placement and incarceration costs (Florida Department of Juvenile Justice, 2010; Maryland Budget and Tax Policy Center and Advocates for Youth, 2008).

The costs of post-adjudication settings, such as detention, incarceration, and other related residential facilities, cost is more than $240 per day on average (over $88,000 annually) for each youth; excluding costs for youth in adult correctional facilities (American Correctional Association, 2008). Notably, over 38 percent of youth confined to juvenile correctional institutions were convicted of a non-person and non-violent offense, primarily court order violations, status offenses (truancy, curfew violations, and others), public order offenses, and/or drug-related offenses. Over 25 percent of youth in detention centers are being held because they did not follow their probation and supervision plans; hence, they violated court orders and were remanded or sentenced to the facility (Sickmund, Sladky, and Kang, 2010). Presumably youth who have committed such low-level and non-violent offenses are unlikely to pose a serious safety threat to either their communities or themselves.

Tallies of costs incurred over time for youthful offenders do not provide encouraging news. In one review of 500 offenders, total lifetime estimated cost was over $1.1 million dollars per youth (DeLisi & Gatling, 2003). A second review of 500 youthful offenders found that those who became involved with the juvenile courts at an early age averaged over thirty-four total offenses over time and incurred approximately $220,000 in costs by age seventeen. However, the smaller group of more serious and chronic offenders within this population, comprising only 10 percent of the juvenile court population, averaged over 142 offenses per youth over time and incurred approximately $800,000 in costs by age seventeen (Welsh et al., 2008). Most recently, in a review of over 27,000 youthful offenders, it was estimated that by diverting just one serious or chronic youth away from ongoing delinquent activities, between $2 million and $5 million could be saved over the youth's lifetime (Cohen and Piquero, 2009). These reviews reinforce the need for, or at least for the fiscal benefit, of identifying early which individuals are most at risk for serious or chronic youthful offending.

From Serious Youthful Offending to Adult Incarceration: The Ultimate Dead-end

Most youth in the general population have no contact with the juvenile justice system. In fact, even when youth do have contact (e.g., truancy pick up or arrest for traffic violation) - a majority, 54 percent of males and 70 percent of females - never have a second contact (Puzzanchera, 2009). The concern, though, is for youth who do have additional interactions with the system, thus increasing their formal involvement with the juvenile courts. Within the youth population who are formally involved with the juvenile courts, often adjudicated delinquent, there is an even smaller subset of repeat and continual offenders. For this subset there is significant risk that their offending behaviors may continue into young adulthood and criminal court involvement. In addition, as noted, a large number of youth under the age of eighteen are already involved with the criminal courts through automatic or prosecutorial transfers to the adult system. This subset of the juvenile delinquent population, often referred to as serious, chronic, or violent youthful offenders, is the group most at risk to continue these offending patterns into adulthood and to be incarcerated as adults (Degue and Widom, 2009; Howell, 2003; Snyder, 1998).

A number of factors predict involvement with the adult criminal courts, mostly related to the onset and persistence of juvenile offending behaviors. The youngsters most at risk are those whose offending behaviors start early and continue through late adolescence; who commit more offenses, primarily person and violent offenses, and are more frequently adjudicated delinquent; and who have an escalation of offenses over time (Loeber and Farrington, 1998; Tolan and Gorman-Smith, 1998; Tracy and Kempf-Leonard, 1996). In some juvenile court settings, youth who were incarcerated in juvenile facilities, compared to those who received lighter sentences and were not incarcerated, were three times more likely to be incarcerated eventually in adult facilities (De Li, 1999).

If these more serious or chronic youthful offenders do not desist these negative patterns, but continue their involvement with the criminal courts as adults, their prospects are bleak. Imprisonment of youth with adult offenders attempts to address a number of public policy goals, including community safety, personal retribution, and discouragement of reoffending. Unfortunately, this last goal is most often not met (Pew Center on the States, 2011b; Spelman, 2000; Trulson et al., 2011). Recidivism, typically measured as a return to a jail or prison facility, and presumably important in assessing the impact of incarceration, is discouragingly high. A recent report on over 80 percent of the states, representing almost 90 percent of all released state inmates, found that 44 percent of those inmates were returned to prison within three years (Pew Center on the States, 2011b). Such high recidivism rates to adult incarceration facilities have remained fairly stable over the past two decades, with the most common offenses that lead to reincarceration being robberies, burglaries, larceny, stolen property, and weapons charges (Beck and Shipley, 1989; Langan and Levin, 2002).

Ex-prisoners face significant and substantial barriers to reintegration and successful re-entry to their communities upon release from adult incarceration facilities (Pager, 2003; Western, Kling, and Weiman 2001). Incarceration may perpetuate criminal activities because of socioeconomic harm caused by the imprisonment on offenders, their families, and communities (Hirshfield and Piquero, 2010). Employment is a primary link for the ex-prisoners successful reentry into the community (Bellair and Kowalski, 2011), yet there is often a mismatch within the communities to which the offenders return between employment opportunities and the ex-prisoners' vocational skill set. Often there are not enough low-level jobs in the communities where the ex-prisoners return, leaving few if any alternatives to crime (Ihlanfeldt and Sjoquist, 1998; Soloman, Visher, LaVigne, and Osborne, 2006). Beyond work and employment difficulties, other well-established risks impact ex-prisoners' likelihood of reoffending and recidivism. Risk factors for reoffending include: being a younger adult offender, male, and single; having low educational attainment; having an increased number of convictions; and having an earlier age of onset for offending behaviors (Baumer, 1997; Gendreau, Little, and Goggin, 1996; Uggen, 2000). The failure to complete high school is commonly identified within the juvenile courts as a risk factor for chronic offending (Mears and Aron, 2003); this association has also been made within the adult prison population (Sampson and Laub, 1993).

There are problems also within the adult incarceration facilities. Over the past few decades as the punitive and "tough on crime" approach expanded the number of adult jails and prisons, this same philosophy simultaneously decreased many of the education or rehabilitative programs available to those incarcerated (Gordon and Weldon, 2003; Lynch and Sabol, 2001; Petteruti and Walsh, 2008; Pew Center on the States, 2011a; Vacca, 2004). Jails and prisons are violent and traumatizing places for many inmates, with high levels of physical assaults (Stephan and Karberg, 2003; Wolff et al., 2007). Difficulties encountered while incarcerated may impose new learned behaviors on prisoners, increasing antisocial activities because of the experience (Dodge and Pettit, 2003). In addition, the disproportionate minority confinement problem found within juvenile detention and incarceration facilities is a problem in adult incarceration facilities as well. Minorities are significantly overrepresented in jails and prisons, up to three times more frequently than might be expected from their community populations (Glaze, 2010; Minton, 2011).

If these serious offending and incarceration outcomes are to be improved, it is vital to prioritize efforts in decreasing the number of youth who commit violent and chronic offenses. Knowing that a majority of this youthful offender population struggles with the effects of maltreatment victimization, mental health problems, substance abuse issues, and/or learning and academic difficulties, it is important to identify these problems and appropriately intervene with treatment and rehabilitative efforts.

Summary

Most children and youth never become involved with the juvenile or criminal justice systems. However, those who do often share common delinquency risk factors and background experiences. While these risks and experiences do not necessarily portend later delinquency, because many youth are resilient to the impacts, it is important to minimize the harmful influences for those most vulnerable. For some youth, involvement with the juvenile courts may lead to detention, incarceration, and possibly the adult criminal justice system - all harmful outcomes.

2

Linking Disorders to Delinquency

Maltreatment victimization, mental health disorders, substance abuse, and related school/education problems are associated with profound difficulties for many children and youth. As reviewed in Chapter 1, these experiences and disabilities are often linked to later or subsequent offending and delinquent behaviors, which for some youth becomes an offending recidivism cycle, a negative outcome with serious repercussions. This link from child and youth disabilities to delinquency is most evident within the juvenile detention and incarceration facilities. Within these facilities a majority of youthful offenders have been identified with at least one of these disabilities or maltreatment experiences, though many youth have combinations of these problems before, during, and after release from detention or incarceration (Garland et al., 2001; Mallett, 2009; Rosenblatt, Rosenblatt, and Biggs, 2000). Detention, and in particular incarceration, facilities provide a bleak backdrop for youth struggling to come to terms with adolescence.

Much of the epidemiological research identifying incidence rates of disorders, maltreatment, and related problems within delinquent populations is from studies of detained and incarcerated youth, highlighting the need for more comprehensive studies across other facets of the juvenile justice system. In particular, in order to better understand the pathway to the high disability rates found in the more secure facility settings, it would be pivotally informative to policy makers and stakeholders to have reviews of youths' first contacts with the juvenile justice system through to any formal involvement and confinement (Mallett, 2006; McReynolds et al., 2008). Nonetheless, the prevalence rates of youth within these facilities who suffer from disability and maltreatment victimization prevalence rates is alarming, all the more so when compared to overall prevalence of these conditions among youth in their home communities (see Table 2.1).

Table 2.1 Youth Disability and Maltreatment
Victimization Prevalence Rates

Type	Detained / Incarcerated Youth Population (%)	General Youth Population (%)
Maltreatment victimization	26-60	1
Special education disabilities (learning disabilities and emotional disturbances)	28-45	4-9
Mental health disorders	35-80	9-18
Substance abuse	30-70	4-5

In the general population, most children and youth do not suffer from nor experience any of these disabilities, maltreatment victimizations, or negative conditions and experiences. If a child or youth does have one of these difficulties, it most often is a singular experience, that is, only one mental health problem or one learning disability (Mallett, 2003). Only a small percentage of children and youth will ever be diagnosed with a mental health disorder (9 to 18 percent), have an active substance abuse problem (4 to 5 percent), be a victim of maltreatment (less than 1 percent), or have a special education disability (4 to 9 percent), of which a majority of these are learning disabilities or emotional disturbances (New Freedom Commission on Mental Health, 2003; Substance Abuse and Mental Health Services Administration, 2008a, 2008b; U.S. Department of Education, 2010; U.S. Department of Health and Human Services, 2010). However, for decades, reviews of detained and incarcerated youth have found significantly higher incidences of these disorders and maltreatment victimizations within this population—from two (some mental health disorders) to as many as sixty times (for maltreatment victimization) the rates found in the general youth population (Chassin, 2008; Grisso, 2008; Mears and Aron, 2003; Teplin et al., 2006; Washburn, et al., 2008).

A review of the higher percentages of identified problems for detained and incarcerated youth compared to their non-detained and non-incarcerated peers highlights the link to serious offending, though only correlation, not causation, has been shown so far. Additionally, the high prevalence rates of disabilities of detained and incarcerated youth become more complex and more difficult to unravel because of frequent comorbidities. Court-involved youth often have multiple disabilities and/or disorders occurring both over time and at the same time, a situation that may greatly compound the negative outcomes (Dembo et al., 2008). The comorbidity conundrum is an under-investigated phenomenon, but one that may greatly affect serious and chronic offenders. Correlative links between each of these disability and maltreatment experiences and offending, as well as delinquency, will be explored next, along with the comorbidity of these difficulties.

Maltreatment Victimization

Child and youth maltreatment victimization may entail a wide range of harmful treatment, from physical, sexual, emotional or psychological abuse, to neglect. Such maltreatment has increasingly been found to evoke serious, long-lasting negative repercussions for many of the victims. Some refer to these experiences as chronic trauma, acute trauma, and/or complex trauma. Broader definitions of maltreatment note that victimization over time complicates recovery, though for some children and youth just one instance of victimization can be sufficiently traumatic to induce symptoms (Buffington, et al., 2010; National Child Traumatic Stress Network, 2008).

Over the past two decades, approximately 800,000 to 1 million children and youth nationwide each year are victims of reported and substantiated maltreatment. The majority of which are neglect cases (ranging from 50 to 80 percent, depending on the year), followed by physical abuse (17 to 27 percent), sexual abuse (9 to 17 percent), and psychological abuse (4 to 7 percent). The victims of such maltreatment do not differ in terms of gender. Males and females are equally at risk. However, they are disproportionately younger (under the age of ten, with adolescents comprising only 20 percent of current victims) and minority children (African-American, American Indian, and Pacific Islander) (Administration for Children and Families, 2010, 2011).

Many of the youth involved with the juvenile courts have maltreatment histories; that is, they are past victims of physical, sexual, or psychological abuse, or neglect. When care is taken to identify such histories, between 26 and 60 percent of formally juvenile court-involved youth have been found with these maltreatment histories (Bender, 2009; Ford et al., 2007; Mallett and Stoddard-Dare, 2009; Sedlak and McPherson, 2010; Stouthamer-Loeber et al., 2002; Tuell, 2002). Though maltreatment is a significant risk factor for later juvenile court involvement, it is important to highlight that a large majority of children and youth who are victims never become involved with the juvenile courts (Yun, et al., 2011; Widom, 2003). However, victims of maltreatment are significantly overrepresented among youth involved with the juvenile courts and, in particular, among youth who are detained and incarcerated (Currie and Tekin, 2006; Lemmon, 2006).

The correlation between maltreatment and juvenile delinquency is a serious concern. Research is gradually revealing how victimization experiences may contribute to children's and youth's pathway into delinquency. Yet this remains a complex matter because of the differential impact of maltreatment, maltreatment victimization types and diverse harmful outcomes, and because a number of maltreatment outcomes are, in their own turn, also significant serious youthful offending risk factors.

Maltreatment Differentiation

In studies relating maltreatment to juvenile offending and delinquency, maltreatment types have typically been classified and measured across three categories: physical abuse, sexual abuse, and neglect. Psychological or emotional abuse and neglect are more recently added categories. Children and youth who have been maltreated are more likely to engage in offending and delinquent behaviors compared to children and youth without a maltreatment history. Due to the significant differences of outcomes of offending acts (e.g., arrest, conviction, delinquency adjudication), including whether official records or youth self-reports were used, the link between certain maltreatment types and delinquency may be underestimated (Maxfield, et al., 2000).

This link was first identified in the late 1980s when it was discovered that maltreated youthful offenders (physical abuse, sexual abuse, and neglect victims) had not only a significantly greater chance of being arrested, but also a greater likelihood of being arrested a year earlier than did non-maltreated youthful offenders (Widom, 1989). Additionally, these maltreated youth were more likely to be formally supervised by the juvenile court for more serious offending behaviors than were their non-maltreated peers (Loeber and Farrington, 2001; Smith and Thornberry, 1995). All three maltreatment types have been linked to later antisocial behavior, violent crimes, and juvenile court involvement (Lemmon, 2009; Manly et al., 2001; Widom and Maxfield, 2001; Yun, et al., 2011; Zingraff et al., 1993). While neglect has been found to be more often associated with later delinquency, living in poverty and living in a single-parent household were also factors that contributed to the delinquency outcome (Weatherburn and Lind, 1997; Weeks and Widom, 1998). However, studies have found that all types of maltreatment are associated with criminal offending even in the presence of these other risk factors (Lemmon, 1999; Zingraff, et al., 1993). It is not yet clear which type or types of maltreatment are most independently predictive of youthful offending; however, studies increasingly point to neglect and physical abuse as most closely linked, with sexual abuse less closely linked (Loeber and Farrington, 2001; Smith and Thornberry, 1995).

Research is clear, however, and disconcerting, that repeated maltreatment no matter the type (physical abuse, sexual abuse, or neglect) has a key impact on youthful offending behavior. Such repeat victimization predicts the initiation, continuation, and severity of delinquent acts (Hamilton and Browne, 1998; Lemmon, 2006; Verrechia et al., 2010), and is associated with serious, chronic, and violent offending behaviors (Hamilton, Falshaw, and Browne, 2002; Kelly, et al., 1997; Smith and Thornberry, 1995). In addition, children who are maltreated during later childhood and adolescence (Stewart, et al., 2008) are at even higher risk of committing violent and delinquent acts (Ireland, et al.; Johnson-Reid and Barth, 2000; Smith, et al., 2005). Comparatively, children who are persistently maltreated from childhood to adolescence may be no more at risk than those youth not maltreated, though it is not understood why this may be the case (Stewart, et al., 2008; Thornberry, Ireland, and Smith, 2002).

Within juvenile court populations, females are more likely than males to have been victims of sexual abuse, and are equally likely to have experienced physical abuse (Acoca, 1998; Hennessey et al., 2004; Shelton, 2004). The cumulative impact of maltreatment, in addition to other risks often associated with this maltreatment, such as substance abuse and school difficulties, may affect females more negatively than males (Howell, 2003; National Center for Child Traumatic Stress, 2009). However, research findings are not sufficiently conclusive to posit that maltreatment effects for females are greater when compared to males in delinquency development (Zahn et al., 2010).

No definitive answer has yet emerged linking the various maltreatment experiences to specific delinquency outcomes. However, studies consistently find that persistent or recurring maltreatment, as well as maltreatment that occurs during early adolescence, is strongly associated with serious juvenile offending. Still more evidence is needed to more strongly link victimization with risk of offending so that stakeholders and policy makers can make increasingly informed preventative and interventive decisions.

Maltreatment Outcomes and Serious Offending Risks

Another complex concern about delinquency risk factors centers on the number of maltreatment effects that are subsequently also risk factors for serious youthful offending. Children and youth who have been maltreated will have higher risks for certain harmful outcomes, and some of these harmful outcomes themselves are also correlated with increased risk of offending. These include mental health and substance abuse problems, running away from home (which is considered a status offense), and school difficulties (Hawkins et al., 2000).

Mental Health and Substance Abuse Problems

Mental health and substance abuse problems are often outcomes of child and youth maltreatment. Physical abuse of children often results in depression and post-traumatic stress disorder (Dykman et al., 1997; Kilpatrick et al., 2003); sexual abuse is associated with post-traumatic stress disorder and other anxiety difficulties; and neglect also often leads to anxiety disordersnd related problems (Turner, Finkelhor, and Ormrod, 2006). In turn, increasing evidence links these and other mental health difficulties to later youthful offending behaviors and delinquency, though such link may be direct or indirect, perhaps with interceding problems (Widom and White, 1997).

Running Away from Home

Running away is both an outcome of maltreatment at home and a precursor to delinquent behaviors and activities. The act itself can be prosecuted as a status offense for youth, bringing the youth under juvenile court supervision. Many youth run away, or are "kicked out," from abusive or unsafe home environments. Some of these youth return, some stay away for extended periods of time, and some become homeless. These runaway youth are at much higher risk for school difficulties and truancy due to these disruptions, while youth who experience homelessness are much more likely than non-homless youth to commit drug and/or violent crimes (Baron, 2003; Chesney-Lind, 2003).

School Difficulties

Children and youth with maltreatment victimization histories, compared to those without similar histories, are less successful in both primary and secondary school. Depending on when the maltreatment occurs the child's development and school performance may be differentially impacted (Leiter, 2007; Veltman and Browne, 2001).

Cognitive and language delays in primary school are greater for maltreated children versus non-maltreated children from lower socio-economic backgrounds, and much greater when compared to non-maltreated children from higher socio-economic backgrounds (Wiggins et al., 2007). On average, maltreated children enter school one-half year behind on academic performance (Smithgall et al., 2004) and have poorer academic performance and functioning at ages six and eight (Kurtz et al., 1993; Zolotor et al., 1999). These children also have higher absenteeism rates that may be affecting or complicating these negative outcomes (Lansford et al., 2002; Leiter, 2007). An increased severity of maltreatment may also have a harmful impact on children's verbal abilities and verbal intelligence quotient (Perez and Widom, 1994). The more serious or pervasive the maltreatment, the greater the risk for the child's decline in school performance, including absenteeism and lower grades. Experiencing maltreatment at an earlier age may lead to behavior problems and increased placement into special education programs (Leiter and Johnson, 1997).

Maltreated children, and particularly children in foster care, are more likely to be diagnosed with a special education disability during earlier school years: between 30 and 50 percent in some populations (Frothingham et al., 2000; Goerge et al., 1992; Scarborough and McCrae, 2009). Children in foster care also have poorer academic achievement compared to their peers; they are often behind in grade level and in reading and mathematics ability (Burley and Haplern, 2001; Conger and Rebeck, 2001; Hyames and de Hames, 2000).

For older secondary-age youth, maltreatment negatively affects their academic, social, and related outcomes (Coleman, 2004). Older adolescents, particularly those with longer histories of maltreatment victimization, are often three or four grade levels behind in reading abilities and repeat at least one grade significantly more often than non-maltreated adolescents, making their chances of high school completion much less likely (Slade and Wissow, 2007). Similarly, youth who have experienced foster care placement are particularly at risk, with a much higher percentage not completing high school compared to their non-maltreated peers (Courtney et al., 2004). Youth with maltreatment histories who do not complete high school, youth in foster care who are truant or change schools often, and youth aging out of the child welfare system are at high risk for becoming involved in offending and delinquent activities. Without effective supports or efforts to complete their secondary school education, as young adults this group typically finds that their employment and independent living options limited (Lederman et al., 2004; Lipsey and Derzon, 1999; Ryan et al., 2007).

Special Education Disabilities

Youth and Juvenile Court Populations

Special education disabilities include a wide range of physical, education, and emotional impairments, including mental retardation (developmental delays), deafness and other hearing impairments, blindness, autism (spectrum), speech and language problems, orthopedic problems, traumatic brain injury, emotional disturbances, and specific learning disabilities. Youth with special education disabilities are not common in the general population, accounting for at most 9 percent of school-aged children and youth (ages six to twenty-one). The most common of these education-related disabilities is a specific learning disability, affecting 4 percent of school-aged children and youth (ages six to twenty-one). Because learning disabilities are often not remedied, older youth populations account for a larger percentage of the total population count of learning disabilties. Among older youth, learning disabilities account for a higher percentage of all special education disabilities: 14 percent for youth ages six to eleven, but 26 percent for youth ages twelve to seventeen (U.S. Department of Education, 2009; 2010).

The incidence of youth with special education disabilities is much higher among juvenile court populations, particularly in detention and incarceration facilities, than in the youth population overall. It is estimated that between 28 and 43 percent of detained and incarcerated youthful offenders have an identified special education disability (Casey and Keilitz, 1990; Kvarfordt, Purcell, and Shannon, 2005; Morris and Morris, 2006; National Center on Education, Disability, and Juvenile Justice, 2001; Rozalski, Deignan, and Engel, 2008; Wang, Blomberg, and Li, 2005; White and Loeber, 2008). Among youth with special education disabilities within incarceration and detention facilities, 48 percent had an identified emotional disturbance, 39 percent had a specific learning disability, 10 percent had mental retardation, and three percent had other health impairments (Quinn et al., 2005). Incidences for incarcerated youth with disabilities have not changed significantly over time (Rutherford, Nelson, and Wolford, 1985). The two most common special education disabilities are of primary concern here because they are most prevalent in detention and incarceration facility populations: specific learning disabilities and emotional disturbances (Burrell and Warboys, 2000; Leone et al., 1995; SRI International Center for Education and Human Services, 1997).

Learning Disabilities and Emotional Disturbances

A lack of consistent definitions across systems that address some of the special education disability impairments of at-risk children and youth furt her complicates an already difficult situation. For instance, within school systems and in special education disability laws mental health problems are defined as "emotional disturbances," rather than a diagnoses or specific disorders recognized within the youth mental health sector (American Psychiatric Association, 2000). When a child or youth is identified within school special education departments as having an emotional disturbance, for all practical and intervention purposes, this is equivalent to a mental health diagnosis, a more serious and impairing problem than many disorders, such as some behavioral or anxiety difficulties. However, emotional disturbances significantly impair the functioning of children and youth, both at home and in school. Presumably at some point these children and youth will be identified by the youth mental health system as having ongoing difficulties comorbid with mental health disorders (Reddy, 2001; Theodore, Bray, and Kehle, 2004). In fact, this small subset of children and youth with such emotional disturbances are the most likely to fail in school and least likely to complete high school, yet this group is among the most under-identified and untreated of child clinical populations (New Freedom Commission on Mental Health, 2003; Reddy and Richardson, 2006). As with children and youth who have experienced maltreatment, those with learning disabilities, mental health and emotional problems, and issues related to those conditions have an increased risk of delinquency as well. First, attention will be focused on learning disabilities and delinquency. The linkage of serious mental health problems with delinquency will be addressed in the next section.

A learning disability is defined by federal law as "a disorder in one or more of the basic psychological processes involved in understanding or in using language, spoken or written, that may manifest itself in an imperfect ability to listen, think, speak, read, write, spell, or do mathematical calculations" (Code of Federal Regulations, 2011). It may include related conditions such as brain injury, dyslexia, perceptual disabilities, minimum brain dysfunction, and developmental aphasia; however, it excludes learning problems stemming from environmental, economic, or cultural disadvantage. Learning disabilities vary in impact across children and youth, are diagnosed on a continuum from mild to severe, and can appear differently in various academic or nonacademic settings (Council for Learning Disabilities, 2011). Of interest and concern, because of the linkage of these disabilities with juvenile court populations, is that certain minority youth are at higher risk for learning disabilities: Hispanics are almost 20 percent more likely; African-Americans more than 40 percent more likely; and American-Indians more than 80 percent more likely (U.S. Department of Education, 2010). And, as mentioned earlier, there are often risk factors that are comorbid between and among these disabilities. Similarly, risk factors that increase the likelihood of having a learning disability include living in poverty, male gender, poor family functioning, being adopted, and lower household education attainment; these are also risk factors for juvenile delinquency (Altarac and Saroha, 2007).

From Learning Disabilities to Delinquency

Children at risk for academic failure in elementary school often have unidentified special education and learning disability needs, and are subsequently at increased risk for later violent behaviors (Hawkins et al., 2000). More broadly, youth with unidentified learning disabilities may be disproportionately represented among those youth who are suspended, expelled, and/or drop out of high school (Keleher, 2000). Suspensions, expulsions, and drop-outs are all risk factors for delinquent offending activities, often serious offending (Hawkins et al., 2000; Sum et al., 2009).

Learning disabilities are correlated with delinquency. Reviews have found that youth with learning disabilities, compared to those youth without such learning disabilities, have two to three times greater risk of being involved in offending activities (Matta-Oshima, Huang, Jonson-Reid, and Drake, 2010; Wang et al., 2005; Zimmerman, Rich, Keilitz, and Broder, 1978), as well as higher recidivism rates (Katsiyannis and Archwamety, 1997). Youth with learning disabilities were found to be at an increased risk of being arrested while in school, as well as within one year after they finished school (Doren, Bullis, and Benz, 1996). However, this link has not been consistently identified within delinquent populations, nor does it serve as a precursor to delinquent activities. Continued investigation is imperative (Cornwall and Bawden, 1992; Malmgren, Abbott, and Hawkins, 1999; Pearl and Bryan, 1994; White and Loeber, 2008). Still and all, this link from the schools to the juvenile courts, as well as to detention and incarceration facilities, has gained the attention and concern of many policy makers and stakeholders. This pathway, often called the school-to-prison pipeline, may be funneling youth with learning disabilities in disproportionate numbers into the juvenile justice system (Federal Advisory Committee on Juvenile Justice, 2010; Fenning and Rose, 2007).

Mental Health and Substance Abuse Disorders

Youth Population

Most of the children and youth in the general population with an identified mental health or substance use problem are considered to have mild or moderate impairments (Kessler et al., 2005; Substance Abuse and Mental Health Services Administration, 2008a). A smaller subset of this youth population, between 5 and 10 percent, develop serious emotional disturbances that cause substantial impairment in functioning at home, at school, and/or in the community. This group of children and youth with serious emotional disturbances do not differ significantly in terms of age, ethnicity, or gender from the general youth population (Friedman, Katz-Leavy, Manderscheid, and Sondheimer, 1996; Substance Abuse and Mental Health Services Administration, 2008b). However, these severely impaired youth have challenges accessing mental health services, have trouble in school settings, and are often formally involved with the juvenile courts (Armstrong, Dedrick, and Greenbaum, 2003; Bazelon Center for Mental Health Law, 2003; Simpson et al., 2005). In fact, this small group of youth who are considered seriously emotionally disturbed typically have long histories of multiple mental health disorders that will normally persist into adulthood, and make up an estimated 15 to 20 percent of the youth in juvenile justice detention and incarceration facilities (Cocozza and Skowyra, 2000; MacKinnon-Lewis, Kaufman, and Frabutt, 2002).

Youth Detention and Incarceration Facilities

Youth mental health disorders are much more common within detention and incarceration facilities than in the general youth population. Common mental health disorders found within youth correctional facility populations includes depressive disorders (between 13 and 40 percent), psychotic disorders (between 5 and 10 percent), anxiety disorders (up to 25 percent), attention-deficit hyperactivity disorder (ADHD) (up to 20 percent), disruptive behavior disorders (between 30 and 80 percent), and substance use disorders (between 30 and 70 percent) (Abram et al., 2003; Atkins et al., 1999; Kinscherff, 2012; Goldstein et al., 2005; Grisso, 2008; Mallett, 2006; Pliszka et al., 2000; Shufelt and Cocozza, 2006). Gender and race differences appear across these disorders for this population.

Females in juvenile detention and incarceration facilities are at higher risk than males for mental health difficulties, with up to two-thirds of males and three-quarters of females meeting criteria for at least one mental health disorder (Huizinga et al., 2000; Teplin et al., 2002; Wasserman et al., 2002). Both conduct disorder and ADHD are prevalent in delinquent male populations (Moffitt et al., 2001), while depression, anxiety, and post-traumatic stress disorder, often related to maltreatment victimization, are prevalent in delinquent female populations (Teplin, et al., 2002). One review found that 29 percent of females versus 11 percent of males in detention and correctional facilities were diagnosed with major depression; however, equal rates of conduct disorder, over 50 percent, were found for both males and females (Fazel, Doll, and Langstrom, 2008). A unique review of youth entering the juvenile courts at intake found what may be expected, in light of other epidemiology literature: lower rates of mental health disorders for youth entering the juvenile courts compared to incarcerated youth; higher rates for youth entering the juvenile courts compared to the general population; and females reporting higher rates of mental health problems than males in most categories (McReynolds et al., 2008).

Prevalence and patterns of mental health and substance disorders also appear to differ across race in populations of incarcerated youth. In one review of these populations, 82 percent of Caucasian males, compared to 70 percent of Hispanic males and 65 percent of African-American males, met criteria for a mental health disorder, including a substance abuse disorder. For females, 86 percent of Caucasian females, compared to 76 percent of Hispanic females and 71 percent of African-American females, met criteria for a mental health disorder, including a substance use disorder. Similar patterns were found across gender by race for substance use disorders. Significantly more Caucasian males met criteria for a substance use disorder than did non-Caucasian males. Similarly, more Caucasian females met criteria for a substance use disorder than did non-Caucasian females (Teplin et al., 2002). This was also found in other prevalence rate studies where Caucasian youth reported more mental health problems than did minority youth, with female Caucasian youth most likely to report a problem, and African-American youth, either gender, least likely to report a problem

(Cauffman, 2004; Domalanta et al., 2003; Vaughn et al., 2008; Wasserman et al., 2005).

From Mental Health Problems to Delinquency

Mental health difficulties and disorders are linked to later youth-offending behaviors and delinquency adjudication, though it is not clear if this link is direct or if these difficulties lead to other risk factors, poor decisionmaking, or the interaction of various other risks (Grisso, 2008; Heilbrum, Goldstein, and Redding, 2005; Mallett, et al., 2009; Moffitt and Scott, 2008; Shufelt and Cocozza, 2006). Still, reviews have consistently found that children and youth who are involved with mental health services have a significantly higher risk for later juvenile court involvement (Rosenblatt et al., 2000; Vander-Stoep, Evans, and Taub, 1997; Westendorp et al., 1986).

In reviews that investigated the link from specific childhood mental health difficulties to juvenile court involvement, a number of pathways have been established. Developmental studies have found behavioral and emotional problems to be predictive of later delinquency and substance abuse (Dishion, Capaldi, and Yoerger, 1999; O'Donnell et al., 1995). Early childhood aggressive behaviors have been found predictive of later delinquent behaviors and activities (Kashani et al., 1999; Tremplay and LeMarquand, 2001). Attention and hyperactivity problems are linked to later high risk taking and more violent offending behavior (Elander et al., 2000; Hawkins et al, 1998; Kashani et al., 1999). Antisocial behaviors and emotional problems in early childhood are markers for later delinquent activities (Wasserman, Keenan, Tremblay, Cole, Herrenkohl, Loeber, and Petechuk, 2003). In addition, childhood depression and ADHD have been linked to later delinquency, evidenced through physical aggression and stealing behaviors (Goldstein et al., 2005; Loeber and Keenan, 1994; Moffitt and Scott, 2008; Ryan and Redding, 2004).

For youth who are formally involved with the juvenile courts and detained or incarcerated, a number of pathways from earlier mental health problems have been identified. Adolescent mental health and delinquent populations were found to have risk factors for detention or incarceration that included being African-American or Hispanic (a potential tie-in with the disproportionate minority confinement problem), having a diagnosis of alcohol problems or conduct disorder in middle school, reported use and abuse of substances, and receiving prior mental health services (Scott, Snowden, and Libby, 2002; Watts and Wright, 1990). Other reviews have substantiated an increased risk of juvenile justice system detainment for minorities, drug users, and public mental health insuranced youth (Mason and Giggs, 1992; Westendorp et al., 1986), though the questions remain whether drug use is a predictor of delinquency or if delinquency predicts drug use (Brunnelle, Brochu, and Cousineau, 2000; Wierson, Forehand, and Frame, 1992). Youth who received mental health system services prior to juvenile court involvement were at risk, compared to peers not involved with the juvenile courts, for drug and/or alcohol abuse and conduct disorder, and had been physically abused (Evans and Vander-Stoep, 1997; Rosenblatt, et al., 2000). These two populations - youth with emotional disturbances and youth involved in the juvenile justice system, - differ little across service delivery systems. In other words, these populations intersect, sharing members and have similarly identified needs and problems (Melton and Pagliocca, 1992; Teplin et al., 2002).

Suicide

Many mental health and substance abuse problems place youth at high risk for suicidal ideation, attempts, and completions (Douglas et al., 2006; Gould et al., 2003; Wilkes et al., 1994). Serious mental health problems have been found to affect more than one in four youth involved in the juvenile justice system (Shufelt and Cocozza, 2006). Suicide-related difficulties are challenging and often ongoing for the youth and their family; they are more common than often realized. Suicide is the third leading cause of death among youth ages ten to twenty-four years (Child Trends, 2010); with 1,000 completed suicides annually for youth aged twelve to seventeen (Centers for Disease Control and Prevention, 2008a; Substance Abuse and Mental Health Service Administration, 2010c). Many more young people contemplate suicide and others make attempts that are not fatal. Of the nearly three million youth aged twelve to seventeen who received mental health services in 2009, more than 20 percent reported seeking services for suicide-related problems (Substance Abuse and Mental Health Services Administration, 2010b).

Risk factors associated with suicide among the youth population include a family or individual history of suicide, a history of depression, serious alcohol or drug abuse, loss, easy access to lethal methods, and incarceration (Centers for Disease Control and Prevention, 2008a). Since incarceration is a risk factor, it follows that youth suicides and suicide attempts are more common within these facilities than among the general youth population.

Researchers have identified both a higher risk for youth while within these incarceration facilities and also a higher lifetime risk of suicide attempts after these incarcerations. A national study of court-ordered juveniles in placement found that 110 completed suicides occurred between 1995 and 1999. Of the seventy-nine cases with complete information, 42 percent of the suicides took place in secure juvenile court facilities and training schools, 37 percent in detention centers, 15 percent in residential treatment centers, and 6 percent in reception or diagnostic centers (Hayes, 2009). A similar review of youth in juvenile detention facilities in the 1980s found a suicide rate that was almost five times higher than for youths in the general population (Memory, 1989). In addition, thoughts of suicide have been reported by as many as half of incarcerated youths (Esposito and Clum, 1999), while large reviews of youth in custody, found that between 25 and 30 percent reported these suicidal thoughts (Putnins, 2005; Sedlak and McPherson, 2010). Researchers have begun to analyze how facility characteristics may be related to suicide attempts and deaths (Gallagher and Dobrin, 2005; 2006). One review found that facilities that house larger populations of youth that had locked sleeping room doors had the highest risk of suicide (Gallagher and Dobrin, 2006).

Because the youthful offender population is disproportionately minority and male, it is important to note that adolescent males are more likely to die from suicide attempts, as well as use more violent means than females, though adolescent females are more likely to report attempting suicide (Centers for Disease Control and Prevention, 2008a; Penn et al., 2003). Native American/Alaskan Native and Hispanic youth have been found to have the highest rate of suicide deaths (Centers for Disease Control, 2008b) and suicidal ideation (Graham and Corcoran, 2003), while Caucasian adolescent females reported more incidents of suicide or self-injury than their African-American counterparts (Holsinger and Holsinger, 2005). In an additional review of detained youth, Caucasian males were over three times more likely than their African-American counterparts to have committed suicide (Kempton and Forehand, 1992).

However, predicting suicide risk is difficult, for risk factors vary in their impact and intensity. Not only incarcerated youth, but also youth who are simply involved formally with the juvenile justice system, are at higher risk for suicidal behavior than non-involved youth (Epstein and Spirito, 2009; Evans, Hawton, and Rodham, 2004; Flisher et al., 2000; Rutter, 2007; Thompson, Ho, and Kingree, 2007). Even when other risk factors - age, ethnicity, gender, alcohol and drug problems, depression, and impulsivity - were accounted for, delinquency was still related to suicidal ideation and attempts up to one year later and to ideation up to seven years later (Thompson et al., 2007). Youth with an arrest history are more likely to report a suicide attempt than youth without an arrest history (Tolou-Shams et al., 2007). In addition, demonstrating the impact of comorbid problems, young people in juvenile justice facilities who have experienced maltreatment as children are more than twice as likely to have attempted suicide as their peers who had experienced maltreatment but were not in these facilities (Croysdael et al.,, 2008). Additionally, those who committed suicide had experienced rates of maltreatment two to ten times greater than the general youth population (Hayes, 2009). In a stark finding, 63 percent of youth who had completed suicide between the years from 1996 to 1999 in Utah had previous contact with the juvenile justice system (Gray, Achilles, Keller, Tate, Haggard, Rolfs, et al., 2002). Clearly, the risk of suicide for youth involved with the juvenile courts is significant; however, comorbid mental health problems and maltreatment victimizations have an impact.

Comorbidity of Risks and Disabilities

It is quite evident that these childhood and youth disabilities, maltreatment victimizations, and related difficulties and effects are often interrelated or comorbid. These difficulties can last for weeks or perhaps for years, often greatly affect child and youth development and may combine with other challenges, leading to additional complicated problems. They may also predispose a youth to additional negative outcomes. Comorbidity within the child and youth population has been alternatively defined as the presence of more than one mental health disorder (Costello et al., 2004; Grisso, 2008), the presence of a mental health disorder (often depression and conduct problems) and a substance abuse problem together (Goldstein et al., 2005; Green and Ritter, 2000; Lexcon and Redding, 2000; Wasserman et al., 2009), an emotional disorder and involvement with the juvenile justice system (Roenblatt et al., 2000), psychiatric disorders prevalent across at-risk youth-caring systems (Garland et al., 2001), substance abuse problems and learning disabilities (National Center on Addiction and Substance Abuse, 2000), maltreatment and delinquency (Center for Juvenile Justice Reform, 2011; Petro, 2008), and combinations of maltreatment, mental health problems, and delinquency (Teplin et al., 2002; Mallett, 2009).

However comorbidity is defined, the various combinations of these disabilities and difficulties have made antecedent or concurrent youth-offending activity and delinquency outcomes very difficult to understand. The complexities of how these difficulties affect children and youth, when and for how long they are experienced, and in what combinations have rarely been investigated. However, when such comorbid phenomena have been studied, difficult and complicated youth and family problems have come to light. In one review of five at-risk youth-caring systems—mental health, child welfare, alcohol and drug, juvenile justice, and public schools—it was found that over 54 percent of all children and youth from all systems met criteria for at least one mental health diagnosis, with attention and disruptive behavior disorders being the most common (Garland et al., 2001). In a separate investigation of delinquent and juvenile court-supervised youth, it was found that 32 percent had an identified special education disability, 39 percent had an identified mental health disorder, 32 percent had an active substance abuse problem, 56 percent had been victims of maltreatment, and over 40 percent had comorbid problems, with higher disability prevalence rates found for youth who were detained or incarcerated (Mallett, 2009). In a similar review of one jurisdiction's mental health system and juvenile court, 20 percent of youth receiving mental health services had a recent arrest record, while 30 percent of youth arrested received mental health services (Rosenblatt et al., 2000). And in a unique study of the mental health problems of youth transferred from the juvenile court to the adult criminal court in Chicago, over 43 percent of the youth had two or more psychiatric diagnoses (Washburn et al., 2008).

Additional investigations have supported linking these disabilities and difficulties. Children served within the community mental health system were three times more likely to be referred to the juvenile courts than youth not receiving community mental health services (Vander-Stoep, et al., 1997); almost 40 percent of youth referred for mental health services had prior juvenile justice system contact (Breda, 1995); and over 44 percent of youth were concurrently receiving community mental health services and were formally involved with the juvenile court (Bryant, Rivard, and Cowan, 1994). The combination of ADHD and conduct disorder greatly increased the likelihood of serious and chronic youthful offending (Barkley, 1996), as did the combination of anxiety or depression and a substance use disorder during adolescence (Frick, 1998). Substance abuse frequently co-occurs with other mental health problems and disorders within the juvenile offender population, with depressive symptoms often comorbid with substance abuse (Neighbors, Kempton, and Forehand, 1992). There are also strong associations between learning disabilities and subsequent struggles with substance abuse in youth (Fox and Forbing, 1991; Kress and Elias,

1993; Pandina, Johnson, and Labouvie, 1992; Weinberg and Glantz, 1999).

Of significant concern are the youth who are seriously emotionally disturbed, identified with multiple mental health disorders and related problems that continue into young adulthood. This group almost always has contact with the juvenile justice system, represents up to 20 percent of youthful offenders within incarceration facilities, and continues to have offending problems and eventual involvement with the adult criminal courts (Cocozza and Skowyra, 2000). It is estimated that one of every ten youth who are seriously emotionally disturbed has both an impairing mental health disorder and an active substance abuse problem—a dual diagnosis which is particularly difficult to address in treatment (Chassin, 2008).

Summary

A majority of youth formally involved in juvenile court have at least one, if not more than one, significant disability or maltreatment experience.   This is particularly true in juvenile detention and incarceration facility populations. These mental health disorders, education-related disabilities, and trauma experiences often have direct correlations to delinquent behaviors. The challenge to stakeholders, though, is addressing youth with multiple and comorbid difficulties, for this group is most at risk for incarceration and involvement with the adult criminal justice system.

3

Primary School–Aged Children

Many of the factors linked with later juvenile court involvement are rooted in childhood, making it critical to investigate this developmental time period. Chapters 3 and 4 should be utilized in tandem, as they are organized to address two separate developmental time periods: first, primary school-age children (ages three to eleven) and then secondary school-age youth (ages twelve to seventeen). However, as is becoming evident, these disabilities and victimizations that are being discussed pose a number of challenges in terms of delinquency prevention. Although Chapter 3 addresses the earlier developmental time frame for children, the information and programming discussed may be equally relevant to secondary school-age youth given the current lack of clarity regarding the onset of many of the issues under review. Additionally, the difficulties encountered first in earlier childhood may very well continue into adolescence, and may be complicated then because of comorbid difficulties. While what is included in Chapter 3 is indeed focused on children, discerning the impact may not be so easily categorized by a developmental timeframe. However, it is widely known that the earlier a difficulty or disability is identified in children, the better the chance that harm can be minimized and outcomes improved; hence, striving to understand onset and occurrence of these matters is important. If the etiology and scope of the problems are fully identified and understood, more effective steps can be taken by policy makers and stakeholders in delinquency prevention.

Onset and Occurrence: Maltreatment Victimization

Federal and subsequent state laws direct the investigation and reporting of certain specific acts defined as maltreatment victimizations: physical abuse, sexual abuse, neglect, and emotional/psychological abuse, the latter being a more recent category established in the 1990s (Wiig,

Spatz-Widom, and Tuell, 2003). Longitudinal data on child and youth maltreatment has been collected by the U.S. Department of Health and Human Services for three decades. In 2008, over 3.3 million reports of abused or neglected children and youth were fielded by children's services protection agencies, with 772,000 of those substantiated. Seventy-one percent of those cases were deemed to be neglect, 16 percent were for physical abuse, 9 percent for sexual abuse, and 7 percent for emotional or psychological abuse (the total is greater than 100 percent due to multiple types of maltreatment in some cases). For three of every four of these children and youth, there was no prior history of maltreatment victimization (U.S. Department of Health and Human Services, 2010). However, it has been strongly hypothesized that investigated and substantiated cases of maltreatment are just the identified portion of a most underreported phenomenon, with some estimates of maltreatment affecting perhaps over eight million of this country's children and youth (Finkelhor et al., 2005).

Victims vary in terms of age, gender, and race. Children younger than eight years old are at higher risk than older children for substantiated cases of any of these maltreatment types, with the highest risk for those younger than one year of age. This may be due to increased time the child spends in the home, higher care needs and subsequent stress, and less involvement with daycare or school. The infant to age twelve child population accounts for approximately three of every four substantiated maltreatment victimization cases; though, youth older than twelve are still at risk, accounting as they do for the remaining 25 percent of cases (National Child Abuse and Neglect Data System, 2010). Looking at rates per 1,000 for subsets of these age groups highlights the greater risk for the youngest children and the decreasing vulnerability as children grow: 21.7 per 1,000 maltreatment victimization were for infants less than one year; 12.4 per 1,000 for two-year-olds; 11.0 per 1,000 for four to seven-year-olds; and 9.2 per 1,000 for eight to eleven-year-olds. Overall, rates of maltreatment victimization are higher for females than for males, but not significantly, making their maltreatment risk fairly equal. However, some minority children, including African-American, American Indian, Alaska Native, and multiracial children, are at higher risk for maltreatment than their Caucasian counterparts (Centers for Disease Control and Prevention, 2010; Magruder and Shaw, 2008; U.S. Department of Health and Human Services, 2010). Why some minority children and youth are overrepresented in maltreatment victimization populations is controversial, with some identifying racial bias as the cause (Sedlak and Broadhurst, 1996), while others find no racial bias but poverty, neighborhood instability, and social context to be explanatory (Coultin et al., 1995; Korbin et al., 1998; Sedlak and Schultz, 2005).

As noted, these maltreatment rates may be under reported; broader reviews and definitions of the trauma experience may be important in identifying the true extent of the problem (Fergusson, Boden, and Horwood, 2008; Finkelhor, 2008; Finkelhor and Wells, 2003). Expanded definitions, including additional trauma measures, may include assaults, harassments, and other direct and indirect witnessing of violene or victimization (Baum, 2005; Dong et al., 2004); all known risk factors for youthful offending and delinquency.

In fact, a representative national survey that used more broadly defined maltreatment categories found increased prevalence for most children and youth, with over 18 percent of the population identified as victims of maltreatment or violence trauma over their lifetime. When sexual victimization definitions were expanded to include harassment as well as assaults, the victimization rate rose to almost 10 percent of the child and youth population. Both physical abuse and emotional abuse (without expanded definitions) were reported by almost 12 percent over their lifetimes. While older children were found to be at higher risk for physical abuse, no gender differences were identified. This finding that older children were at higher risk is counter to the officially identified cases, causing some cause for concern about the underreporting of maltreatment and subsequent harms. Additionally, older children were found to be at higher risk for psychological or emotional abuse, again counter to the officially reported cases, and females were at higher risk for this outcome than males. Of interest were the significantly higher rates reported by the fourteen- to seventeen-year-old age group, youth who may be involved with the juvenile courts and have other related difficulties. Within this older age group, victimization rates over their lifetimes were significantly higher: girls sexual assault rates were over 18 percent, physical abuse rates were almost 19 percent for both boys and girls, and emotional abuse rates were over 22 percent for both boys and girls (Finkelhor, et al., 2009).

Addressing the Problem of Maltreatment Victimization

Significant efforts over the past two decades have focused on designing and evaluating interventions and methods for the prevention and treatment of childhood maltreatment (Child Welfare Information Gateway, 2011; Wiebush et al., 2001) in the hopes of circumventing the pathway from maltreatment to delinquency and serious offending. Clearly the old adage that an ounce of prevention is worth a pound of cure has obvious applicability when applied to both fiscal responsibility and, above all, to children's lives and futures (Mikton and Butchart, 2009).

Early Identification and Assessment

A number of decision-making and assessment instruments and models have been developed to assist the child welfare system in identifying those families most at risk of maltreating their children. Three of these have been found effective. First, the Family Assessment Approach was designed for at-risk families that were not found to have maltreated their children, but who pose high risks for doing so in the future. This assessment approach utilizes family and community resources in devising a strengths-focused plan on eliminating conditions that place a child at risk within the home (Siegel and Loman, 2006). Second, the Structured Decision-Making (SDM) model is a set of assessment tools that identifies key decision points within child protection agency cases and provides interventive directives. These areas of assessment include response priority, safety, risk factors (individual, family, school, and community), and family strengths and needs (Children's Research Center, 1998, 1999; Michigan Family Independence Agency, 1996; Wagner and Bell, 1998; Wiebush et al., 2001). Similarly, the third, the CIVITAS/CCCC Core Assessment focuses on the same domains as the SDM model, including medical needs, family and social areas, life history and traumatic events, behavioral and emotional difficulties, and academic/cognitive challenges, and provides risk and interventive directives (Conrad et al., 1998).

Prevention Approaches

Home Visiting Programs

Home visiting programs, delivered through a multitude of different methods and with various professional providers, share common intervention goals. These goals include providing parents with the following: education, information, access to other services, support, and direct instruction on parenting practices (Brooks-Gunn, Berlin, and Fuligi, 2000; Howard and Brooks-Gunn, 2009). They also share a common perspective that altering parental practices can have long-term benefits for child development, though this may not directly prevent child maltreatment (Kendrick et al., 2000; Sweet and Appelbaum, 2004).

Such in-home programs, often delivered by nurses or related paraprofessional staff, may focus on one primary role or service, or may offer more complete family support services. In some cases the home visitor is focused on being a source of support, while, in other cases, the paraprofessional may serve as an information and referral source or role model to the parents. There are three primary types of home visiting programs, each with a leading program model: the Nurse-Family Partnership (Olds et al., 1986), Healthy Families America (Harding et al., 2006), and Early Head Start (Howard and Brooks-Gunn, 2009).

These three program types differ in service delivery. The Nurse-Family Partnership works primarily with low-income, first-time mothers prenatally up to two years of age, teaching health behaviors and developmentally appropriate skills. Healthy Families America uses trained paraprofessionals from the prenatal period up to five years of age, who provide services such as parenting skills, child development to disadvantaged mothers, and other preventative maltreatment efforts. Early Head Start, a federally funded program, provides both in-home parent training and center-based early care and education, utilizing paraprofessionals and teachers (Bilukha et al., 2005; Howard and Brooks-Gunn, 2009).

These home-visiting programs appear to have a significant impact on reducing a number of child maltreatment risk factors (home environment, maternal parenting, and child development), although, except for a few reviews of the Nurse-Family Partnership model (Olds, 2007; Olds et al., 1997), a direct decrease in reported child maltreatment incidents has not been established (Howard and Brooks-Gunn, 2009; Mikton and Butchart, 2005). However, in addition to these three models of home-visiting programs, the U.S. Department of Health and Human Services has identified two programs that have been found effective in addressing the risk for future child maltreatment. These programs are designed similarly to the Nurse-Family Partnership: the ChildFirst program, which provides a care coordinator to provide assessment, consultation, and intervention services; and the Project 12-Ways/Safecare program, which provides parent training in specific risk areas with specialized staff (U.S. Department of Health and Human Services, 2012). It is important to note that in order to be effective in reducing maltreatment risk, home-visiting programs must be appropriately designed and delivered (Gomby, Culross, and Behrman, 1999; Guterman, 1997). The Nurse-Family Partnership has shown significant returns on investment: for every dollar invested in the program a $3benefit to future costs of maltreatment victimization efforts has been estimated (Aos et al., 2011).

Parent Training/Education Programs

Parents and caregivers are often the perpetrators of children's maltreatment (U.S. Department of Health and Human Services, 2010). Often they lack certain parenting abilities, child-rearing knowledge, or the psychological makeup to be positive caregivers but can improve with intervention and mediation (Belsky, 1984). Education and training programs are often utilized within children's service agencies when supervising parents and their children or when working with parents who are at risk for abusive or neglectful behavior (Dore & Lee, 1999; Sanders, Cann, and Markie-Dadds, 2003). These programs share core foundation curriculum planning that child maltreatment can be reduced if parents modify their attitudes on child rearing, improve skills in working with their children, and rely less on coercive parental techniques. In addition to these foundational foci, the programs may also offer anger management, stress control, emotional management, and even psycho-educational mental health services to parents because provision of such interventions has been found to correlate with decreases in abusive or neglectful parental behaviors (Barth, 2009; Lundahl, Nimer, and Parsons, 2006).

Evidence of the effectiveness of training and education programs for parents is mixed because of differential outcomes and lack of longer-term follow up, though a number of models have shown reductions in child maltreatment incident rates. In one meta-analysis of twenty-three programs, measuring a wide variety of outcome variables, an impact on reported attitude and child-rearing behaviors by the parents was identified immediately following parent training and education program completion (Lundahl et al., 2006). Unfortunately, the number of programs that were evaluated and measured the direct impact on child maltreatment incidents is limited (Barth et al., 1983; Gershater-Molko, Lutzker, & Welsch, 2002), and additional evaluation is required to ascertain these programs' effectiveness. Moreover, when programs try to address a wide array of maltreatment risk factors the impact on maltreatment reduction is often diluted or negligible (Klevens and Whittaker, 2007).

Within the parent training and education programs, a number of effective components have been identified: early intervention, clearly articulated model or program, strong theory base, interventions with multiple components (e.g., group work, individual sessions, and office-based and in-home programming), and longer duration with follow up (Moran, Ghate, and Van Der Merwe, 2004; Thomas and Zimmer-Gembeck, 2011). Also, a number of programs have shown effectiveness with reducing maltreatment risk and offer a variety of intervention techniques. The Family Connections program works with at-risk parents and grandparents to prevent maltreatment by using in-home training and service provider coordination (DePanfilis, Dubowitz, and Kunz, 2008). The Triple P (Positive Parenting Program), based on social learning theory, incorporates various intervention techniques and five levels of intervention: (1) a media campaign to inform and identify parents, (2) specific topic training, (3) childhood development and behavior problem programming, (4) serious child behavior and mental health problem programming, and (5) significant family dysfunction focus and work (Daro and Dodge, 2009; Sanders, et al. 2003a; Sanders, Cann, and Markie-Dadds, 2003b). Parent-Child Interaction Therapy, also based on social learning theory, teaches and coaches parenting behavior-management techniques to regulate parents' own emotions, maintain limits in parenting, and work with disruptive children (Timmer et al., 2005). The Incredible Years Program utilizes specific behavioral techniques and sequential learning steps in different settings with parents and children to improve strength-based skill building (Wulczyn, Webb, and Haskins, 2007). Two of these programs - Triple P and Incredible Years - have also been assessed as to their cost/benefit impacts. The Triple P was found to return between $4 and $10 dollars for every dollar invested, and the Incredible Years Program to return $4 dollars for every dollar invested (Aos, et al., 2011).

Family/Parent Support Groups

Family and parent support group programs, of which there are a variety of types, have gained increased recognition in the prevention and treatment of child and youth maltreatment (Falconer et al., 2008; Thomas et al., 2003). They address a number of key risk factors identified primarily with neglect and physical abuse of children (Leventhal, 2005). Family support groups provide formal peer-supported and facilitator-led programming, and typically meet on a regular, often weekly, basis. These groups also support the formation of informal networks among parents and family members involved, through which to augment and continue the preventative efforts begun in the program (Stagner and Lansing, 2009). These formal and informal groups try to improve communication within the families, as well as in parent-child interactions, and to reduce related negative behaviors (Dunst, 1995).

Some of these programs are affiliated with child care centers or formal programs, such as Head Start or Early Head Start, and show promise in improving parents' attitudes and behaviors in interactions with their children (Daro and McCurdy, 2007). In particular, the Strengthening Families Initiative builds upon existing child care centers and early intervention programs to help families avoid contact with the child welfare system (Casey Family Programs, 2001). A number of evaluations have found that group-based parental support and education programs were more effective for some families than were home-visiting services (Layzer and Goodson, 2001). Others have found some encouraging evidence that parental functioning improves in highly structured and led groups (Falconer et al., 2008). Groups modeled on the Alcohol Anonymous twelve-step model (Parents Anonymous groups) showed improvement by all parents, but, in particular, with those parents who were at high risk for perpetrating child maltreatment (Polinsky et al., 2010). Though the evidence is encouraging, ongoing and rigorous reviews are important to ascertain the overall effectiveness of these widely used preventative and interventive groups (Barth et al., 2005; Kaminski et al., 2008).

Substance Abuse and Dependence: Parents

Substance abuse, dependence, and addiction are a significant problem for many families involved with child protection service agencies. While the definitions of substance use problems vary across epidemiological reviews (Testa and Smith, 2009), when using the most narrow, specific diagnosis (substance abuse disorder), between 11 and 14 percent of parents/caregivers investigated for child maltreatment had substance abuse problems, increasing to 18 to 24 percent among substantiated cases (Semidei, Radel, and Nolan, 2001; Sun et al., 2001). The prevalence of parental/caregiver substance abuse was found to be more than twice as likely for children and youth who were placed into foster care (Besinger et al., 1999; Famular, Kinscherff, and Fenton, 1992; McNichol and Tash, 2001; Smith and Testa, 2002; U.S. General Accounting Office, 1998).

Parent and caregiver substance abuse problems have often been linked to neglect of children, and families with substance abuse problems face between a three and four times higher risk for maltreatment (Chaffin, Kelleher, and Hollenberg, 1996; Kelleher et al., 1994; Magura and Laudet, 1996). However, often these families face additional challenges and risks beyond substance abuse, with significant comorbid problems with housing, domestic violence, low education attainment, and/or mental health (Marsh et al., 2006; Tracy, 1994). Two key concerns challenge the child welfare system regarding parental substance abuse and dependence. First, not many parents are accurately identified as substance abusing or dependent; and, second, when the problem is identified, successful connection of parents to treatment often falls short of preventing maltreatment recidivism due to substance abuse (Drake, Johnson-Reid, and Sapokaite, 2006; Guo, Barth, and Gibbons, 2006; Littell and Tajima, 2000; Rittner and Davenport-Dozier, 2000). Improved integration of parent and caregiver treatment with child welfare involvement is essential for children and youth at risk for maltreatment, and in particular to prevent maltreatment recurrence. Once these improvements occur, effective substance abuse treatments and relapse prevention must be closely monitored during children's services supervision, including through long-term follow-up procedures.

Child Sex Abuse Prevention Programs

Reported and identified sexual abuse of children has decreased over the past two decades by over 50 percent (Finkelhor, 2008). Explanations for this include improved public recognition and awareness of the problem, the impact of federal and state laws mandating how to manage known sex offenders, or the impact of education and intervention strategies (LaFond, 2005; Velazquez, 2008; Zwi, 2007). The challenge in continuing this trend of identifying and decreasing sexual abuse victimization is the lack of clear evidence behind any one strategy showing any one strategy directly improves outcomes (Finkelhor, 2009). It is unknown which one of these, or combination of these, prevention and intervention efforts might be the best recommendations.

Public concern and media attention have prompted legislation in state houses and Congress alike, including increased sexual offender registration, community notification of sexual offender residences, residency restrictions around children and schools, longer criminal sentences, and civil commitments that also lengthen incarceration sentences. Yet evidence is insufficient to fully gauge such legislation's impact (Conklin, 2003; Duwe & Donnay, 2008; Loving, Singer, & Maguire, 2008; Prescott and Rockoff, 2008; Vasquez, Maddan, and Walker, 2008). Some of these enforcement and supervision strategies look to be counterproductive and illogical. For example, requiring residency restrictions for a convicted sex offender only targets a small percentage of offenders. Considering that most abusers are probably never caught or identified, and when identified, a majority of them are a family member or family friend, these efforts may be misguided or provide a false sense of security to the public (Bolen, 2001; Finkelhor, 2009; Snyder, 2000).

Other efforts to reduce sexual abuse have included treatment of offenders, both adults and juveniles, as well as education and training programs for children to increase their awareness and self protection against predation. At this point, mental health treatment has been shown to have some limited impact with adult offender and significant impact with juvenile offenders (Finkelhor, 2009; Hanson et al., 2002). It should be noted that one-third of identified sexual offenders are juveniles, often delinquent youth who are developmentally immature in these actions or exploring behaviors inappropriately with other teenagers or children (Hunter, 2009). This may explain why the treatment outcomes appear to be much better for the juvenile sexual offender population. Alternatively, education and training programs for children, which aim to increase their awareness and protective reactions, have demonstrated success and warrant continued investigations, though it is unclear if future victimization is decreased (Finkelhor, Asdigian, and Dziuba-Leatherman, 1995; Zwi, 2007).

Public Education and Information

Public awareness activities may be important in promoting positive parenting and decreasing maltreatment victimizations, at least in terms of increasing the reporting of these childhood maltreatment acts. Through the use of a variety of media outlets, such as public service announcements, press releases, information brochures, and television/radio documentaries, initiatives can be highlighted that not only promote positive parenting and improve child safety but also share protocols for reporting suspected victimizations. Examples of these efforts include the prevention of shaken baby syndrome, the Stop It Now Program, and the Prevent Child Abuse America efforts (Cohn, 1997; Kaufman, 2010; Thomas, et al., 2003).

Programs for Maltreatment Victims

There are two categories of maltreatment victims: those identified and supervised by child protection agencies and those whose victimizations are unknown or hidden. Researchers speculate that a majority of maltreatment victims remain unidentified or unknown, which leaves them vulnerable to continuing maltreatment and its short- and long-term effects (Finkelhor, et al., 2005). For those children and youth identified and supervised by child protection agencies, a variety of measures or interventions are utilized during this supervision timeframe. These include the initial safety measures and decision making required to keep the child safe from further victimization, and, if harmful maltreatment effects are apparent, then programming measures are also initiated. Interventions vary according to the victimization type or effects and may include individual or family counseling/therapy with a wide array of intervention techniques, such as, for example, play, behavioral, or psycho-dynamic therapies (Stagner and Lansing, 2009). These interventions are aimed at short-term impact and stabilization of crisis situations, and are important in addressing such difficulties as childhood traumatic stress reactions, attention and focus problems, immediate school issues, and other related childhood concerns. In particular, finding safe environments for the victims to reside and recover is paramount, but additional opportunities for children to recover from the trauma are often necessary (Koball et al., 2011; Thomas et al., 2003).

Elements of effective programs for children and youth with maltreatment and delinquency risks have been identified. These recommended components include the following: thorough individualized assessment, including risk and protective factors; addressing the entire context of child/youth and family functioning; provision of parental supports and parenting education; a focus on improving the parent-child interaction; involving a multimodal intervention approach; utilization of community supports as available; emphasis on behavior skills development; coordination and integration with school, juvenile court, child welfare, and mental health systems; and a focus on long-term outcomes, including follow-up and relapse prevention (Wiig, Spatz-Widom, and Tuell, 2003).

However, as reviewed earlier, for many victims, both identified and not identified, maltreatment effects often span broad areas of functioning and may be long term in impact (Hawkins et al., 2000). Such victimizations often lead to mental health problems (trauma, anxiety, depression, and stress-related issues), increased risk for substance abuse and dependence for adolescents, difficult home situations and increased run away incidents, poorer school performance during both primary and secondary school, high risk of school failure, and increased risk of a number of special education disabilities (both learning and emotional problems) (Chesney-Link, 2003; Kilpatrick et al., 2003; Leiter, 2007; Mallett, 2011b; Scarborough and McCrae, 2009; Slade and Wissow, 2007). Addressing these difficulties, while utilizing additional preventative and interventive programming, is dependent on when the symptoms or difficulties occur and which at-risk child and youth-caring system or support is available. These various systems (child welfare, mental health, schools, and juvenile courts) are reviewed and discussed in later chapters.

Onset and Occurrence: Learning Disabilities

Children with learning disabilities are not normally identified until
school age, whereby federal and state law requires public and private
school systems to address these learning disabilities (Herr and Forness,
2003; Mears and Aron, 2003). A key reason for not identifying children
with learning disabilities before the age of seven is because the
diagnosis requires a history of neurological impairment to be known and
documented (Harrison, 2005; Streiner, 2003). However, most learning
disabilities are identified by the end of primary school, both because
earlier identification has led to service provision for the majority of
children with learning disabilities and fewer resources utilized in
identifying these disabilities within the older youth age group (Mears
and Aron, 2003). The U.S. Department of Education reports on school-
age children and youth from six to twenty-one found that the number of
learning disabilities identified over the past two decades has remained
stable at approximately 4 percent of the child and youth population (U.S.
Department of Education, 2009). Interestingly, the number of minority
children and youth identified with learning disabilities has increased
over this same time period, though the reasons for this remain unclear
(Gamm, 2008; Reschley, 2002).

Children who are older, either who enter primary school at an older
age than their peers because of birth date month or who are older by
grade level, are less likely to be evaluated for a learning disability
(Dhuey and Lipscomb, 2010). However, there is little to no correlation
of family socioeconomic status with the likelihood for disability
evaluation (Elder and Lubotsky, 2009). Once chosen for evaluation,
though, older children are as likely as younger children to be diagnosed
with a learning disability (Dhuey and Lipscomb, 2010). Because of
these trends, there is a higher percentage of youth than children who are
diagnosed with a learning disability during any given year. Within the
school-aged child and youth population learning disabilities are more
prevalent among the older youth: while the six to eleven-year-old group
has a learning disability prevalence rate of 7 percent, and the twelve- to
seventeen-year-old age group has a learning disability prevalence rate of
10 percent (Pastor and Reuben, 2008).

More specifically, in the most recent reporting year (2007), the
following rates represent the percentage of school-aged children and
youth who were identified with learning disabilities and received
services to address these difficulties (see Table 3.1):

Table 3.1 Child and Youth Identified with Learning Disabilities and Receiving Services

Age	Learning Disability Identified, 2007 (%)
6	< 1
7	2.5
8	4.8
9	6.9
10	8.5
11	9.5
12	10.1
13	10.5
14	10.8
15	10.9
16	10.3
17	8.9
18	8.9

Source: U.S. Department of Education (2010). Digest of education statistics, 2009. National Center for Education Statistics, Washington D.C.

Aggregated by age group, the categories include: ages three to five, 10.3 percent; ages six to eleven, 40.9 percent; ages twelve to seventeen, 44.3 percent; and ages eighteen to twenty-one, 4.6 percent (U.S. Department of Education, 2010). Under current federal law, learning disability services, which include primarily transitional, vocational, and educational support, are provided through age twenty-one (Mallett, 2011b).

Addressing the Problem of Learning Disabilities

It is vital to identify children with learning disabilities, for without knowing the problem exists, no services or programming efforts can be pursued. Schools districts are obligated by federal law to locate and evaluate all children who may have a learning or other special education disability (Mallett, 2011b). Children, those identified and those not identified by the school districts, with learning disabilities are at high risk to fall significantly behind in reading and writing skills, deficiencies that are often not improved upon in secondary school and that often lead to other education-related problems (deBettencourt and Zigmond, 1990; Jenkins and O-Connor, 2002; Shaywitz et al., 1999; Zigmund, 1990).

Children with learning disabilities are also at higher risk for classroom and academic difficulties. Children who underachieve in the classroom, who are behind in reading and writing abilities, and who are placed into remedial classrooms are at higher risk for secondary school failure and school dropout, deviant peer friendships, and serious offending behaviors (Jenkins and O'Connor, 2002; Mears and Aron, 2003; Patterson, DeBaryshe, and Ramsey, 1989). However, these potentially harmful outcomes are not inevitable, for some children and youth are resilient or find ways to cope with learning problems and impairments, sometimes with little to no assistance (Hamilton & Browne, 1998). Yet for many children who suffer from the comorbidity of learning disabilities linked to earlier maltreatment victimization, the challenges are significant in recovering from the victimization and its potential academic and social repercussions, in combination with learning problems (Veltman and Browne, 2001).

Though children do not typically outgrow learning disabilities because they are often developmentally related, ways exist to ameliorate and address many of the difficulties that affect the child's school and academic abilities (Hamre and Pianta, 2005; Semrud-Clikeman and Schafer, 2000). There is strong evidence that a number of school-based teaching programs help students who are behind in academic performance or at risk of failing a grade, as are many children with reading problems and/or learning disabilities. The first area is the classroom setting and interactions between teachers and children, when teachers gain knowledge of how to offer effective instruction that can ameliorate a number of these risks (National Institute of Child Health and Human Development, 2003; Pianta et al., 2002). The second area includes school-based interventions that address related learning disability risk factors for these students (Greenberg et al., 2003; Wilson, Gottfredson, and Najaka, 2001). An example of an effective in-class literacy intervention is Read 180. This program combines individual and small-group direct instruction along with computer-based intervention to improve reading abilities, with widely implemented successful results (Institute of Education Services, 2009). Programs that are offered during non-school hours (after school and summer) have also shown success in improving reading and learning results, with a number of important components found necessary in the interventions: quality staffing, access to and sustained child/youth participation, and strong partnerships with families, schools, and related community stakeholders (Harvard Family Research Project, 2008; Lauer et al., 2006).

Children with learning disabilities may significantly benefit from either in-class or out-of-the-classroom tutoring and instruction. These tutoring program models may be highly or minimally structured, and may use professional or volunteer tutors (Fashola, 2001). A review of twenty-eight non-professional volunteer tutor programs (all studies used a comparison group with a one-month tutoring duration minimum) for school-aged children (K-8) found positive impacts on reading and language outcomes; specifically oral fluency, overall reading, writing, and letter and word identification improved. There were no significant differences between volunteer tutor type, grade level, or program focus (Ritter et al., 2007).

Reviews of tutoring programs that used certified teachers (professionally trained) are less definitive, although the reviews show a growing evidence base. In one review of five tutoring programs, including both professional and non-professional tutors, the reading improvements for children were significant (Wasik and Slavin, 1990). A meta-analysis of twenty-nine tutoring programs that included both adult non-professional and adult trained-professional volunteers also demonstrated that these programs were effective at improving reading abilities for elementary school children (Elbaum et al., 2000). Additionally, the Reading Recovery tutoring model has been found effective in improving participants' alphabetic skills and general reading achievement outcomes. This model uses certified teachers, takes place during the school day, and is designed for the lowest 20 percent achieving first-grade students, with the tutoring discontinued when the student consistently reads at the grade-level average, normally between twelve and twenty weeks (U.S. Department of Education, 2010).

Onset and Occurrence: Mental Health Disorders

Over the past three decades, but particularly since the early 1990s, there have been significant epidemiological studies of child and youth mental health problems; prior to this time knowledge was scant about the occurrence of these difficulties. While these reviews include no national survey of child and youth mental health problems in the United States (though these have been completed in Britain and Canada), there have been enough reviews, including over 40,000 child and youth observations, from which to extrapolate the prevalence and epidemiology findings to the population (Costello, et al., 2004; Costello, Egger, and Angold, 2005a).

Between 3 and 20 percent of children have an identified psychiatric disorder that impairs their functioning at a moderate to significant degree (Reddy et al., 2008). Disruptive disorders are some of the most commonly identified problems with eighteen percent prevalence rates; this includes lower rates in younger children, more often oppositional defiant disorder, and higher rates for older primary school-age children, more often conduct disorder (Almqvist et al., 1999; Costello et al., 1996; Narrow et al., 1998; Nock et al., 2007). Conduct disorder is characterized by persistent violation of age-appropriate societal rules, a disregard for others' rights, violation of expected behavioral expectations, and persistence of these behaviors for a minimum of six months (American Psychiatric Association, 2000; Goldstein, et al., 2005). ADHD has the opposite prevalence trends, with almost all diagnoses made prior to the age of twelve, though for many children the difficulties continue into the secondary school age period and even beyond. All three of these disorders—conduct, oppositional defiant, and ADHD—are significantly more common in boys than girls (Debar et al., 2001; Fombonne et al., 2001; Gomez-Beneyto et al., 1994; Sawyer et al., 2002).

Major depression is not common for children twelve years old and younger, accounting for less than 2 percent of all cases. However, depression rates rise dramatically within the secondary school-age population, and impacts between 4 and 5 percent of this group (Costello et al., 2002; Fergusson & Horwood, 2001; Giaconia et al., 1994; Kroes et al., 2001; Simonoff et al., 1997). Depressive disorders, including major depression, have been found to be more prevalent within Caucasian youth populations than African-American youth populations (Angold et al., 2002).

However, anxiety disorders, affecting between 1 and 3 percent of the child and youth population, differ in that they impact both the primary and secondary school-age populations equally, though with different diagnoses for each group. Separation anxiety and some related anxiety difficulties are more often found in primary school-age children, while panic disorder, agoraphobia, social phobia, overanxious disorder, and generalized anxiety disorder are more often found within secondary school-age youth. Girls are slightly more often diagnosed with certain anxiety difficulties, primarily post-traumatic stress disorder and obsessive-compulsive disorder (Costello et al., 1996; Heyman et al., 2001; Meltzer, Gatward, and Goodman, 1999; Merikangas, 2005; Rappaport et al., 2000; Verhulst et al., 1997).

Comorbidity, the concurrent prevalence of more than one difficulty, and in this case more than one mental health disorder, is discouragingly common for children and youth. The presence of one mental health disorder may often increase the risk for other mental health difficulties, making the impact on the child or youth more difficult to deal with, and for professionals to address (Angold, et al., 2002). A number of mental health disorders are often found to be comorbid for this population: ADHD with conduct disorder - in one review 30 to 50 percent of children with an ADHD diagnosis also received a conduct disorder diagnosis (Lexcen and Redding, 2000); ADHD with anxiety disorders; ADHD with depression (a surprising combination, considering the symptoms); conduct disorder with depression, and/or anxiety disorders; and depression with anxiety disorders (Costello et al., 2004; Giaconia et al., 1994; Siminoff, et al., 1997; Verhulst et al., 1997). Considering that ADHD is most commonly identified in younger primary school children, and many of these symptoms and difficulties lasts into secondary school, this disorder's comorbidity with other disruptive disorders can pose significant risks for later school and community-related problems (Cocozza and Skowyra, 2000).

Addressing the Problem of Mental Health Disorders

Attention-deficit Hyperactivity Disorder

ADHD is characterized by symptoms of hyperactivity, inattention, and/or impulsivity that impair in a number of functioning areas: at home, at school, or in the community (American Psychiatric Association, 2000). More specifically, symptoms include child disorganization, impulsivity, hyperactivity, and attention problems (Lexcen and Redding, 2000). There are three primary subtypes with corresponding focal symptoms: inattentive, hyperactive-impulsive, and combined. Children with primarily inattention symptoms may be easily distracted, forget things, have difficulty focusing on one thing, become bored quickly with uninteresting tasks, have trouble completing school work, appear not to listen when spoken to, have difficulty quickly processing information, and struggle to follow directions. Children with hyperactivity may talk nonstop, fidget constantly, have trouble sitting during school or home activities, be in motion at all times, and have difficulty with quiet tasks. Children with impulsivity may be impatient, act without regard to consequences, show emotions without restraint, have trouble waiting, and may often interrupt others' activities (Howe, 2009; National Institute of Mental Health, 2008).

A number of intervention modalities, across many domains, have been identified as useful or effective in treating or managing symptoms of ADHD. Psychosocial interventions include classroom-based behavior modification, social skills training, and cognitive-behavioral skills training, as well as home-based/parent training, with varying degrees of success (Wierson, et al., 1992).

Behaviorally-focused efforts aim to help a child change targeted behaviors and may include organizing tasks, completing school work, or managing and monitoring his or her own behaviors or emotions (National Institute of Mental Health, 2008). Medication has also been widely prescribed to address the difficult and bothersome symptoms of ADHD, including antidepressants and stimulants, but also more powerful psychiatric drugs including neuroleptics and adrenergic agonists (Brown and LaRosa, 2002; Conners, 2002; Steingard et al., 1993). Medications do not cure ADHD, but control the symptoms, and in some reviews show short-term effectiveness in up to 75 percent of cases, though these medications should be closely monitored for impact and side effects. Often the use of medications conjointly with behavioral therapy, counseling, and/or academic supports may be most effective (Connors et al., 2001; MTA Cooperative Group, 1999). This combination of interventions may be important because medication alone does not significantly improve upwards of 30 percent of children's ADHD symptoms nor does it impact many children's long-term symptoms (Barkley, 1990).

Anxiety Disorders

Many children respond to a number of interventions that assist in decreasing or managing their anxiety symptoms and disorders, though segments of this population are still unresponsive and continue to struggle with these problems into adolescence, even after intervention (Muris and Broeren, 2009). Many outcome studies on a range of interventions used to address anxiety problem symptoms in children report two with the greatest impact: cognitive-behavioral therapy and pharmacotherapy. The evidence, though, is stronger for the effective impact of cognitive-behavioral therapy versus pharmacotherapy; thus, this should be utilized as an initial treatment. In fact, in many reviews child-focused cognitive-behavioral therapy has reduced anxiety in a majority of children (Barrett, Dadds, and Rapee, 1996; Podell and Kendall, 2011; Walkup, Albano, Piacentini, Birmaher, Compton, Sherrill, et al., 2008). When children do not respond well to these initial efforts, then pharmacotherapy, in particular Selective Serontonin Reuptake Inhibitors (SSRIs), can be recommended in addition to cognitive behavioral therapy. It should be cautioned, though, that while this combination of interventions improves the symptoms in the short term, there are side effects and tolerance buildup, often in reaction to the pharmacotherapy regimen (American Academy of Child and Adolescent Psychiatry, 1997; Barrett, 1998; Birmaher et al., 2003; RUPP Anxiety Group, 2001).

A variety of behavioral and cognitive-behavioral therapies incorporate components that have found to be effective in working with children with anxiety disorders (Salloum et al., 2009). These components include exposure therapy (including systematic desensitization), cognitive restructuring, psycho-education on anxiety and its effects, contingent reinforcement, and modeling (Amaya-Jackson and DeRosa, 2007; Barrett, et al., 1996; Chambless and Olleneick, 2001; Kendall and Suveg, 2006; Wade, Treat, and Stuart, 1998). Through the use of these components, children learn to recognize anxious feelings and reactions to anxiety, develop a coping plan for these situations, clarify cognitions in anxious situations, and reinforce these new skills and behaviors (Suveg et al., 2006).

Behaviorally-based Disorders

Parent management training, also called parent training and family training, has been found effective in working with children who have behaviorally-based and/or aggression problems, and particularly demonstrates short-term improvements in the development of pro-social behaviors and in minimizing maladaptive behaviors. Parent management training involves teaching parents how to respond consistently and more positively to their children while changing maladaptive interaction habits within the relationship that lead to continued aggressive or antisocial behaviors. In doing so, this training, based on social learning theory, utilizes operant conditioning procedures to reduce these problem areas (Bernazzani and Tremblay, 2006; Farrington and Welsh, 2003; Froehlick, Doepfner, and Lekmkuhl, 2002; Kazdin and Weisz, 1998; Mape, Turner, and Josephson, 2001). It is important to provide interventions as early as possible because of the increased chance of stemming behavioral disorders and minimizing later intransigence of any adverse behaviors (Mears and Aron, 2003; Robins, 1978). In one review, parent management training was found to significantly decrease recidivating behavior problems in younger children by 50 percent, compared to children whose parents' lacked such training. The latter had only a 33 percent decrease (Piquero, Farrington, Welsh, Tremblay, and Jennings, 2008).

A related parent management training program type, sometimes called behavioral parent training, is also based in social learning theory but has a stronger focus on behavioral management. In this, the emphasis is on the importance of observing and modeling the behaviors and attitudes of others to help the child with behavior problems. Here the programs teach broad behavioral principles for producing and reinforcing positive child behaviors which can be adapted in the home environment through the use of rehearsing and coaching (Dretzke et al., 2004). Reviews of these programs have found them of high quality and effectiveness in decreasing children's behavior problems (Barlow and Parsons, 2002; Richardson and Joughin, 2002; Serketich and Dumas, 2006). Further, a number of meta-analyses supported these findings, with results showing effectiveness of behavioral parent training programs in a number of areas: working with children with conduct disorders (Gould and Richardson, 2006); improving overall child and parent functioning levels, in particular with older children (ages nine to eleven) (Serketick and Duman, 1996); in terms of decreasing classroom disruptions (Stage and Quiroz, 1997; Wilson, Lipsey, and Derzon, 2003); and modifying behavior problems (Maughan et al., 2005).

Because children with behaviorally-based disorders and problems often struggle in the home, school environments, and community, programs or interventions addressing multiple locations may be necessary. Interventions that focus on behavioral and cognitive behavioral orientation treatment when working with children with behavioral problems and emotional disturbances have been found to have positive impacts (Beard and Sugai, 2004; Robinson and Rapport, 2002). Interventions include behavioral therapy, individualized therapy, social skills training, medication, and art/play therapy, with the social skills training and token economies (a behavioral approach) being two of the more common (Reddy et al., 2008). In particular, the Promoting Alternative Thinking Strategies (PATHS) Curriculum is an effective school-based, multi-year program that decreases aggressive behaviors through teaching children developmentally-based lessons and instructions on emotional literacy, self-control, interpersonal problem-solving skills, and positive peer relations (Greenberg, Kusche, and Mihalic, 2006).

Summary

The earlier and more effectively these risks, difficulties, and disabilities are addressed, the less chance youth have for later juvenile court involvement. As reviewed in this chapter, identifying childhood maltreatment is the first step to efficiently addressing the potential harmful impacts of this victimization. If maltreatment is prevented then subsequent mental health, school, peer, and related problems are avoided (Weibush, et al., 2001). If special education disabilities and particularly learning disabilities are identified and addressed early, many later school difficulties and failures may be averted (Keleher, 2000). If serious mental health problems and substance abuse disorders are identified early and addressed in either the school or home environment, risks for youthful offending behaviors may be greatly reduced (Cocozza and Skowyra, 2000; MacKinnon-Lewis et al., 2002).

Most of these difficulties can be identified during childhood, because many of these problems manifest symptoms during this developmental time period. If not addressed, often one problem that was manageable at this earlier age may lead to additional or related comorbid problems, making interventions or delinquency prevention efforts more difficult and/or less effective (Mears and Aron, 2003). It is widely acknowledged that, as the number of difficulties increases for children and families, these risk factors and problems become cumulative and harmful outcomes snowball, including delinquent activities and formal juvenile court involvement (Chassin, 2008; Child Welfare Information Gateway, 2011; Howell, 2003; Teplin, et al., 2006; Weinberg and Glantz, 1999).

4

Secondary School–Aged Youth

Chapters 3 and 4 should be utilized in tandem, as they are organized to address two separate developmental time periods: first, primary school-age children (ages three to eleven) and, then, secondary school-age youth (ages twelve to seventeen). However, as is becoming evident, these difficulties that are linked to delinquency and incarceration pose a number of challenges in identification, onset, and eventually prevention and treatment. Although Chapter 3 addressed an earlier developmental time frame, the information and programming discussed there is also relevant in this chapter because the onset of disabilities in question is often unclear. Chapter 4 focuses on older children and youth in middle and high school, though their difficulties may well have occurred or impacted the individual at a younger age, but may not have come to the attention of a youth-caring system until secondary school. So although these chapters are thus organized by time period, discerning the impact of these disabilities and maltreatment victimizations may not be so easily categorized.

Onset and Occurrence: Maltreatment Victimization

Adolescents account for nearly one of every four substantiated child and adolescent abuse and neglect cases, with some minority groups - African-American, American Indian, Alaska Native, and multiracial youth - at higher risk for maltreatment victimization (National Child Abuse and Neglect Data System, 2010). While this age group, compared to children, consists of a smaller percentage of the abuse and neglect victims, they are at greater risk, than children, for psychological or emotional abuse because of these maltreatment experiences, with girls at especially high risk (Centers for Disease Control and Prevention, 2010; U.S. Department of Health and Human Services, 2010). When maltreatment definitions are expanded beyond the publically identified abuse and neglect cases to include additional trauma experiences, such as violence, assaults, and witnessing these events, adolescents aged fourteen to seventeen have been found to have significantly higher lifetime prevalence rates of these problems: emotional abuse rates of over 18 percent and physical abuse rates of over 19 percent (Finkelhor, et al., 2009). These cumulative maltreatment rates are often found to be comorbid with other difficulties (Mallett, 2009).

Addressing the Problem of Youth Maltreatment Victimization

Identification and Assessment

During later childhood and adolescence although fewer reported maltreatment victimizations are identified, trauma experiences tend to be more extreme, including such experiences as violence, witnessing violence, and related crime victimizations (National Child Abuse and Neglect Data System, 2010). Identifying these maltreated youth is imperative because their risk of harmful outcomes, including serious offending behaviors, is greater at this crucial developmental juncture (Hawkins et al., 2000). Of significant concern, and public policy attention, is the issue of youth who are involved concurrently with child service protection agencies and with the juvenile courts. Youth so involved are increasingly labeled dually-involved, dually-adjudicated, or crossover youth (Halemba et al., 2004; Petro, 2006). These youth are often transferred between the courts and child service protection agencies for supervision or adjudication issues. As previously mentioned, youth who have been maltreated and involved with child service protection agencies are at a heightened risk for later offending behaviors and subsequent formal juvenile court involvement, making dual adjudication more likely (Center for Juvenile Justice Reform, 2011), but the connection is bi-directional, with some jurisdictions finding that 10 percent of youth who left the juvenile justice system entered the foster care system after their release (Cusick, Goerge, and Bell, 2009).

Dually-adjudicated youth are more likely to be minorities, primarily African-American, and female when compared to the formally-involved juvenile court population. Most have been placed out of the home, and a smaller subset has experienced numerous out-of-home placements over time. They often perform poorly in school, have high absenteeism rates, and are more likely than their non-dually involved peers to be held in juvenile court detention facilities (Halemba et al., 2004; Herz and Ryan, 2008; Ryan, et al., 2007).

Substance Abuse and Dependence: Parents

Parental substance abuse is common among youth who are maltreatment victims. Between 11 and 24 percent of investigated and substantiated maltreatment cases stem from parents' substance abuse (Semidei et al., 2001; Sun et al., 2001). Older maltreated youth are more likely than younger maltreated children to spend time in a foster care placement, an outcome that is more than twice as likely linked to parent or caregiver substance abuse or dependence problems when compared to parents or caregivers who are maltreating their children but are not abusing substances (Besinger et al., 1999; McNichol and Tash, 2001; Smith and Testa, 2002; U.S. General Accounting Office, 1998). Neglect is more likely than other forms of maltreatment when parents or caregivers are substance abusers (Chaffin, Kelleher, and Hollenberg, 1996; Magura and Laudet, 1996). In addition, parents and caregivers with substance abuse problems often have other risk factors for perpetrating maltreatment, including housing instability, domestic violence situations, and/or mental health disorders (Marsh et al., 2006; Tracy, 1994).

An effective approach to parental substance abuse is in involving the family in treatment. One intervention for families with teenage youth, the Strengthening Families Program, has been found to have a significant impact on decreasing parents' alcohol and drug use (Kumpfer et al., 2010). This program utilizes cognitive-behavioral, social learning, and/or family systems theory in involving the whole family with parent and youth skills training. Components that have been found effective across many similarly situated family strengthening interventions (Kaminski et al., 2008; Kumpfer, Alvarado, and Whiteside, 2003).

Treatment Foster Care

Treatment foster care is a more intense and structured foster care setting that is designed for children and youth with more serious adjustment difficulties within their home, school, and community environments. One type of treatment foster care is the Multidimensional Treatment Foster Care program, a foster family-based intervention that provides youth with programming designed to improve functioning and school outcomes, decrease mental health and behavioral difficulties, and avoid placement recidivism to residential care and/or juvenile court facilities

(Casey Family Programs, 1994; Chamberlain, Leve, and DeGarmo, 2007). This program was designed specifically to address the problems of youth at high risk for residential, out-of-home care through a long-term, intensely supervised foster home placement utilizing close supervision and predictable environments (Chamberlain, 1998; Clark et al., 1993; Foster Family-based Treatment Association, 2004). The foster care parents are carefully trained and supervised to provide these placements and are the primary providers of interactive treatment. The foster homes utilize behavior management systems, a therapeutic and highly structured environment, and coordinated efforts across other youth-caring systems, including schools, mental health agencies, and others as needed (Chamberlain, 1998, 2003). Most often the youth placed into these foster homes are maltreatment victims who also experience subsequent severe mental health and/or antisocial behavioral problems, often leading to juvenile court involvement (Davis, Foster, and Whitworth 1984; Webb, 1988).

Treatment foster care is less costly than comparable residential facility placements and often than juvenile court detention or incarceration facility placements (Almeida et al., 1989; Chamberlain, 1990). These placements may be most effective with the twelve- to eighteen-year-old age group (Hahn et al., 2004). Outcomes that have found significant improvement for involved youth include more positive behaviors, increased social skills, and more positive psychological adjustment (Reddy and Pfeiffer, 1997). Though the impact appears significant for many youth in these programs, reviews and evaluations thus far are too few in number and have varied too greatly in design to allow any broad generalizations, though ongoing efforts should be pursued with optimism (MacDonald and Turner, 2007). Evidence is increasingly finding that treatment foster care is significantly effective for youthful offenders in decreasing their violent activities, felony convictions, and incarceration placements. The intense collaboration between child welfare, juvenile courts, and treatment agencies has been identified as a key program component to decreasing delinquency and recidivist outcomes in a cost-effective manner (Chamberlain, 1998; Hahn et al., 2005). In a number of evaluations, treatment foster care produced between $5 and $14 dollars in taxpayer savings for every dollar spent on the program (Aos et al., 1999; Aos, et al., 2011).

Onset and Occurrence: Special Education, Learning Disabilities

Learning disabilities are more prevalent in older youth populations, with 10 percent of the twelve- to seventeen-year-old age group identified, compared to only 7 percent of the younger than twelve age group (Pastor and Reuben, 2008). As identified earlier (see Table 3.1), those identified with learning disabilities remained at 10 percent for youth aged twelve to sixteen, and then slightly decline for the seventeen- to eighteen-year-old age group (U.S. Department of Education, 2010).

Assessment and Identification of Learning Disabilities

Assessment and identification are undoubtedly the most significant aids to addressing any learning disability among secondary school-aged youth. A large percentage of youth with learning and other related special education disabilities are identified as children, typically between the first and fifth grades. However, there is general agreement that, because of the time frame necessary to accurately diagnose some disabilities, many children go unidentified as they enter secondary school (Mears & Aron, 2003; White and Loeber, 2008). The reasons for this are varied but may be because the learning difficulties have not come to significantly impair the child or youth's functioning, the family and school personnel are not identifying or routinely looking for these difficulties, or the school district's special education budget may be underfinanced and does not have sufficient personnel or resources to both identify and then address these disabilities (Burrell and Warboys, 2000; Mallett, 2011b).

This may be occurring even though the identification of learning disabilities has been required by federal law since 1974 (Individuals with Disabilities Education Act) for all students in public and private schools. Once evaluated to determine that the youth has a learning, or other related special education disability, school districts are required to have an Individualized Education Plan (IEP) in effect at the beginning of each academic year. The IEP Team, which includes the school personnel and family, considers the youth's present level of educational performance, special education needs, services to be delivered, objectives to be met, timelines for completion, and progress assessment when developing how best to address the learning disability (Mallett, 2011b). These are important functions in addressing the problems that impact youth with learning disabilities, and sometimes these supports are pivotal in academic progress, grade passage, and high school graduation.

Why the Learning Disabilities to Delinquency Link?

Why are youth with learning disabilities at significantly higher risk for offending behaviors and formal juvenile court involvement? The answer has not yet been fully explicated, though it appears to be complex. However, there are three competing hypotheses: school failure, susceptibility to delinquent behaviors, and differential treatment from authorities. Depending on further research and results, which may vary from one juvenile court jurisdiction to another because of the different youth populations served and differing school districts, appropriate steps could be pursued locally to address the problem.

School Failure Hypothesis

The school failure hypothesis suggests that school failure for youth with learning disabilities is a precipitating step that leads eventually to juvenile court involvement. Intermediary steps may include rejection by peers, lower self-worth because of academic difficulties, and school dropout, leading to increased engagement with delinquent peers and activities (Malmgren, et al., 1999; Morris and Morris, 2006). What is not clear, though, is whether the disabilities themselves are the reason for school failure or if there are other factors, such as family structure or functioning, negatively influencing peers, poor neighborhoods, and emotional difficulties, which may influence this outcome (Cruise, Evans, and Pickens, 2010). School failure is correlated with many negative outcomes. If learning disabilities are shown to be causal, then efforts should be put in place to assure the identification of these disabilities and education curriculum appropriate to minimizing failure. If learning disabilities are correlated to other risk factors such as poor peer choices or low family functioning, then those intervening influences should be appropriately addressed.

Interventions that can lower the risk of school dropout have posed challenges, considering the multiple factors that contribute to a decision to discontinue education. Risk factors for dropout include family difficulties, low-income status, negative peers, grade retention, low parental educational status, changing schools often, urban location, and unidentified school-related learning problems (Balfanz and Legters, 2004; Bridgeland, DiIulio, and Morison, 2006; Hammond et al., 2007). While no one risk factor is paramount in a youth's decision to drop out of school, more than one plus combinations of difficulties often make this outcome significantly more likely. In addition, youth who drop out of school often do not do so in the moment, but consider doing so over a significant period of time; in other words, the decision to dropout is often a process and not an event-centered circumstance (Gleason and Dynarski, 2002; Ingel et al., 2002; Rumberger, 2004; Schargel, 2004).

Programs that address multiple risk factors in a strategic, long-term manner show the greatest impact on decreasing youth school dropout rates. These programs often combine youth skill-building, family outreach, academic support, and larger system organization - schools, communities, and youth-caring systems (Battin-Pearson et al., 2000; Catalano, et al., 1999; Lehr et al., 2004). Although few programs offer all these interventions, some effective programs that address a number of risk factors and problems include the Adolescents Transition Program, Big Brothers Big Sisters, Brief Strategic Family Therapy, Families & Schools Together (FAST), Midwestern Prevention Project (Project STAR), PATHS, Schools & Families Educating Children (SAFE Children), Strengthening Families Program, Job Corps, and The Incredible Years Program (Schochet, Burghardt, and McConnell, 2006; 2008; Hammond et al., 2007).

Many of these programs and interventions involve parents and other caregivers with the youth's school work and activities. Youth tend to be more successful in school when their parents or caregivers are involved, showing improved attitude toward school, higher motivation and academic achievement levels, and higher school completion rates (Barnard, 2004; Harvard Family Research Project, 2010; Hill and Tyson, 2009; Jeynes, 2007).

Interventions that address low or poor family functioning are diverse, and many effective strategies are also discussed under the mental health disorders section later in this chapter. Working with the youth generally entails working with the family. Addressing family functioning is driven by the assessment and identification of the precipitating and presenting problems, which are then prioritized and addressed so as to develop the most appropriate treatment or clinical plan (Miley, O'Melia, and DuBois, 2006; Zastrow and Kirst-Ashman, 2006).

A number of family-focused interventions and programs have been found effective at improving family dysfunction, poor family relationships, low school commitments, negative peer choices, and youth behavioral problems (Brook et al., 1998; Hawkins, Arthur, and Catalano, 1995; Henggeler, 1989; Kumper and Alvarado, 1995). Programs that use multiple modalities in working with the family, including behavioral parent training, family therapy, and youth social skills training, have been found most effective compared to programs that focus only on the youth or parents/caregivers (Kumpfer, 1999; Szapocanik, 1997).

Some multiple modality programs with effective outcomes in improving poor family functioning include strategic family therapy, structural family therapy, behavioral family therapy, Strengthening Families Program, Multi-systemic Therapy (MST), and Functional Family Therapy (FFT) (Alexander et al., 1998; Henggeler et al., 2006; Howell, 1995; Kumpfer, et al., 2010; Molgaard, Spoth, and Redmond, 2000). These family-focused interventions range from low to very high in structured intensity, though the cost and time commitment of higher-intensity programs can be significant. For example, FFT, a short-term ninety-day, intensive intervention, requires many stakeholders to be involved in a very structured way across numerous youth settings, including home, school, and community, and may cost upwards of $3,000 per youth to complete (Alexander et al., 2002). However, the long-term impact and cost-benefit return may be four to seven times this investment, arguably making the program expenditures worthwhile (Aos, 2004; Aos et al., 2001).

Susceptibility Hypothesis

The susceptibility hypothesis proposes that youth with learning disabilities have cognitive, neurological, and intellectual difficulties that contribute to delinquent behaviors. Thus, in addition to their learning disabilities, youth may also be afflicted with low social skills, impulsivity, suggestibility, and a lower ability to predict the consequences of their behaviors. In particular, influence from negative peers and an inability to understand outcomes of negative decisions may have a key role in delinquency activity involvement (Brier, 1989; National Center on Education, Disability, and Juvenile Justice, 2001). If this hypothesis is proven, then a focus on earlier identification of these problems is important, and signs of impulsivity and low social skills may be symptoms to identify during this process. A number of these symptoms, especially low social skills and poor choice of peers, can be addressed by certain programs and interventions.

Interventions for the improvement of youth social skills may be stand-alone or part of other broader intervention efforts. Social skills encompass a range of behaviors and abilities that are related to social interactions and competence, including cooperation with others, friendliness, helpfulness, and self-control (Kavale and Forness, 1996). Interventions aim to increase more normalized behaviors through listening, anger control, emotions management, and other related techniques (Funderburk, Schwartz, and Nye, 2007). Research demonstrates that such programs show some improvement for some children and youth, but improved efficacy in research designs and evaluations is necessary (Forness and Kavale, 1996; Kavale and Forness, 1995; Kavale and Mostert, 2004).

Interventions to assist in positive peer choices are varied and may also be part of broader programming efforts. Evidence supports highly structured after-school programs positively affecting youth social skills and lessening the impact of negative peers. However, to be effective, these programs must focus on character development, have high staff-to-youth ratios, provide one-on-one training, have low attrition by building strong relationships between staff and youth, be long term, and address a broad range of youth difficulties across gender, age, and problem areas (Dodge, Dishion, and Landsford, 2006; Durlak and Weissberg, 2007; Gottfredson, Cross, and Soule, 2007; Zief, Lauver, and Maynard, 2006). An intervention that provides a majority of these program components is the Strengthening Families Program, which has been shown to effectively reduce the impact of negative peer influence in the use of alcohol, cigarettes, and marijuana during middle and high school, while also improving peer resistance skills (Molgaard et al., 2000).

Differential Treatment Hypothesis

The differential treatment hypothesis suggests that while youth with learning disabilities are no more involved with delinquent activities than their non-disabled peers, they are more likely to be identified by school personnel, arrested, and formally be involved with the juvenile courts. This explanation places the responsibility for this disparity on reactions by school, police, and juvenile court personnel to working with youth with learning disabilities. For example, school personnel may be more aware of these youth because of their disability status, and if the youth act out in disruptive ways, staff may be more likely to take punitive action and refer the disruptive youth to the police and courts, whose personnel in turn may repeat this pattern (Keilitz, Zaremba, and Broder, 1979; U.S. Department of Education, 2001a). If this hypothesis is proven, then at the point of identified differential treatment, broad system-wide reviews of why this is occurring should be undertaken. Correcting for these systematic biases should include a wide cross-section of stakeholders to assure a thorough analysis.

Onset and Occurrence: Mental Health Disorders

As reviewed earlier, between 3 and 20 percent of children and youth have an identified psychiatric disorder that impairs their functioning from a moderate to significant degree. Conduct and oppositional defiant disorders are the most often diagnosed mental health problems for adolescents, with boys being more frequently affected (Simonoff, et al., 1997). Other common mental health disorders and related problems, often correlates of trauma, found in the adolescent population include anxiety disorders, depressive disorders, and hyperactivity (Costello, et al. 1996; Cuffee et al., 1998; Lewinsohn, Rohde, and Seeley, 1998; Oldehinkel, Wittchen, and Schuster, 1999; Perkonigg et al., 2000; Romano et al., 2001). Anxiety disorders include a number of different diagnoses, with generalized anxiety disorder most prevalent in youth (Costello, Egger, and Angold, 2005b). Adolescents with ADHD often have impaired school functioning and performance; their social relationships decrease in quality and quantity; and their long-term prognoses are poor in improving symptom reductions (Barkley, 2002; Barkley et al., 1990). Although attention-deficit problems pose more cognitive functioning problems for affected youth, the symptoms may appear similar to those of conduct disorder, with functional impairments often exacerbating the behavioral problems (Aronwitz et al., 1994; Forehand et al., 1991).

Mental health difficulties and disorders often begin in primary school, yet continue for many youth into secondary school. Some of these disorders, such as ADHD, may become a comorbid problem with other later youth difficulties, including disruptive disorders (conduct and oppositional defiant) as well as depression and anxiety disorders (Melzer et al., 1999; Verhulst et al., 1997). An earlier onset of mental health disorders is associated with an increased risk of having one or more comorbid mental health disorders (Giaconia et al., 1994).

Though disruptive disorders are the most prevalent disorders among adolescents, depression and related disorders are also common, and suicidality is often present in teens with depressive disorders (Douglas et al., 2006; Gould et al., 2003). Rates of depression disorders increase as youth get older, causing significant distress at any given time for between 4 and 5 percent of youth (Costello et al 2002; Fergusson and Horwood, 2001; Giaconia et al.,1994; Kroes et al., 2001). Major depression appears to be more prevalent among Caucasian than African-American youth, though this remains unexplained (Angold et al, 2002).

Similarly, anxiety disorders are found in between 2 and 4 percent of the youth population, with panic disorder, agoraphobia, social phobia, overanxious disorder, and generalized anxiety disorder most frequently diagnosed among secondary school-age youth. Post-traumatic stress disorder and obsessive-compulsive disorder are the most common anxiety diagnoses among secondary-aged girls (Heyman et al., 2001; Meltzer et al., 1999; Rappaport et al., 2000; Verhulst et al., 1997).

Addressing the Problem of Mental Health Disorders

Most youth with mental health disorders or serious emotional disturbances neither access nor receive treatment (U.S. Surgeon General, 2001). Among youth who do access services, though, there are confounding disparities that affect these youth and their families. Many disorders, even when identified, often do not lead to treatment, particularly depression. Barriers to treatment are unclear; however, as youth reach young adulthood, their chances for accessing treatment for depression improve (Olfson et al., 1998). Youth who have public health insurance coverage have increased access to mental health services in comparison to youth who have private health care coverage. The impact of Medicaid has a significant influence on improved access, both by the provision of health care coverage to impoverished youth but also because mental health care is often more widely available compared to private health plans (Burns et al., 1995; Witt, Kasper, and Riley, 2003). In addition, minority youth, primarily African-American, Hispanic, and Native American, receive fewer mental health services than Caucasian youth, though reasons for this have not yet been determined (Elster et al., 2003; Friedman et al., 2004). When mental health services were initiated through child welfare, juvenile courts, schools, or pediatric primary care providers, however, access for African-American youth was found to equal that for Caucasian youth (Angold et al., 2002).

Attention-deficit Hyperactivity Disorder

Although most children with ADHD continue to have symptoms into adolescence, some youth are not even diagnosed until this later developmental stage (Barkley, 2002). Late identification is more common among youth with attention problems (that is, difficulties in focusing on tasks, organizing, completing school work, and processing information) than it is among youth with disruptive problems (that is, impatience and violating social norms). Youth with ADHD often have increased difficulty as academic and social expectations rise in secondary school. Interventions often utilized with these youth include behaviorally-focused strategies and medication.

Behaviorally-focused strategies have been found effective when they utilize clear standards, completion of specific tasks, positive reinforcement, easily understand instructions, and any follow-up supervision that may be necessary in both the home and school environments (Howe, 2009; National Institute of Mental Health, 2008). Behavior modification techniques show some signs of positive impact for many youth with ADHD symptoms, though this appears to be less effective compared to stimulant medication alone. However, the combination of behavior modification techniques and stimulant medication has generally seen better short-term outcomes than either treatment alone. However, many youth build up resistance to these stimulant medications, decreasing their symptom reduction impact (American Academy of Child and Adolescent Psychiatry, 1997; Fabiano et al., 2000; Jenson et al., 2001; Pelham, Wheeler, and Chronis, 1998).

Behaviorally-based Disorders

The epidemiology and development of conduct disorder has numerous influences, including individual youth characteristics, economic (e.g., the impact of living in poor neighborhoods), and environmental difficulties (family troubles, conflict, etc.) - each area often addressed through different strategies (Kazdin and Weisz, 1998). Cognitive-based parent training, focused on teaching practical skills to caregivers to address conflict, improve communication, and address interpersonal problems, has been found effective. Cognitive-behavioral treatment interventions more broadly utilized with both youth and their families have demonstrated effectiveness in reducing aggressive and antisocial behaviors (Barkley, Edwards, and Robin, 1999).

In fact, cognitive-behavioral treatments have been found to be some of the more efficient treatments for conduct disorder and related violent youth behaviors (as well as anxiety problems). These interventions improve positive behavioral and other psychological outcomes (Andreassen et al., 2006; Baer and Nietzel, 1991; Connor, 2002; Durlak, Furhman, and Lampman, 1991; Farrington, 2002; London Department of Health, 2001; Turner, MacDonald, and Dennis, 2007). Cognitive-behavioral interventions are designed to identify cognitions - thoughts, expressions, perceptions - and to then alter cognitions that are distorted in order to reduce maladaptive or dysfunctional thinking, attitudes, or behaviors (Foa and Meadows, 1997; Lipsey and Landenberger, 2006; McGuire, 2000). Such approaches may include social skills training, parenting skills training, teaching problem-solving skills, behavioral contracting, anger management, and related efforts (Dodge, 1993; Rapp and Wodarski, 1997; Rapp-Palicchi and Roberts, 2004).

Other programs and interventions that also utilize some cognitive behavioral components have demonstrated positive effects on youth conduct disorder symptoms, including FFT and MST. Both of these techniques use a framework of modifying youth behaviors and cognitions, family (in FFT), and multiple systems (in MST), with an emphasis on the larger family or system groups as the focal area needing change rather than only on troubled youth. MST is designed for youth with severe psychological and behavioral problems through short-term (four to six months), multi-faceted (using techniques from structural family therapy and cognitive-behavioral therapy), and home- and community-based interventions (Henggeler et al., 2006; Henggeler et al., 2002; Sexton and Alexander, 2000). Research has shown that MST reduces recidivism significantly, with an almost four-to-one return on investment (Aos et al., 2001; Aos et al., 2011). However, a thorough review of the available research on MST found it to be only as effective as other comparable or usual interventions for youth with emotional or behavioral problems; further research must determine if MST outperforms less expensive alternatives in important ways with any youth subgroups (Little, Popa, and Forsythe, 2005). This may be particularly important for smaller juvenile court jurisdictions with more limited rehabilitative budgets.

FFT, a short-term program of engagement with the family, is designed to motivate the youth and family members to alter ineffective, acting-out youth behaviors. Interventions with eleven- to eighteen-year-old youth with behavioral disorders lasts from eight to thirty hours, depending upon problem severity level, through various engagement and treatment phases (Alexander et al., 1998), and FFT has been found to significantly decrease out-of-home placement offending behavior recidivism (Alexander et al., 2002; Aos et al., 2011; Howell, 2003).

Schools can have an impact on aggressive youth behaviors as well. Many youth report troubles dealing with violence, bullying, and related problems within their schools, leading a majority of school districts to offer some sort of preventative programming (Gottfredson et al., 2000). Most of these programs use social processing and cognitive-behavioral techniques to inform and educate youth on improving problem-solving skills, consequential thinking, aggressive cue identification, and response options (Crick and Dodge, 1994; Shure and Spivack, 1982). These preventative and interventive programs are offered in both a universal format - to all students in a classroom - or on a selective, individualized basis - youth who are identified as having aggression or violence problems. Meta-analyses of these two social skill development formats have found that both universal and selective programming significantly decrease youth aggressive and disruptive behaviors, and that the affect for some youth was long-term (Wilson and Lipsey, 2006a, 2006b).

Depression and Suicide Prevention

Numerous approaches have been utilized over the past two decades to decrease the symptoms and impact of youth depression and related disorders: various individual and group therapeutic modalities, psychopharmacology, and public education, among others. While some of these interventions, primarily psychopharmacology, are important in stabilizing the most serious depressive symptoms, including suicidal ideation and behaviors, others do not appear to be effective in achieving symptom reduction goals, including therapy, psychotherapy, and psychoanalysis (March et al., 2004).

A smaller set of interventions may be helpful for some youth with significant depression problems (Curry and Wells, 2005). Interventions that are more likely to be effective include cognitive-behavioral approaches attuned to youth and focused on increasing social activities, on problem-solving abilities, on cognitive restructuring, on psycho-education for parents and youth, and on mood and emotion regulation. However, little long-term follow-up research has been done to date, so whether or not lasting effects are achieved is not yet known. Also, when working with youth with multiple or comorbid problems that significantly complicate treatment planning and coordination efforts, care should be taken because similarly few long-term intervention outcomes are known (Brent and Poling, 1997; Clark et al., 2001; Kaslow and Thompson, 1998; Lewinsohn et al., 1990; Reinecke, Ryan, and DuBois, 1998). In one review of studies that assessed universal service delivery programs when compared to selective interventions for preventing and treating youth depression, more positive effect was found with the specific youth interventions. In other words, selecting and working with youth who are at an elevated risk for depression was more effective than broader interventions - for example school- or classroom-based (Horowitz and Garber, 2006).

A number of risk factors correlate with suicidal behaviors, though a youth with an increased risk will not necessarily develop suicidal tendencies. Risk factors include depression and other related mental health problems (substance abuse with a comorbid mental health problem), a prior suicide attempt, a family history of suicide or family violence, firearms in the house, and incarceration (March, et al., 2004; National Institute of Mental Health, 2011; Substance Abuse and Mental Health Services Administration, 2009). When working with youth a number of suicidal behavior signs or symptoms can be identified, thus allowing immediate and concerted preventative actions. These signs include feelings of hopelessness or worthlessness, a decline in or lack of family or social activity participation, changes in sleeping or eating patterns, feelings of rage or need for revenge, consistent exhaustion, low concentration abilities at home and/or school, regular or frequent crying, lack of self-care, reckless or impulsive behaviors, and frequent physical symptom problems (Centers for Disease Control and Prevention, 2009; National Institute of Mental Health, 2011).

Of concern is the effect of comorbid difficulties and problems that increase the risk for youth suicidal behavior. As the number of risk factors increases for youth, the risk increases; however this is complicated by the impact of other mental health or substance abuse problems (Shaffer et al., 1996). Depression, and in particular unipolar depression, disruptive behavior disorders (conduct and oppositional defiant), and substance abuse are strongly linked to suicide risk; however, anxiety disorders have not been established as contributing to such risk (Conner and Goldston, 2007).

The National Registry of Evidence-Based Programs, supported by the National Institute of Mental Health, has identified a number of suicide prevention programs found effective in working with at-risk youth or their caregivers in group and community settings. These include the following: CARE (Care, Assess, Respond, and Empower), a high-school based program utilizing motivational counseling and social support; CAST (Coping and Support Training), a twelve-week program focused on life skills and social support delivered by teachers in a group setting; Emergency Department Means Restriction Education, an adult caregiver program that helps to minimize access to youth suicidal risks within the home, for example firearms and prescription drugs; Lifelines Curriculum, a school-wide prevention program that focuses on available resources and decreasing the stigma of suicidal behaviors; and Reconnecting Youth: A Peer Group Approach to Building Life Skills, a school-based prevention program that teaches skills to build resiliency against suicide risk factors and early substance abuse or emotional problems (Substance Abuse and Mental Health Services Administration, 2011).

Onset and Occurrence: Substance Abuse

Substance abuse and alcohol problems are uncommon prior to adolescence, with onset normally occurring during the early teen years. While only a small number of youth, between 4 and 5 percent, are diagnosed during any one year with an active substance abuse disorder (Substance Abuse and Mental Health Services Administration, 2008a), many other youth use these substances and are at risk. In 2010 over 10 percent of youth aged twelve to seventeen self-reported current illicit drug use; this rate represents a slight decline from the previous decade. The most common substances used were marijuana (over 7 percent); psychotherapeutics, including pain relievers, tranquilizers, sedatives, and stimulants (over 3 percent); inhalants (1 percent); and hallucinogens (1 percent) (Substance Abuse and Mental Health Services Administration, 2010c). However, the rate of alcohol use by youth is substantially higher than drug use although this does not often receive as much focus. Alcohol is often the first substance tried and most often used by most youth (Johnston et al., 2011). Youth drinking is ten times higher among eighteen-year-olds compared to twelve-year-olds, with significant binge drinking by one in four high school seniors (Johnson et al., 2011; National Institute on Alcohol Abuse and Alcoholism, 2011).

The use of illicit drugs and alcohol (as noted) increases as youth get older. This increase is seen in a review of the past thirty-day illicit drug usage reports, which show the following rates of use: 4 percent of twelve- to thirteen-year olds, over 9 percent of fourteen- to fifteen-year-olds, over 16 percent of sixteen- to seventeen-year-olds, and 23 percent of eighteen- to twenty-year-olds. The usage rate among eighteen- to twenty-year-olds is the largest for any age group. The trend is similar for heavy alcohol use, with the following usage rates: only 3 percent of twelve- to thirteen-year-olds, 12 percent of fourteen- to fifteen-year-olds, 25 percent of sixteen- to seventeen-year-olds, and 49 percent of eighteen- to twenty-year-olds. Over the past decade there were no significant differences in illicit drug use rates based on race or ethnicity, though illicit drug usage rates among Caucasian and Hispanic-American youth have significantly risen from 2008 to 2010. In addition, Caucasian youth older than twelve reported a significantly higher use of alcohol than do other ethnic groups (Substance Abuse and Mental Health Services Administration, 2010c). However, as discussed earlier, substance abuse and dependence rates are significantly higher in the youthful offender population, and in particular those detained and incarcerated (Brunelle et al., 2000; Huizinga et al., 2000; National Institute of Justice, 2003; Teplin et al., 2002).

Addressing the Problem of Substance Abuse: Parents

Parental substance abuse is a significant risk factor for subsequent child neglect and/or abuse, which is then related to the increased risk for youthful offending behaviors (Chaffin et al., 1996; Kelleher et al., 1994; Magura and Laudet, 1996). However, more than half of substance-abusing parents who are involved with children's service agencies do not receive a referral or assistance in accessing substance abuse treatment, either because the problem was not identified or follow-through was not supervised (Child Welfare League of America, 2001). It is important that child protection service agency personnel identify which parents need such assistance and find effective ways to engage and connect the parents to appropriate treatment (Berry, Charlson, and Dawson, 2003; Dore, Doris, and Wright, 1994). When youth exhibit problem behaviors, and the parents have a substance abuse problem, it is critical to utilize family interventions. For example, FFT or the Focus on Families Program that directly address the parents' problems and relapse concerns, as well as the negative impact and influence that substance abuse is having on the family, including the identified youth (Dusenbury, 2000; Ferrer-Wreder et al., 2003; Office of Juvenile Justice and Delinquency Prevention, 2011).

Addressing the Problem of Substance Abuse: Youth

Program Efforts

Substance abuse prevention programs should target the enhancement of protective factors and the reduction of risk factors; they should focus on all types of drug abuse and program characteristics should be designed to be appropriate and effective for the intended community population (Hawkins et al., 2000; Johnston, O'Malley, and Bachman, 2002). Risk factors correlated with youth substance abuse include early aggressive behavior, lack of parental supervision, substance use by a caregiver, drug availability, deviant peers, lack of caring adult relationships, traumatic life events, mental health difficulties, academic failure, poor social skills, and poverty; protective factors are often the minimizing or elimination of these risk factors (Frischer et al., 2007; National Institute on Drug Abuse, 2003; Spooner, 1999).

Families play a key part in reducing the risk of substance abuse, which can be strengthened through skills training, education, and increased involvement among family members (National Institute on Drug Abuse, 2003). Parental skills training can improve rule-setting, monitoring, and consistent disciplinary actions (Kosterman et al., 1997); drug education and information can improve family discussions about substance abuse (Bauman et al., 2001); and specific family-focused interventions can improve parenting behaviors (Spoth et al., 2002). Schools can also play an important preventative role by increasing youth academic (study habits, self-efficacy) and social abilities (peer relationships, drug resistance skills) (Botvin et al., 1995; Scheier et al., 1999). Communities can also have an impact on high-risk families by targeting populations in multiple settings (home, schools, faith-based centers, etc.) through the use of consistent messages about the risks for and problems of substance use (Chou et al., 1998; Dishion et al., 2002). These efforts, and the use of empirically-supported preventative efforts, can be cost-effective, saving many more dollars in youth and family treatment compared to later treatment costs. Cost-effective programs include the Midwestern Prevention Project (MPP); the Strengthening Families Program: For Parents and Youth 10-14; Guiding Good Choices; and the Skills, Opportunity, and Recognition (SOAR) Program (Aos et al., 2001; Hawkins et al., 1999; Pentz, 1998; Pentz, Mihalic, and Grotpeter, 2006).

Preventing or inhibiting substance use is easier and less costly that later treatment, and avoids the difficulty of substance abuse and addiction, along with their many associated problems; let alone the costs and difficulties in successful recovery from substance dependence. Many efforts are pursued by numerous stakeholders in preventing substance use and abuse, and a number of these programs have been found to have a significant impact. Such programs are offered in three formats: (1) universal, to all youth within a certain environment, for example a school classroom; (2) selective, to those families at high risk; and (3) indicated, identifying certain youth at high risk (National Institute on Drug Abuse, 2003). Universal programs with significant preventative impact include the Caring School Community Program (U.S. Department of Education, 2001b), PATHS (Greenberg and Kusche, 1998), Classroom-Centered Intervention (Ialongo et al., 2001), SOAR Program (U.S. Department of Education, 2001b), Guiding Good Choices (Koball et al., 2011), Life Skills Training (Botvin et al., 2003; Office of Juvenile Justice and Delinquency Prevention, 2011), Project Alert (U.S. Department of Education, 2001b), Project STAR (Chou et al., 1998), Project Towards No Drug Abuse (Sussman, Rohrbach, and Mihalic, 2004), and the Strengthening Families Program: For Parents and Youth 10 to 14 (Spoth, Redmond, & Shin, 2001). Effective selective programs include Focus on Families (Catalano et al., 1999), Strengthening Families Program (Kumpfer et al., 2002), and Coping

Power (Lochman and Wells, 2002), while effective indicated programs include Project Towards No Drug Abuse (Sussman, Dent, and Stacy, 2002) and Reconnecting Youth (Eggart et al., 2001).

Mentoring Programs

Mentoring programs are one of the most common interventions utilized in working with at-risk youth across many problem areas: aggression, delinquency, antisocial behavior, substance abuse, school failure, and others (Dubois et al., 2002; Rhodes, 2002). However, they are often designed with limited focus on the outcomes at which the efforts are being directed. In other words, once the youth risks are known, a program provides for a non-family member adult to take on a mentoring role, and the intervention is typically designed to grow into a long-term relationship between the youth and the mentor; however, the specific outcomes of import are often not identified. Nonetheless, the goals of the programs are often to minimize risk factors that lead to problems by utilizing the mentor's sharing skills, abilities, experiences, and knowledge that may assist the mentee, providing guidance and advocacy, and sometimes taking on a quasi-parental or guardian role (Dubois and Karcher, 2005; Jekielek et al., 2002; Rhodes, 2002). Research has shown that there is significant comorbidity across the problem areas that mentoring programs try to address; for example, youth with aggression or delinquency problems are often involved with substance use or abuse. Hence, it is possible that this intervention may directly or indirectly positively affect youth substance abuse problems.

Many reviews of mentoring programs have been completed, with generally significant positive outcomes. These reviews have found significant decreases in youth delinquent activities, improved school performance, lower levels of aggression, and other related improvements (Aos et al., 2004; Hall, 2003; Lipsey and Wilson, 1998; Rhodes et al., 2002). The more effective mentoring programs are those that provide training and ongoing mentor supervision, expectations of more time involved with the mentee, program-sponsored activities, parent support and involvement, and supplemental services (Herrera et al., 2007; Jolliffe and Farrington, 2007). In particular, one review of mentoring programs that specifically targeted youth substance abuse problems found a substantial positive effect. However, this review found that limited information is available on how mentoring programs are designed and operate as well as on how service delivery might be connected to desired youth outcomes (Tolan et al., 2008).

Substance Abuse Treatment

Among youth ages twelve to seventeen, at most 5 percent have been estimated to be in need of substance abuse treatment; however, at most, one in ten of these youth in need of treatment actually access services (Substance Abuse and Mental Health Services Administration, 2010a). Reasons identified for this chasm between identification and treatment services include concerns that interventions do not work for youth and because of high drop-out rates and substance abuse recidivism (Austin et al., 2005). However, this does not need to be the case, for a number of programs have been found effective (Rowe and Liddle, 2006). Family-based therapies have shown promise, with recommendations for additional investigations to identify the specific techniques that are most successful (Kowalski et al., 2011). Components of family-based therapies found to be effective include comprehensive interventions, parent support, and individualized youth and family care (Hogue and Liddle, 2009; Waldron and Turner, 2008). These multi-component programs target the risk factors and triggers that led the youth to abuse substances (Office of Juvenile Justice and Delinquency Prevention, 2011).

Cognitive-behavioral therapy is one of the most reviewed and researched interventions for substance use and abuse and has shown promising youth outcomes (Becker and Curry, 2008; Vaughn and Howard, 2004; Waldron and Turner, 2008). A related intervention is motivational interviewing, though it is designed more to move individuals toward addressing their issues than actually treating the substance abuse itself. This brief intervention is based on the philosophy that youth want their substance use behavior to end, but are not able to act on this willingness (Prochaska and DiClemente, 1984). Motivational interviewing is a psychological intervention that tries to enhance a youth's motivation to change, and to decrease their ambivalence about doing so (Miller and Rollnick, 2002). Despite significant use of this intervention with youth, the evidence has found motivational interviewing to be ineffective as a stand-alone technique (Dunn, Deroo, and Rivara, 2001). However, when used in conjunction with cognitive-behavioral therapy, and, in particular, when addressing cannabis abuse, it is very effective (Bailey et al., 2004; Carroll et al., 2006; Dennis et al., 2004).

When youth with substance abuse problems pose a safety risk to themselves or require a more intense intervention, a residential treatment setting may be in order. Unfortunately, outcome evaluations of such facilities are few, although, reviews that exist show improvements in substance dependency and addiction for many residents (Jainchill et al., 2000; Mock et al., 2001; Morral, McCaffrey, and Ridgeway, 2004; Spooner, Noffs, and Mattick, 2001; Vaughn and Howard, 2004; Winters et al., 2000). To be effective, treatment and program efficacy was identified as important if decreased youth substance use and dependency were to be maintained after residential facility placement (Orlando, Chan, and Morral, 2003).

Summary

Youth who become involved with the juvenile justice system and, in particular who are repeat offenders are at high risk for formal juvenile court supervision and incarceration. Youth who are formally involved with juvenile court and are subsequently detained or incarcerated are also most likely suffering from maltreatment victimization, school and learning problems, and/or mental health/substance abuse difficulties (Grisso, 2008; Mallett, 2011b; Teplin et al., 2006). Addressing these difficulties and disabilities is an integral part of breaking a youth's recidivist offending cycle, a pattern that often predicts adult offending and incarceration (Degue and Widom, 2009; Puzzanchera, 2009). Fortunately, as reviewed in this chapter, there are effective prevention and intervention programs that decrease or even eliminate offending behaviors, both for low-level youthful offenders and for more serious or violent youthful offenders.

5

Addressing Low-level Offenders

Most youth who have an initial contact with law enforcement and the juvenile courts do not have a second contact. Nonetheless, contact with the juvenile justice system provides an important opportunity for the juvenile courts and related youth-caring systems to identify and assist youth with disabilities and maltreatment histories. These contacts are often for low-level offenses: misdemeanors or status offenses. Misdemeanors may entail assaults, thefts of property, traffic offenses, possession of illicit substances, and other similar acts. Status offenses are acts that are legal for adults but illegal if committed by a youth (less than the age of majority, which is eighteen in most states) and include truancy, curfew violations, and underage drinking. This early involvement with the juvenile justice system for youth with disabilities and/or maltreatment histories provides an opportunity for increased identification and, if appropriate, treatment of these difficulties, as well as an opportunity for improved and coordinated efforts across youth-caring systems and the juvenile courts.

Pathway to the Juvenile Court

The pathway a youth takes to the juvenile court begins with committing an offense and subsequent interaction with law enforcement. Most police contact with youth is unofficial (10 to 15 percent of cases). A majority of the cases in which there is an official contact and arrests are made are for non-criminal offenses: public disorder, traffic offenses, and non-violent crimes; only about one-fourth of the cases are for violent offenses (Sickmund, Sladky, and Kang, 2010). Options for police when deciding on how to handle a youth offense include the following: questioning, warning, and community release; taking the youth to the police station and recording the offense; a referral to a diversion program; issuing a citation and making a formal referral to the juvenile court; or taking the youth to a detention center or group home (Lawrence and Hemmens, 2008). Many factors are influential at this decision-making point, including the youth's profile, the police officer's perspectives, organizational policies, specific offense and circumstances, and community pressures (Martin, 2005).

This first point of contact can be a pivotal time for youth with disabilities and/or maltreatment histories. A decision to release a youth or to make a referral for diversion services may provide far greater opportunities for assistance, compared to a formal juvenile court referral, detainment, or group home placement. In fact, most youth who are arrested one time are not arrested a second time, so generally either inaction or informal actions by the police and juvenile court seem to be appropriate because of the lower recidivism rate for first-time offenders (Sickmund et al., 2010). However, though keeping youth and the community safe are factors that weigh most heavily in making the decision for a formal juvenile court referral, still and all, youth with disabilities and maltreatment victimizations appear to be more often, than their non-disabled peers, formally involved with juvenile court (Children's Defense Fund, 2009; Mulvey, 2011).

The concern at this early and often low-level first offense is that youth with disabilities, in particular those with learning problems and mental health symptoms, are at significantly higher risk for later and deeper juvenile court involvement, as is evidenced by the disproportionate number of these youth within detention and incarceration facilities. However, police and court personnel training for identifying these types of problems is all too often a low priority, incomplete, or not a focus of concern at all (Rosado, 2005).

Diversion

Diversion is an important option for first-time or low-level youth offenders because most of the youth in this population do not pose any serious threat of reoffending. Beyond this, many youth may be effectively assisted because of the diversion efforts in thwarting or decreasing offending behaviors. In some cases, as previously discussed, disability needs can be identified when youth are diverted by law enforcement officials before arrest, during juvenile court intake, or even after adjudication (Roush, 1996). The term "diversion" has come to mean a number of different things for youthful offenders, including: non-arrest and release back to the community, addressing the identified problems through rehabilitative means, and any attempt to divert from the juvenile justice system (Bynum and Thompson, 1996; Griffin and Torbert, 2000; Kammer, Minor, and Wells, 1997; Lemert, 1981).

Diversion is particularly helpful for youthful offenders with disabilities: first, to identify the problems and, next, to lead to possible alternative intervention. In particular, when diversionary services result in youth voluntarily accessing available and effective community-based services, results are likely to be optimum (Kelley, Schulman, and Lynch, 1976). Diversionary programming may be offered by a juvenile court or a community-based agency, and may entail a wide array of alternatives, depending on the youth need, including mental health or drug court, teen (or youth) court, truancy intervention programs, respite, shelter care, mentoring, curfew enforcement programs, parent-training, restorative justice models, and other alternatives. A number of examples may be useful.

The Project Back-on-Track is an after-school diversion program designed for low- and mid-level youthful offenders (domestic violence, assault, drug and property offenses) to divert from further juvenile court involvement. This multi-faceted program curriculum involves the youth and family for four weeks, with the provision of youth and group therapy, parent support groups, community service projects, psycho-educational sessions, and youth empathy-building sessions. Youth participate in thirty-two hours of programming (two hours per day, four days per week), while parents participate for fifteen hours. One-year followup evaluations found the program significantly decreased the recidivism rate for participants when compared to non-participating youthful offenders with similar offending histories (Myers et al., 2000; Office of Juvenile Justice and Delinquency Prevention, 2011).

The Girls Circle Program is a strengths-based group that works with girls ages nine to eighteen through the integration of cultural theory, resiliency practices, and skills training to assist in diversion from offending behaviors. The program consists of an eight- to twelve-session curriculum, normally held weekly, led by a facilitator who follows a six-step format of gender-specific themes, motivational interviewing techniques, and identified improvement areas (coping with stress, sexuality, drugs or alcohol, decision-making, relationships, trust, etc.). Long-term followup studies of program participants found significant improvements in decreasing alcohol abuse and use, attachment to school, self-harming behavior, social support, and self-efficacy (Irvine, 2005; Office of Juvenile Justice and Delinquency Prevention, 2011).

The Indianapolis Restorative Justice Program is designed for first-time youthful offenders (assault, criminal mischief, disorderly conduct, shoplifting, and theft offenses) who are fourteen years of age or younger and have no pending charges. A conference including all stakeholders - offender, victim(s), family members, and supporters of the offender (i.e., teachers or coaches) - is convened to discuss the harm, give voice to the victim, and have the youthful offender understand the impact of the offense. From there a restorative plan to repair the harm is agreed upon, often including restitution, community service, or other appropriate alternatives. Youths who participated in the program were significantly less likely to be re-arrested at both six- and twelve-months post completion; however, re-arrest rates at twenty-four-months post completion were not significantly different than similarly situated, non-participating youthful offenders (McGarrell and Hipple, 2007; Office of Juvenile Justice and Delinquency Prevention, 2011).

The Multidisciplinary Team Home Run Program of San Bernardino County, California, is a case management intervention designed to identify the youthful offender's difficulties and provide intense family and individual treatment. The treatment planning process includes the family, school personnel, and other relevant individuals in the youth's life. This strengths-based and goal-oriented program targets first-time youthful offenders who are seventeen or younger and at risk for more serious criminal activity. The case management team includes the probation officer, public health nurse, licensed therapist, social service practitioner, and volunteers who coordinate, make appropriate referrals, and incorporate, as necessary, interventions such as restitution, restorative justice, community service, counseling, and group therapy (Office of Juvenile Justice and Delinquency Prevention, 2011; Schram and Gaines, 2005).

Mentoring programs have received extensive attention over the past decade as a preventative measure for at-risk youth (Office of Juvenile Justice and Delinquency Prevention, 1998; Tolan et al., 2008). Significant evidence supports mentoring as a stand-alone intervention that is effective for many youth who may become involved with the juvenile courts. Mentoring, particularly programs based on the Big Brothers Big Sisters model, has been shown to be effective for a wide range of youth difficulties. Program participants show significant improvements, when compared to non-involved at-risk youth, in academic behavior, attitudes, and performance, as well as improved relationships with parents and peers (McGill, Mihalic, and Grotpeter, 1998; Novotney, Mertinko, and Baker, 2000). More specifically, in a review of thirty-nine mentoring programs, while most programs were found effective in producing positive outcomes for youth, mentors with a professional background generally promoted more effective outcomes than did mentors without a professional background. While it is known that the relationship between the mentor and youth is most important, beyond this, the specific processes or program structures still need to be identified to know which specific program factors are more effective and why they are more effective (Tolan et al., 2007). This being noted, a key role that a mentor may have, particularly if professional or professionally-trained, is in helping to identify youth disabilities, maltreatment histories, and related difficulties that are unknown or not addressed.

Evidence of the impact of diversion programs has been mixed, though, with some programs having an impact on reoffending rates while other programs do not. Research indicates that a diversion program can most likely be effective in decreasing future reoffending if the program is intensive, comprehensive, and offered long-term (Sheldon, 1999). One of the key roles diversion may play is the opportunity to further screen youth for disabilities, something that is not always apparent without proactive attention.

Risk and Disability Identification

Screening is a brief process used to identify problems that are in need of further attention or assessment. Youthful offenders may benefit from screenings for the problems that have been under discussion and, because of their higher risk, may, in fact, require more thorough assessment (Grisso and Barnum, 2000). Screening efforts can occur at any point during the juvenile justice process, but are likely best performed as soon as a youth is involved with the system. Screening may initially identify youth problems related to mental health, substance use, family troubles, school difficulties, trauma, and other related or comorbid difficulties, allowing for further informed review, planning, and investigation (Hoge, 1999). Knowing that many youth disabilities and related problems are both risk factors for ongoing offending behaviors, as well as barriers to improved functioning in the community, identification is a vital first step toward improved functioning and prevention of deeper involvement with the juvenile justice system (Heilbrun et al., 2000).

Youth with mental health, trauma, substance use, and learning problems pose significant challenges. Identifying these youth has met with various barriers as previously discussed, including inadequate screening and assessment, inadequately trained juvenile justice personnel, and insufficient numbers of juvenile justice personnel to deliver appropriate services even after identification. One way to address these problems is through an expanded use of informal intake, a process whereby screening of youthful offenders and diversion to community resources with appropriate services occurs on a regular basis (Kelly et al., 1976; Mears and Aron, 2003; Rapp-Palicchi and Roberts, 2004).

Screening and Assessment

Within the juvenile justice system, professionals make a series of judgments on youth's risk of harm to themselves and the community and their amenability to treatment. While significant empirically-supported screening and assessment instruments are available, which can help inform these decisions, a less coherent and haphazard decision process is all too often the norm in determining the balance of youth's dangerousness, blameworthiness, and likely future behavior. Both tradition within the juvenile justice system and lack of resources weigh the system toward such decision making. With almost a million youth formally involved annually with the juvenile courts, verified and standardized assessments cannot be completed for the entire youthful offender population. In fact, there is little evidence that because of the necessary cost and personnel expenses, assessments, as compared to screenings, at this earlier point of entry into the juvenile justice system improve service identification or delivery (Mulvey and Iselin, 2008; Sickmund, Sladky, and Kang, 2010). However, even so, there are ways to identify youthful offenders within this population who show signs of certain disabilities and problems, and designate them for further assessment in an efficient process (Mears and Aron, 2003).

There are two types of screening methods: actuarial and clinical. An actuarial method utilizes tools that allow the practitioner to quickly complete a screening based on a number of objective criteria, often leading to a final point or scale score that measures the outcome of interest - for example, risk of reoffending, suicidal ideation, or alcoholism, among others (Marshall and English, 2000; Miller and Lazowski, 2001). A clinical method develops a coherent view of the pertinent outcome through the construction of a theory of why the event happens by gathering information from multiple parties of interest (Mulvey and Iselin, 2008). For decades the juvenile justice system has utilized the clinical method for assessment of youth and future risks. However, the use of actuarial screening tools, as well as the combined use of both of these methods, has greatly increased over the past fifteen years in the hopes for improved predictive outcomes, as well as improved process efficacy and efficiencies (Chapin and Griffin, 2005; Webster, Hucker, and Bloom, 2002).

As mentioned, screening youthful offenders early in their encounters with the juvenile justice system often allows nonprofessional staff to assist in identifying the subset of the youthful offender population that may be in greater need of a broader assessment and/or diversion or treatment. Screenings should follow a standardized procedure with utilization guidelines as early as possible during youth processing. This would allow the often limited juvenile justice resources to be used more appropriately in making assessments and ultimately accurate recommendations for the youth and their families. However, utilization and reliance only on actuarial instruments may not always be supported within the juvenile justice system, which sees it as contradictory to its individualized youth assessment and planning philosophy (Mulvey and Iselin, 2008; National Center for Mental Health and Juvenile Justice, 2007). Though this tradition is a strong influence on juvenile court personnel, increased screening efforts for youth with disabilities and/or maltreatment histories can lead to improved outcomes.

Risk of Harm/Reoffending

Risk assessments in juvenile courts most often measure the risk of reoffending or re-arrest as the outcome variable, and many instruments can reliably measure this outcome (Turner and Fain, 2006; Wiebush et al., 1995). For juvenile courts, this is almost always the key area of preventative focus. Often risk assessments, calculated by combining the number of risk factors known to impact recidivism, utilize a final score that directs juvenile justice professionals toward a recommended level of intervention (Baird, 1991). These assessments commonly measure offending history, substance use/abuse, peer delinquency, family problems, and school related problems in determining a youth's overall risk of recidivism (Schwalbe, 2008).

A number of assessment tools have an acceptable level of reliability and predictive validity. Many use interviews, rating-type scales, and/or self-reporting, including the Structured Assessment of Violence Risk for Youth, Early Assessment Risk List, and the Antisocial Process Screening Device (Falkenbach, Poythress, and Heide, 2003; Frick and Hare, 2001; Webster, Muller-Isberner, and Fransson, 2002). However, it is most often recommended that each local juvenile court jurisdiction develop its own risk assessment instruments based on its unique youth and family population. This individualized assessment screening process is rarely possible because of the time, planning, and resources required; thus, many jurisdictions use previously developed assessments from demographically similar juvenile court districts. However, in doing so, there may be matching or measurement validity problems that can lead to inaccurate predictions about youth offending (Annie E. Casey Foundation, 2006).

Mental Health and Substance Abuse

Mental health screenings of youthful offenders have recently become the norm in many juvenile court jurisdictions, and, in particular, in detention centers, though still more progress in performing these screenings is strongly recommended. Mental health screening is a brief process that can be administered by nonprofessional staff using a standardized tool, often used as a triage assessment to identify a potentially serious mental health problem, suicide risk, or re-offending risk. Quick initial screenings can identify those with need for further diagnostic assessments, which are individualized, comprehensive evaluations by clinicians (Grisso, 2005; National Center for Mental Health and Juvenile Justice, 2007; Vincent, 2012).

A number of screening tools are utilized both to predict future risk and to identify specific problem areas that may be intertwined with the youth's offending behaviors. Such standardized screening tools can assist in identifying risk for offending, as well as past and current social and family histories, mental health concerns, and other related problems. Commonly used instruments include the Massachusetts Youth Screening Instrument (MAYSI-2) and the Youth Level of Service/Case Management Inventory (Y-LSI) (see Figure 5.1). The MAYSI-2 is a fifty-two-item standardized instrument with seven subscales used to identify mental health needs of youth (Grisso et al., 2001), while the Y-LSI is a forty-two-item checklist with eight subscales, including offense history, family circumstances/parenting, education, peer relations, substance abuse, leisure/recreation, personality/behavior, and attitudes/orientation (Schmidt, Hoge, and Gomes, 2005). These tools have been most often used in making decisions on youth detention, in identifying other needs and presenting problems that may need to be addressed but are outside the scope of the juvenile courts' diversion, supervision, or programming options.

In addition to these combined screening tools, many other standardized evaluation options are utilized in the youth mental health and substance abuse fields (Williams, 2008). Two of the more rigorously validated screening tools, based on current psychiatric nosology definitions (American Psychiatric Association, 2000), include the Behavioral and Emotional Screen System (BESS) and the Diagnostic Interview Schedule for Children Version 4 (DISC-R). Both of these require a larger time investment because they include reports from youth, parents, or guardians, and, for the BESS, from teachers as well. The BESS is used to identify behavioral and emotional strengths and weaknesses for adolescents through secondary school ages and can screen for a variety of behavioral and emotional disorders that can lead to adjustment problems. The DISC-R is a comprehensive, structured interview that assesses for over three dozen youth mental health disorders (Kamphaus & Reynolds, 2011; Shaffer, Lucas, and Fisher, 2011). Because of the increased suicidal behavior risks for youth involved with the juvenile justice system, the use of the Suicidal Ideation Questionnnaire (SIQ) may be important. The SIQ is a twenty-five-item, self-report screening instrument used to assess suicidal ideation in adolescents (Reynolds, 1988).

Substance use and abuse are not only risk factors but also, often, offenses for youth; therefore, it is important to know if offenders have or are at risk of developing these problems. A number of reliable screening tools are available that are appropriate to utilize with the youth population (see Figure 5.1), including the Adolescent Substance Abuse Subtle Screening Instrument (SASSI-3), Global Appraisal of Individual Need-Short Screen (GAIN-SS), and the Michigan Alcohol Screening Test (MAST) (Grisso, Vincent, and Seagrave, 2005). The SASSI-3 is a psychological screening measure that can identify adolescents with chemical dependency, substance abuse, and substance use disorder (SASSI, 2001). The GAIN-SS can be used to quickly and accurately identify youth who may need a more thorough assessment for substance use disorders, as well as internalizing or externalizing psychiatric disorders (Dennis et al., 2006). The MAST is a twenty-five-item structured screening tool that can be used to detect an alcohol problem, though it may under-identify youth who are unaware of this potential problem (Selzer, 1971).

Maltreatment and Trauma

Identifying, or uncovering, maltreatment and trauma histories is often difficult if relying on youth interviews and family reports (Steen et al., 2005). In addition, maltreatment and trauma may impact youth differently and at different developmental time periods; screening and assessment therefore must be continued over time to correspond with

Figure 5.1 Mental Health and Substance Abuse Screening Tools

Massachusetts Youth Screening Instrument (MAYSI-2)
Youth Level of Service/Case Management Inventory (Y-LSI)
Behavioral and Emotional Screen System (BESS)
Diagnostic Interview Schedule for Children Version 4 (DISC-R).
Suicidal Ideation Questionnaire (SIQ)
Adolescent Substance Abuse Subtle Screening Instrument (SASSI-3)
Global Appraisal of Individual Need - Short Screen (GAIN-SS)
Michigan Alcohol Screening Test (MAST)

development and accounting for changing circumstances or symmptoms (Buffington et al., 2010). Trauma screenings are available that can provide assistance in identifying youth with maltreatment histories including the Traumatic Events Screening Inventory (TESI), the Child Welfare Trauma Screening Tool (CWTST), and the Trauma Symptom Checklist for Children (TSCC). The TESI is a structured clinical interview that assesses the youth's and parents' reports of past or current traumatic events, including maltreatment; the CWTST assesses for trauma and mental health needs for children and youth; and the TSCC is a self-report symptom inventory that identifies behavioral and mental health disorders that are often the outcome of maltreatment, and includes measures that assess directly for chronic traumatic stress (Ford et al., 2007; Igelman et al., 2007).

Once youth with maltreatment and trauma histories are identified, effective interventions can be provided by the juvenile justice system or other community-based providers. Overall, cognitive-behavioral treatments have been studied more frequently than most other modalities and have been found to be effective for traumatized youth (Centers for Disease Control and Prevention, 2008b). Specifically, the interventions with the most empirical support include the Cognitive Behavioral Intervention for Trauma in Schools, Trauma Affect Regulation: A Guide for Education and Therapy, Seeking Safety, Trauma-Focused Cognitive Behavioral Therapy, and Skills Training in Affective and Interpersonal Regulation. In addition, the Trauma Recovery and Empowerment Model (TREM) has been found effective for female youth, an important consideration because of the apparently strong gender differential impact of maltreatment on delinquency (see Figure 5.2). Most of these interventions include a number of the following components: psycho-education, emotional regulation, cognitive processing, family or caregiver involvement, a strengths-based perspective, and personal empowerment training (Cloitre et al., 2002; Cohen et al., 2004; Ford et al., 2005).

Figure 5.2 Trauma Interventions for Youth Maltreatment

Cognitive Behavioral Intervention for Trauma in Schools
Trauma Affect Regulation: A Guide for Education and Therapy
Seeking Safety
Trauma-Focused Cognitive Behavioral Therapy
Skills Training in Affective and Interpersonal Regulation
Trauma Recovery and Empowerment Model

Learning Disabilities

Federal law (the Individuals with Disabilities Education Act) requires that all children and youth, including those who are homeless and wards of the state, be identified for special education disabilities. School districts are required to locate and evaluate all children and youth who may have these difficulties and determine if services are necessary to ensure an appropriate education in the least restrictive environment. However, identifying learning disabilities is not always straight forward, and few appropriate youth screening tools exist, unlike for mental health, substance abuse, and trauma difficulties (Jenkins and O'Connor, 2002; Mallett, 2011b).

There are a number of common signs and symptoms of youth learning disabilities, including the following: misspelling the same word within a single document; reluctance to take on reading or writing tasks, though this could also be a sign of illiteracy; trouble with open-ended questions; weak memory skills; difficulty in adapting skills from one setting to another; slow work pace; poor grasp of abstract concepts;

inattention to details or excessive focus on them; trouble with word problems; slow or poor recall of facts; difficulty making friends; trouble understanding social cues of others; frequent misreading of information; trouble completing applications or forms; easily confused by instructions; and poor organizational skills. Some of these symptoms are common for many youth; the concern is when a youth presents consistently a significant number of these problems and they impair functioning (LD Online; 2009; National Center for Learning Disabilities, 2011).

There are more specific learning disability types that trained evaluators can identify through psycho-educational assessment and related testing. These learning disability types include dyslexia (language and reading disability), dyscalculia (problems with math and arithmetic concepts), dysgraphia (writing disorder leading to illegibility), dyspraxia (problems with motor coordination), central auditory processing disorder (difficulty processing and remembering language-related tasks), non-verbal learning disorders (trouble with non-verbal cues), visual perceptual and visual motor problems (reversing letters, losing place, etc.), and language disorders (trouble understanding spoken language, poor reading comprehension) (Learning Disabilities Association of America, 2011). One of the most overlooked of these difficulties is the non-verbal learning disorders, which is frequently undiagnosed and instead misidentified as behavioral or emotional problems. Unfortunately and ironically, emotional and behaviorally problems indeed are often the outcomes when these disorders are missed and untreated (Thompson, 1996).

Thus identifying youth with these types of learning disabilities may pose significant challenges to front-line juvenile justice system personnel; however, it is imperative to work toward this so these deficits do not further imperil these youths' futures. Though it is easy to overlook or misinterpret the key signs and symptoms, steps can be taken by juvenile court personnel to determine if the youth's school district already has identified the youth's learning disability, and if it is providing appropriate services.

A pivotal time for youth with disabilities in the juvenile court system is at intake. Early identification of youth with learning disabilities and coordination with the school district are crucial for positive outcomes. Court personnel can be effectively trained in interviewing youth and families, gathering educational records, becoming familiar with local educational services at placement facilities (if potential exists), and coordinating the juvenile court activities with the youth's school special education team (Keith and McCray, 2002;

Mallett, 2011b). This information may indicate that the youth's current educational plan needs reassessment or modifications, whether the youth is beginning or continuing offending behaviors.

If formal proceedings within the juvenile court have been initiated, continued coordination with the school district is necessary. If, at intake, learning problems or learning-related disability symptoms are indicated, then working with the school district to pursue an evaluation is important. As previously discussed, youth with learning problems and disabilities who are not properly identified by the school districts are at higher risk for ongoing delinquent activities (National Center on Education, Disability, and Juvenile Justice, 2001). The school districts' responsibility to identify and address youth with learning disabilities does not change when the youth is formally involved with juvenile court, detained, or incarcerated. In fact, federal law protecting and supporting youth with special education disabilities requires important supports for this population, including any necessary transitional and vocational services for those aged fourteen and older, necessary transitional services and financing responsibility for youth aged sixteen and older, and necessary services to address post-secondary needs, independent living, and community participation (Mallett, 2011b).

Comorbidity

Many youth who become involved with the juvenile justice system, including some considered low-level or low-risk offenders, are at risk for continued delinquent behaviors and potentially recidivist offending (Howell, 2003). As reviewed, significant efforts are pursued by many interested stakeholders and the juvenile courts in minimizing this youth recidivism risk. At these earlier contact points and stages of involvement with the juvenile justice system, it is suspected that many youth have mental health, substance use, and trauma experiences that affect their offending behaviors (Bender, 2009; Chassin, 2008; Teplin et al., 2002). However, significantly less attention has been brought to identifying and addressing youth learning disabilities, but also youth with multiple or comorbid difficulties. While significant attention has been paid to the proliferation of mental health disorders, substance abuse, maltreatment victimization histories, and, at times, learning disabilities within the youth detention and incarceration population (Fazel et al., 2008; Ford et al., 2007; Grisso, 2008; Sedlak and McPherson, 2010; Teplin 2006; Wang et al., 2005; White and Loeber, 2008), much less focus on earlier identification and preventative efforts has occurred, let alone the need for coordinating service across youth-caring systems. It is strongly hypothesized that if this smaller group of low-level offenders with multiple disability and trauma histories were identified early, then diversion, coordination, and treatment alternatives might greatly decrease youth's later chances for juvenile detention or incarceration and subsequently decrease their risk for serious or chronic offending.

Summary

Most youth who become formally involved in juvenile court are low-level or first-time offenders, though many suffer from mental health, education, and/or trauma-related difficulties. Multiple standardized assessment tools may assist juvenile court personnel in identifying these youth difficulties, thus allowing the appropriate preventative steps and use of effective interventions to minimize future delinquent activity or behaviors.

6

Addressing Serious and Chronic Offenders

Though most youth are involved in delinquent behaviors for only a short period of time, for a smaller number of youth, delinquency and offending behaviors become repetitive and cyclical. These youth are often considered or labeled serious, chronic, or violent youthful offenders and are the group that is most likely to be detained and/or incarcerated in either youth or adult facilities. These youth are most at risk to continue offending patterns into adulthood (Degue and Widom, 2009; Howell, 2003; Snyder, 1998). However, this offending outcome is in no way a fixed path, for many youth can be deterred or rehabilitated (Holman and Ziedenberg, 2006; Moffitt, 1993). In addition, it should be repeated that many youth have protective factors that build their resiliency to delinquent behaviors (Buffington, et al., 2010; Fraser, 2004; Richters and Martinez, 1993). Detained and incarcerated youth struggle during the significant amounts of time they spend within juvenile institutions with the multitudes of difficulties that have been under discussion, all of which can be correlated with higher risk of recidivism in and out of placement (Garland et al., 2001; Rosenblatt et al., 2000).

However, research over the past two decades offers hope regarding juvenile crime reduction for both community-based and institutional settings, which provide programs that reduce the risk of serious youthful offending, sometimes by 20 to 30 percent (Aos et al., 2001; Greenberg, 2008). Programs that are effective have a number of common components: supportive social contexts and authoritative adults, a focus on changing problem behaviors, and interventions to improve the youth's psychosocial maturity (Scott and Steinberg, 2008). For most youthful offenders, there are opportunities to address these difficulties and disabilities during probation supervision, detention, and incarceration.

Delinquency Adjudication and Probation Supervision

Decisions to involve youth formally with the juvenile courts are often referred to as the traditional processing method, whereby a youth is charged, adjudicated delinquent, and most often placed on probation supervision. This traditional process is grounded in a philosophy of trying to balance public safety with youth accountability. It operates under the premise that early offending often leads to later and greater offending; therefore, addressing the problem with formal juvenile court supervision is most appropriate. In addition, formal supervision may allow the youth to be linked to necessary or preventative services (Brown et al. 1989). An alternate approach is to handle low-level offenders in a non-intrusive manner, so to avoid the labeling and negative peer contact that typically follows when a youth is formally supervised or when juvenile court is involved (Schur, 1973; Dodge et al., 2006). As discussed in Chapter 6, diversion methods have accumulated recent empirical support for their positive impact on deterring youthful offenders. Further, in a unique review of juvenile court probation supervision efforts, formal processing and supervision did not reduce crime or reoffending when compared to diversion. In other words, it did not meet the important juvenile justice policy goal of increasing public safety through decreasing youth recidivism (Petrosino et al., 2010).

It is important to reiterate that youth who are formally involved with the juvenile courts are at high risk for having one, or more, disability or maltreatment-related problem, often a non-identified or non-treated difficulty. It appears that youth with these identified disabilities and maltreatment histories may be at higher risk for more severe juvenile court dispositions, particularly, youth with drug or alcohol abuse disorders (Campbell and Schmidt, 2000; Fader et al., 2001) and youth with prior treatment for mental health disorders (Lyons et al., 2001; Schwalbe, Smith-Hatcher, and Maschi, 2009). Additionally, a youth's race has an aggregating impact on the severity of the juvenile court's disposition as well as the probability of the youth's receiving rehabilitative versus punitive services. Specifically, one of the most common juvenile court dispositions is a referral for treatment service (Breda, 2003), and the need for treatment referrals does not seem to differ because of the youth's race (Martin and Grubb, 1990) in both short-term and long-term detainments (Glisson, 1996; Rogers, Powell, and Strock, 1998). Yet, minority youth are more likely to be detained, and detained youth are more likely to receive additional harsh sanctions including incarceration, yet less likely to receive juvenile court treatment referrals compared to youth who are not detained (Leiber and Fox, 2005; Wu, 1997). The result is that minority youth with disability needs and/or maltreatment histories, compared to similarly situated Caucasian youth, are more likely to be detained but probably less likely to receive treatment referrals from the juvenile courts. If detention and lack of treatment significantly affect the likelihood of future reoffending, then minority youth with disabilities and/or maltreatment histories may be at greater risk once formally supervised by the juvenile court.

Effective Probation Supervision Programs

Given these concerns, steps can be taken on behalf of youth under formal juvenile court supervision. Three of the more successful programs utilized in many probation departments focus on family and youth interactions and behavior skill development: FFT, MST, and Intensive Protective Supervision (IPS). These first two programs, FFT and MST, have been found effective in addressing youth substance abuse and violence problems, and are provided in community-based settings in the effort to avoid a residential or detention placement (Alexander et al., 2007; Greenberg, 2008; Henggeler et al., 2006). Critics focus on high program implementation and continuation costs that may be prohibitive to smaller juvenile court jurisdictions (Little et al., 2005; Willison et al., 2010). The third program, IPS, works with youth who have committed status offenses, such as truancy, underage drinking, and so on. This supervision closely monitors these youth while working with their families and providing links to necessary therapeutic services such as mental health, substance use, and school deficit-related interventions (Sontheimer and Goodstein, 1993).

Orange County, California, has developed its youthful offender probation supervision through a comprehensive three-tier system, with positive outcomes. This department has utilized the concept of graduated sanctions—a system of increased juvenile court responses to increased youthful offender difficulties or non-compliance—in conjunction with a parallel system of intervention and supervision options to develop the 8% Early Intervention Program. This program was developed because the juvenile court identified that this small percent of more serious youthful offenders accounted for a significant amount of juvenile court resources, though many of these youth, it was believed, could be diverted from recidivist outcomes. Youthful offenders in this high-risk "8%" group are referred to an intensive, community-based program (Early Intervention Youth and Family Resource Center); the medium-risk group (22 percent of youth) are probation supervised and linked to community-based programs including, as needed, in-home family services, health screenings, substance abuse and mental health treatment , and educational services; while the low-risk group (70 percent of youth) receives diversion and delinquency prevention programming (Lipseyet al., 2010; Schumacher and Kurz, 2000).

Coordination between juvenile courts and school districts is clearly necessary in working with youth with learning disabilities and related academic and non-academic problems. To date, however, there have been limited community-based agency programs that have advocated on behalf of juvenile court-involved youth with these disabilities, though a few exist. The TeamChild Model is one of a handful of programs that address many of these coordination barriers. This program teams defense attorneys with social workers and other professionals to represent court-involved youth with disabilities who are at risk of or are being detained. Through advocacy and case management efforts during the youth's formal court involvement, the team addresses education (including special education), mental health, vocational, and other needs as problems underlying delinquency and offending. The team works closely with the school districts and educates court personnel on non-justice related areas that affect the youth's decision-making, academic limitations, and related problem areas. While not used extensively, this model has been found effective in several communities including Seattle, Washington (returning $2 in savings for every $1 spent within six months) (Washington State Institute for Public Policy, 1998) and in Cleveland, Ohio (saving $620,000 in placement costs over eighteen months) (Mallett and Julian, 2008).

A significant challenge within juvenile court probation and supervision departments is finding ways to hold youth accountable for their delinquent behaviors while concurrently acknowledging, identifying, and treating the effects of the mental health, substance use, and school-related disabilities with which so many of them struggle. While larger jurisdictions may be in a secure enough position fiscally to handle such needs, smaller juvenile court jurisdictions often simply cannot. Financial realties can lead to some perplexing dilemmas around who pays for services, who must provide services, how the juvenile court judge handles treatment dispositions, contingencies if the problems are related to school and special education, and contingencies if the needed mental health or substance abuse services are not available within the court or community-based youth-caring systems, among others (Mears and Aron, 2003; Models for Change, 2011). These, and related issues are further explored in Chapter 7.

Juvenile Drug and Mental Health Courts

The increased recognition and identification of young offenders disability-related problems over the past twenty years has coincided with a move toward a rehabilitative/therapeutic paradigm within the juvenile courts and has prompted and expanded the number of juvenile drug courts (approximately 500) and juvenile mental health courts (approximately fifty) nationally (Bureau of Justice Assistance, 2003; Office of Juvenile Justice and Delinquency Prevention, 2011). Both juvenile drug and mental health courts selectively divert youthful offenders from the regular juvenile courts to work in tandem with community-based service providers, thereby having the judge oversee the therapeutic treatment of the youth and, often, the family, while maintaining adjudication authority (Cooper, 2001; McNiel and Binder, 2007). However, such courts often lack standardization operation, with projected youth outcomes ranging from substance use elimination, to reduction of delinquent acts, to adhering to a probation plan, to improving school performance, among others (Sloan and Smykla, 2003).

While public and stakeholder support is increasing for diversionary and therapeutic alternatives for youthful offenders with mental health and substance abuse problems, full evaluation of such programs' efficacy cannot be completed because of limited data at this point (Wormer and Lutze, 2010). A majority of the evaluations of the juvenile drug courts have focused on substance use reduction, and the results are inconclusive, showing some reductions in use that are significant but no clear consistency of effect (Belenko, 2001; Hiller et al., 2010; Kirchner and Kirchner, 2007; Latessa, Shaffer, and Lowenkamp, 2002). Juvenile mental health courts, which focus primarily on treatment engagement and on improving community safety, simply have not been evaluated sufficiently to know their impact (Cocozza and Shufelt, 2006; Office of Juvenile Justice and Delinquency Prevention, 2011). Before relying on or expanding these therapeutic juvenile court dockets, research designs must be improved and long-term assessments should be completed.

Intensive Case Management: The Wraparound Model

Intensive case management, also called the wraparound model, is a flexible, multifaceted intervention strategy to maintain youthful offenders in their homes and out of correctional institutions or residential care. These highly structured programs, significantly more intense in supervision and service delivery than traditional case management services, have been found effective with youth with low-level offenses and with a smaller number of youth with more serious offenses (Brown, Borduin, & Henggeler, 2001; Burchard, Bruns, and Burchard, 2002). Though designed differently across jurisdictions, these programs often entail collaborative efforts with community-based agency services. In addition, intensive case management programs develop individualized and specific treatment plans for the youth and family, building in numerous redundant and collaborative safety supports (National Wraparound Initiative Advisory Group, 2003; Office of Juvenile Justice and Delinquency Prevention, 2011). To be most effective, it is important that these services have consistent staff working with the youth and family, use a strengths-based paradigm, and incorporate cultural competence in treatment delivery (Bruns et al., 2004).

   Some studies indicate intensive case management services can be effective for youth with serious emotional, behavioral, and comorbid problems across numerous settings (home, school, and community), tackling the difficult problem of allotting costs among various systems of care through shared cost agreements. Improved youthful offender outcomes include significant reductions in residential and psychiatric facility days, as well as lower arrest rates, which reduce costs of care across both juvenile justice and mental health systems. However, while a number of well established programs, including Wraparound Milwaukee, Clark County Wraparound, Washington Connections Program, and California's Repeat Offender Prevention Program, have demonstrated efficacy, empirical support is not yet well established across a broad array of settings (Kamradt, 2000; Mendel, 2003).

Detention

As discussed previously, it is critically important for detention and incarceration personnel to identify, as early as possible, a youth's disability problems or difficulties. In Chapter 5, a number of screening tools and instruments were listed as effective in identifying youth mental health problems and disorders (MAYSI-2, Y-LSI, BESS, Diagnostic

Interview Schedule for Children Version 4), substance abuse and disorders (SASSI, GAIN-SS, MAST), and trauma problems (TESI, CWTST, TSCC). In fact, studies of the effects stemming from the utilization of one of these mental health screening tools (the MAYSI-2) found that in nine detention centers in three states, staff increased efforts to obtain mental health services and suicide precautions for youth in the facilities (Models for Change, 2011). Unfortunately, this is far from the norm in such facilities (Sedlak and McPherson, 2010).

The detention of youthful offenders is best limited to only those youth who have committed a serious offense and who pose a clear danger to public safety due to a high risk of their reoffending. However, detaining and incarcerating youth in and of itself does little to improve delinquent behaviors or offending outcomes, and, in certain circumstances, it causes harm by negatively affecting youth and increasing their recidivism risk (Loughran et al., 2009; Myner et al., 1998, Winokur et al., 2008). However, when such institutional stays incorporate the identification of youth disabilities and other problem areas, include subsequent rehabilitative efforts, and move away from a punitive framework, youth outcomes can be improved (Annie E. Casey Foundation, 2011). Reviews show that programming that addresses youth mental health problems is more successful than programming that takes a completely punitive only approach; also, these programs have a more positive impact when delivered by mental health professionals compared to detention center staff (Greenberg, 2008).

Within the detention facilities a number of specific programs and interventions have been found effective: aggression replacement training, cognitive-behavioral therapy, and the Family Integrated Transitions Program. Aggression replacement training uses certain cognitive-behavioral techniques to identify anger triggers, improve behavioral skills, and increase youth pro-social skills; cognitive-behavioral therapy focuses on skill building and step-by-step curriculum to affect change; and the Family Integrated Transitions Program uses a combination of interventions (Multi-systemic Therapy, relapse prevention, etc.) to address youth mental health and substance abuse problems and to ease transitions back to the community after detention facility release (Aos, 2004; Glick, 1996; Lipsey and Landenberger, 2006).

Incarceration

While incarcerated many youthful offenders do not receive services that may assist in mitigating their prior offending behavior or address their disabilities. Many, but not all, incarceration facilities use punitive approaches; however, recognition is growing that a rehabilitative approach better achieves important public policy goals of decreasing youth recidivism and, subsequently, increasing community safety. There is evidence that incarceration facilities that identify youth problems and provide disability treatment services can have a significant impact on decreasing youth reoffending (Garrido & Morales, 2007; Holman and Ziedenberg, 2006). The same types of programs that have been found to positively affect incarcerated youth have shown positive results within residential treatment centers as well. Behavior contracting and programming, token economies, level systems, individual counseling, skill building (e.g.e, improving anger management skills), group counseling, education, vocational training, and combinations of these services have shown some effectiveness as rehabilitative interventions. In addition, studies indicate that when such rehabilitative interventions are utilized, they must be well designed, of high quality, and of sufficient duration in order to have an impact (Hoge, 2001; Lipsey, 2009; Lipsey and Wilson, 1998; Weisz, Jensen-Doss, and Hawley, 2006). Some incarceration facilities that have incorporated appropriately designed and implemented therapeutic components have been able to effectively decrease youthful offender recidivism rates (Armelius and Andreassen, 2007; Greenwood and Turner, 2009).

Missouri is often cited as a leading example of how to move away from serious youthful offender incarceration toward a rehabilitative model. Over the past twenty years, the Missouri Division of Youth Services first closed the larger state incarceration institutions (called training schools), divided the state into five regions, and developed a continuum of programs - day treatment, non-secure group homes, medium-secure facilities, and secure care facilities - within each region. None of the secure care facilities hold more than thirty to thirty-six youth; further, youth are placed into even smaller cohorts that live together, receiving individualized, rehabilitative care. Recidivism rates for youthful offenders are less than 10 percent annually (Howell, 1998; Justice Policy Institute, 2009; Mendel, 2003, 2011).

In a corresponding movement away from large facility incarceration, a number of states are shifting their juvenile incarceration facilities toward this rehabilitative and individualized model, including Alabama, New York, California, Texas, Louisiana, Ohio, and Massachusetts (Office of Juvenile Justice and Delinquency Prevention, 2011). More specifically, in Alabama, executive and judicial leadership (initiated through the Juvenile Detention Alternatives Initiative) decreased the state incarceration facility population by 46 percent from

2007 to 2011, thereby reallocating funding to nonresidential, community-based services. In California, coordinated advocacy efforts (Youth Justice Coalition and the National Center for Youth Law) and litigation around dangerous facility conditions have decreased state incarceration facility population by 88 percent from 1996 to 2010; unfortunately, some of this decrease in youth population is explained by a significant increase in transfers of youthful offenders to the adult criminal courts. In New York, a combination of strong state leadership and litigation around lack of quality conditions and mental health care has downsized or closed two dozen youth incarceration facilities, correspondingly decreasing the population by over 73 percent. In Texas, strong advocacy efforts (Texas Criminal Justice Coalition, Texas Appleseed, and Texans Care for Children) and a state reform bill that passed because of abuse by staff that had occurred within the facilities led to a 63 percent reduction in the incarcerated youth population, with many of these dollars being reallocated to the juvenile courts to fund diversion programs (National Juvenile Justice Network, 2011).

However, a majority of serious youthful offenders across the nation are still in large "training schools," commonly known as state jails (Livsey, Sickmund, & Sladky, 2009). As discussed, such facilities generally provide little to no rehabilitative care for youth with disabilities, often do not meet the education, often special education, needs of the youth, and can be overcrowded and unsafe environments (Sedlak and McPherson, 2010). However, if these facilities were to provide appropriate intensive mental health and related disability treatment for youthful offenders with serious problems the results could be positive with a significant cost-benefit return (Caldwell, Vitacco, and Van Rybrock, 2006).

Residential Treatment Centers

Residential treatment centers are an alternative to incarceration for youthful offenders with serious emotional problems or severe behavioral disabilities who are in need of more structure than non-secured, community-based treatment. These structured centers are often operated within the private mental health or substance abuse youth-caring systems and offer an array of mental health/substance abuse services, behavior management, twenty-four-hour supervision, counseling (individual, group, family), and medication management. Residential treatment centers differ significantly from the group homes, commonly used within the juvenile justice system, which provide daily living care and assistance, but infrequent therapeutic treatment services (Mallett et al., 2012). Up to one-third of residential treatment facility residents are serious youthful offenders referred by the juvenile courts. An optimistic sign of at least cross-system collaborative need if not coordination (Hockenberry et al., 2009).

Residential treatment centers have a long established history of providing mental health treatment; however, while outcomes are encouraging, there is still a need for improved evaluation designs, including more frequent and rigorous studies with consistent measurements (Baker, Wulczyn, and Dale, 2005; Foltz, 2004; Lyons and Schaefer, 2000; McCurdy and McIntyre, 2004; Tripodi, 2009). Barriers in research methodology to studying treatment efficacy include difficulties in designing experiments with control groups or utilizing random sampling techniques, but are important to utilize in determining who these facilities are best for and how best these facilities should operate (Blanz and Schmidt, 2000). Still some findings for youth with serious mental health problems are encouraging (Bettman and Jasperson, 2009; Leichtman et al., 2001; Smith et al., 2008). These improved recidivism outcomes were particularly strong in a comparison of residential treatment centers to juvenile justice facilities, with significantly greater reduction in recidivism in the residential treatment centers (Gordon, Moriatry, and Grant, 2000).

Similarly, positive outcomes have been found across a number of distinct measures of residential treatment care, including mental health symptom reduction (Colson et al., 1990; Lyons et al., 2001), orientation to treatment (Mann-Feder, 1996), and improved family and social functioning (Hooper et al., 2000; Larzelere et al., 2001). The positive outcomes were associated with increased family involvement, shorter length of stays in residential placement, and involvement with after-care programming. However, placements longer than two years were associated with more negative outcomes; in other words, regression in negative symptoms and behaviors (Leichtman et al., 2001; Smith et al., 2008). In one thorough review of cognitive-behavioral therapy utilization within residential treatment centers, youth antisocial behaviors decreased by 10 percent compared to youth who did not receive the therapy. In addition, other therapies offered - attention control, stress management training, and discussion groups - within the residential treatment settings were found equally effective, though less evidence is available for comparison (Armelius and Andreassen, 2007).

There are a number of barriers to the juvenile courts utilizing residential treatment centers more frequently for youthful offenders with serious emotional and behavioral difficulties: the sometimes higher costs of residential treatment compared to alternatives, including incarceration; contentiousness regarding financial responsibility for such stays; and the limited number of residential treatment center facilities available in any given community. In many rural and smaller jurisdictions there are no youth residential treatment centers.

However, a number of juvenile court jurisdictions have modified their incarceration facilities away from a punishment model toward a rehabilitative residential treatment center model. Doing so in a cost-effective manner and improving youthful offender outcomes. Such adaptations, most of which incorporate the use of smaller, rehabilitative, and disability-focused facilities, as in Missouri (as discussed earlier), New York, Texas, Louisiana, Massachusetts, and Ohio, can be emulated by other states and jurisdictions.

Developments in Ohio can be informative in moving away from incarceration. Ohio's juvenile institutional placements saw a decrease in average daily census of serious youthful offenders from over 2,000 in 2002 to 823 in 2011, allowing the state to close three of its eight facilities. Within the remaining institutions a culture shift has also occurred, moving away from punishment and control to positive development and treatment, and with youth specialists and not prison guards interacting with the young offenders. In addition, resources have been reallocated from the institutions to the local juvenile courts in order to increase rehabilitative treatment options, delinquency preventative efforts, and juvenile offender re-entry success at the local level. These steps were taken for two reasons. First, a federal class action lawsuit settlement highlighted the poor care that incarcerated youthful offenders received, including a dearth of educational opportunities, inadequate mental health care, unsafe conditions, and lack of due process or redress (*S.H. v Stickrath*; Youth Law Center, 2009). Second, a majority of the serious youthful offenders within the institutions had been identified with mental health problems (many severe), substance use issues, and significant education deficits and/or learning disabilities, and many were not receiving any rehabilitative assistance (Lowenkamp et al., 2010; Ohio Department of Youth Services, 2010; 2011).

Adult Criminal Court and Incarceration

Transferring youth to the adult criminal justice system is controversial for it implies a distinction between a group of serious youthful offenders worthy of juvenile court rehabilitative efforts and a second group that is presumed not rehabilitative, worthy only of punishment, whose disability needs and rights are therefore also neglected (Fagan, 2008; Green, 2005; Marrus and Rosenberg, 2005; Singer, 1996). In addition, there is little evidence that youth transferred to the criminal courts have lower recidivism or offending rates upon release; in other words, harsher punishment does not work better (Bishop, 2000; Lanza-Kaduce et al., 2005; Redding, 2010). Juvenile transfer laws have had an impact on the way offenders are managed within the system and little to no long-term effect on public policy goals of increased offender accountability and public safety; in fact, they worsen the situation for youth offenders with disabilities (Mears and Aron, 2003).

When a youthful offender is transferred to an adult criminal court, neither the need for further schooling nor any school-related disabilities suddenly vanish. However, youth with learning or other special education disabilities will most likely not receive any school- or training-related accommodations while incarcerated in adult facilities, even though most are entitled under federal law to such assistance (Burrell and Warboys, 2000). Youth with mental health problems, and in particular those with the sorts of severe emotional disturbances that are not uncommon among serious youthful offenders, will most likely have neither treatment alternatives nor ongoing care upon release from the adult facilities. Likewise, youth with substance abuse disorders are unlikely to have addiction treatment available within an adult facility, increasing the likelihood that they will resume their abusive lifestyles upon release into their community, which is further correlated with reoffending and recidivism. Because almost all serious youthful offenders who are transferred to criminal court return to their communities, failing to attend to mental health needs and to learning problems and academic barriers undoubtedly makes successful reentry significantly more difficult, if not impossible (Frontline, 2005; Petteruti and Walsh, 2008; Snyder, 2004).

Cost-Benefits of Rehabilitative Efforts

Nationwide, states spend over $5.7 billion annually detaining and incarcerating youth, though a majority of these youth are held for nonviolent offenses and may better benefit from other rehabilitative efforts (Justice Policy Institute, 2009). A number of states have recognized this and have taken steps to readjust fiscal allotments within the system. Ohio created a system that incentivizes the counties to use community-based rehabilitative and diversion efforts rather than state incarceration for many youthful offenders by capping the state allocation and in the process has saved between $11 and $45 in commitment costs for every $1 spent on the Reclaim Ohio program (Lowenkamp & Latessa, 2005). Similar efforts in reallocating Illinois state dollars to the local county jurisdictions has saved an estimated $18 million by decreasing state juvenile incarcerations by over 50 percent (Illinois Department of Human Services, 2008). New York, also by reallocating state funds at the local level, closed six state-run youth residential facilities. A portion of those local funds were made available for diversion and rehabilitative efforts (New York Juvenile Justice Coalition, 2009). Stakeholders in both New York and California are discussing possible further steps toward closing all state-run youth incarceration facilities, with an eventual shift of the responsibility and state resources for youthful offenders back to local jurisdictions.

Washington state has performed extensive cost-benefit reviews of its juvenile justice system over the past decade. The following disability rehabilitative programs, which were also discussed earlier, have a significant positive effect on youthful offenders and have significant returns on investments when cost-benefit ratios were studied. For instance, FFT saved $3 for every $1 dollar invested; Aggression Replacement Therapy saved $6 for every $1 invested; MST saved $7 for every $1 invested; Multidimensional Treatment Foster Care saved $9 for every $1 invested; formal juvenile court supervision with diversion services saved more than $9 for every $1 invested; Intensive Probation Supervision saved $4 for every $1 invested; and, of significant importance, and an important theme in Chapter 7, the coordination of these services within community-based programs for youthful offenders saved more than $25 for every $1 invested (Aos, 2004; Aos et al., 2011; Barnofski, 2009). Clearly stakeholders are increasingly recognizing that dollars spent on treatment and prevention with low-level, and, also, importantly, serious youthful offenders, is important in resolving some of the perplexing problems with high recidivism rates in the juvenile justice system.

Summary

Unfortunately, when youth continue offending behaviors and activities, oftentimes the outcome is placement into detention or incarceration facilities, which typically utilize an ineffective, punitive-only paradigm. However, there are numerous effective rehabilitative (non-punitive) approaches and alternatives in working with these serious offending youth, normally by addressing mental health disorders, education-related disabilities, and trauma-related problems.

7

Shifting from Punishment to Rehabilitation

Children and youth with disabilities and trauma experiences confront many challenges in dealing with these difficulties. For example, a youth may be struggling as a freshman in high school with an unidentified learning disability, leading to both poor grades and negative peer influences. In addition, this youth is a victim of neglect because of his mother's ongoing substance use problems and has the added responsibility of supervising his two younger siblings, leading to school attendance problems and truancy. As has been discussed, youth with these adversities are then also much more likely to find themselves headed into the juvenile justice system, where they are also much more likely to not receive treatment and then to recidivate these behaviors, increasing chances for detention and incarceration. Youth in these positions are in unfortunate circumstances, but also experience a good share of disparity in their school and disability experiences, as well as cumulative unfairness if going down the delinquency adjudication pathway.

However, serious offending does not have to be the outcome for a majority of these children and youth. As reviewed in the preceding chapters, it is possible to prevent many of these difficulties from devolving into debilitating or chronic impairments through earlier identification and effective treatment, thus preventing ongoing difficulties and possible later detentions or incarcerations. Keeping these children and youth out of ever-deepening contact with the juvenile justice system is not a simple task for two reasons: first, the difficulties are often covert; and second, the problems are often comorbid with other challenges as well. When the problems are not identified and tended to during childhood, but manifest themselves into adolescence, there is an increased risk of serious youthful offending. Working with older youth with longer-seated, entrenched problems requires more intense effort and often coordination across numerous youth-caring systems and among many stakeholders to stem youthful offending.

Significant steps have been taken to recognize these multiple and complex problems, to initiate treatment alternatives away from punishment-only options, to coordinate services and supports among the youth-caring systems, and to untangle the most perplexing conundrums in how to pay for the rehabilitation. While it is widely recognized that earlier identification and coordinated interventions for youth with mental health, substance abuse, trauma, and learning disabilities are most effective (Aos, 2004; Aos et al., 2011), such efforts require either additional dollars be reallocated to the diversion and low-level offender stage of the juvenile justice system, or the juvenile courts bear the increased burden of working with serious youthful offenders with comorbid difficulties and more entrenched problems.

Evidence for Moving From Punishment to Treatment

The juvenile justice system is shifting, in fits and starts, from a generation-long punitive model toward a rehabilitative paradigm. The reasons are varied and include, but are not limited to, the poor outcomes from the institutionalizing punishment-only model, states' budgetary restraints and the high costs of institutionalizing youth, changes in spending priorities at the state and local levels, increased identification of effective and non-incarceration alternatives, and shifting public and stakeholder opinions on punishment-only options (Howell, 2003; Mallett et al., 2012; Mulvey and Iselin, 2008). This shift toward rehabilitation, though, poses significant challenges to juvenile courts and juvenile court personnel, not only in reprioritizing policies and procedures, but also because many juvenile justice programs and facilities are ill-equipped to handle the mental health and comorbid youth problems (Kinscherff, 2012).

Public support for treatment and rehabilitation of youthful offenders appears to be growing. National surveys showed overwhelming public approval for a number of changes that focus on prevention and rehabilitation rather than punishment, for an end to the practice of incarcerating youth in adult facilities, and for ongoing efforts to better assist youthful offenders within the juvenile justice system (Campaign for Youth Justice, 2011; National Juvenile Justice Network, 2005).

Some of the strongest supportive evidence for continuing this shift from a punitive to rehabilitative paradigm, particularly for serious youthful offenders, is that youth crime has decreased over the past fifteen years. This decrease in youth crime has occurred even while certain jurisdictions and states have shifted away from punitive models toward youth rehabilitation—diversion, treatment, and other non-punitive measures—thus reinforcing that these changes do not make communities less safe. From 1997 to 2008, the number of youth in juvenile correctional facilities has declined almost 25 percent, with decreases of more than 40 percent in long-term juvenile correctional facilities (Sickmund et al., 2010). Over this same time period all types of juvenile crime—drug, personal, property, and status offenses—have decreased, including an almost 30 percent decline in violent youth offenses (Puzzanchera, 2009). Almost all states that decreased their detention and incarceration rates have simultaneously decreased their juvenile offender arrest rates. But those states that have decreased their correctional facility placements by more than 40 percent have subsequently decreased their juvenile offender arrest rates more than those states that have decreased their correctional facility placements by less significant percentages (Mendel, 2011). Thus, this decrease in juvenile custody populations does not seem to have an impact on juvenile offending rates. This finding is reinforced by the increased recognition that the detention and incarceration of youthful offenders may be part of the problem (Annie E. Casey Foundation, 2011; Dodge et al., 2006; Petrosino et al., 2011).

Systems Collaboration

Some of these improved youthful offender outcomes grow out of better-developed coordination among the systems responsible for working with at-risk youth and youth with disabilities: schools, child welfare, mental health, substance abuse, and the juvenile courts. However, supportive systems are nonetheless still often overwhelmed with the unmet disability needs of at-risk youth. Public schools, the juvenile courts, and community-based youth care agencies may lack the capacity to identify, let alone effectively address, the learning, trauma-related, and mental health problems of youth in their communities. The subset of this at-risk population, those with comorbid disabilities and risk factors, are of special concern to the juvenile courts because of the particular difficulties in treating them and effectively minimizing harmful outcomes (Garland et al., 2001; Sebring et al., 2006).

Children and youth with such complex needs pose significant challenges to the supporting systems that are often designed to address a more narrow set of problems (Spain and Waugh, 2005). Special education programs in schools are regulated by federal and state laws to define the problems; child welfare agencies are charged with identifying and protecting children and youth at risk for maltreatment; mental health and substance abuse agencies utilize psychiatric definitions to identify the child and youth difficulties; and the juvenile courts have the task of protecting both the youth and the community from further or pending offending acts. Sometimes these efforts are aligned toward addressing youth disability needs, but also they are in conflict with battles over the financing of treatment services and over responsibility in caretaking, with fragmentation of services, and with families forced to navigate between or among systems that have separate procedures, language, and expectations (Leone and Weinberg, 2010).

Barriers to coordination across systems can be substantial, and include, but are not limited to, inadequate understanding across systems, too many advocates working at cross purposes on behalf of the youth with disabilities, confidentiality concerns, and information sharing difficulties (Medaris, Campbell, and James, 1997; Stone, D'Andrade, and Austin, 2007; U.S. Department of Justice, 2010; Weinberg, Zetlin, and Shea, 2009). Though vital to coordination efforts, information sharing remains controversial because of concerns among stakeholders as to how certain sensitive information pertaining to matters such as child maltreatment, school problems, or arrest and conviction records may be utilized by other stakeholders (Mears and Kelly, 1999). Still, some significant efforts have been made across some of these systems to improve coordination in achieving improved youth and family outcomes, as reviewed next.

Child Welfare and Delinquency Prevention Coordination Efforts

Public Efforts

The area in which coordination has received the most attention and effort is the link between child welfare and the juvenile court, often referred to as dually-involved, dually-adjudicated, or crossover. These youth, who are adjudicated as delinquent, also have past or sometimes ongoing, maltreatment victimization experiences (Herz and Ryan, 2008; Leone and Weinberg, 2010; Petro, 2008). Numerous stakeholders have prioritized this at-risk population, including a number of federal initiatives.

The Coordinating Council on Juvenile Justice and Delinquency Prevention is an effort by nine federal agencies and other groups to serve, coordinate, and prevent delinquent outcomes for the most vulnerable youth group. Member institutions include the Department of Health and Human Services, Department of Education, Department of Labor, Housing and Human Development, Office of Juvenile Justice and Delinquency Prevention (Department of Justice), Homeland Security and Immigration and Customs Enforcement, Corporation for National and Community Service, and Office of National Drug Control Policy. This policy and stakeholder group is guided by a number of important statutory responsibilities, including coordinating delinquency programs, unaccompanied youth care programs, and missing and exploited children programs; examining how programs can be coordinated among federal, state, and local governments to better serve at-risk youth, with subsequent annual reports to Congress; reviewing practices and programs for adherence to the requirements of the Juvenile Justice and Delinquency Prevention Act; recommending funding proposals that coordinate the Office of Juvenile Justice and Delinquency Prevention Program collaborative efforts; and recommending improved practices for holding youth in custody (Coordinating Council on Juvenile Justice and Delinquency Prevention, 2008).

In addition, the council has established the Shared Youth Vision partnership, a multiagency collaboration developed to integrate systems at the federal, state, and local level in support of the transition of at-risk youth into young adulthood. Sixteen states have received planning grants to pilot collaborative youth-system efforts around information sharing and strategic reform, with initial positive impact (U.S. Department of Labor, 2009a). A number of examples of these state efforts provide some guidance to stakeholders.

In Delaware, important governmental changes have taken place. The state government structure has been coordinated across child- and family-serving agencies, with the Department of Services for Children, Youth, and Their Families overseeing juvenile justice (Division of Youth Rehabilitative Services), child welfare (Division of Family Services), and mental health (Division of Prevention and Behavioral Health Services) (Wilson, Kelly, and Howell, 2012). This unique and enviable state government organization also allows for innovative and collaborative initiatives. One of these is a vocational system for City of Wilmington youth who are aging out of foster care, this addresses the priorities of the Shared Youth Vision framework— alternative education, demand-driven training systems, targeting the neediest youth, and improving service provision. With lessons learned from these efforts, replication is planned for in other areas of the state with targeted at-risk youth populations. Three strategies are being employed: a comprehensive analysis of organizations that serve the target population, searching for service gaps and barriers; creation of an interdisciplinary coalition to strategize and integrate the service delivery system; and improving data collection and sharing to ensure that information is comprehensive and accurate (Leone and Weinberg, 2010; U.S. Department of Labor, 2009b).

Iowa established, prior to the Shared Youth Vision partnership but now working in tandem with this federal initiative, the Iowa Collaboration for Youth Development, a network of ten state agencies committed to improving results among Iowa youth through the adoption and implementation of positive youth development principles and practices at state and local levels. These efforts work with public-private coalitions in both Dubuque and Buena Vista counties to strengthen partnerships, build capacity, and integrate services and resources for youth, ages fourteen to twenty-one, who are involved in or who have aged out of Iowa's child welfare and/or juvenile justice systems. These efforts emphasize youth-engagement by expanding a leadership program for system-involved youth, called Elevate, aimed at educating policy makers, foster parents, human service workers, and juvenile court personnel on the challenges of dually-involved youth. Training and technical assistance developed through this initiative is available to communities throughout the state (Iowa Collaboration for Youth Development, 2010; U.S. Department of Labor, 2009b).

Massachusetts is promoting enhanced coordination of service delivery to the dually-involved youth in two areas of the state: Greater New Bedford and Hampden County. The pilot project is addressing the disproportionate number of youth in state care who drop out of high school. Program directors representing schools, workforce development, juvenile justice, foster care, and mental health have developed a shared understanding of the different youth transition points and are redesigning local programs that address barriers for youth in transition. The pilot sites are improving data collection on youth within the various systems and expanding the use of the Massachusetts Work-Based Learning Plan, a diagnostic and assessment tool. The agencies involved are coordinating ways to better leverage each other's resources to improve youth outcomes (U.S. Department of Labor, 2009b).

While improving systems coordination is possible at the local level, with numerous examples of such success, common difficult challenges include organizational structure that impedes change, adversarial interactions among stakeholders, inadequate understanding of the discrepancies between systems, and legal violations, particularly with child welfare agencies and school districts (Leone & Weinberg, 2010; Petro, 2007; Tuell, 2008). If these barriers are overcome, significant improvements of youth and young adult outcomes can be achieved (Culhane et al., 2011).

Collaborative efforts to coordinate services among youth with comorbid problems are often pursued at the local or county level, where stakeholders and policy makers have many shared interests with this population. One local initiative that collaborates to serve youth in the foster care and juvenile court systems is the Family-to-Family Initiative (sponsored by The Annie E. Casey Foundation) in six California counties. The focus among interagency work groups formed through this initiative is to identify barriers to service coordination and find solutions to these problems, with work group members including representatives from child welfare, county education, school districts, mental health, and probation, among others. Common barriers identified include agency attitudes and organizational structures that impede collaboration; legal violations, often with child welfare and/or the Individuals with Disabilities Education Act regulations; adversarial communications among agency workers; lack of knowledge of other agencies' procedures; and youth placement instability (Leone and Weinberg, 2010; Weinberg, Zetlin, and Shea, 2009). In these counties, work group efforts changed and improved coordination, whereby the work group became the primary place where members collaborated and improved youth outcomes (for example, expedited placement for foster youth into school) (Weinberg et al., 2009).

An important identified component of these public collaborative efforts is information and database sharing. These linkages may include child welfare agencies, juvenile courts, school districts, and mental health agencies, among others, and include both individual and aggregate reporting. Improved information sharing allows all interested parties to be updated in real time as to the functioning and outcomes of the youth. A number of California counties (Sacramento, Fresno, and San Diego) have successfully linked school district, child welfare, and other system databases to allow secure access for authorized users to transcripts, school attendance, disciplinary records, test scores, out-of-home placements, and other important information (California Education Collaborative for Children in Foster Care, 2008).

Private Efforts

Non-governmental efforts to develop a practice model that can be utilized at the local level to coordinate between the child welfare and juvenile justice systems are being led by the Casey Family Programs and the Center for Juvenile Justice Reform. While these practice models have not been in place frequently or long enough for complete evaluation, based on evidence to date there is significant promise in positive coordination efforts and change. This model aims to reduce the number of crossover youth as well as out-of-home or juvenile court placement and includes the following: the timely identification of crossover youth to allow for information sharing between systems, including families as integral parts of the process and decision-making; maximizing services in the prevention of crossover youth; and ensuring that foster care placement bias (the fact that the youth is already placed out of his or her home) does not occur when juvenile court detention or disposition decisions are made. Goals for this practice model include reductions in the following youth measures: placement in out-of-home care, dual-adjudications in child welfare and the juvenile courts, re-entering child welfare from juvenile justice placements, foster care placements progressing to the juvenile justice system; and recidivism, with corresponding increases in interagency information sharing, family involvement, and program evaluations (Center for Juvenile Justice Reform, 2011).

This model approaches change to the current juvenile court processing system in sequential steps. For child-welfare-involved youth who are referred to the juvenile court, diversion meetings with stakeholders from all systems (including child welfare) are held to reduce youth crossing over into formal court processing, with the identification of available diversionary resources an important priority. If a youth is formally involved with juvenile court, then coordination between the child welfare and court personnel must occur. This includes integrating assessments, case plans, family involvement; and, as needed, utilizing evidence-based practices: FFT, MST, wraparound services, and Family Functional Parole. If youth placement is necessary, in either system, then these efforts are coordinated between the workers and stakeholders, identifying the most appropriate options through concurrent planning. These efforts often include other involved youth-caring systems, in particular, the schools and mental health agencies (Center for Juvenile Justice Reform, 2011).

Dismantling the School-to-Prison Pipeline

School districts working with youngsters who have learning and emotional disabilities are directed by the Individuals with Disabilities Education Act. The identification, evaluation, and, when appropriate, servicing of these children and youth are vital in reducing ongoing or long-term difficulties. However, an area of concern that has received appropriate and significant attention over the past decade is the link from these youth with certain school-related disabilities—most often learning disabilities and emotional problems—to the juvenile courts, a phenomenon noted earlier, and called the school-to-prison pipeline. This pipeline refers to a set of school policies and procedures that make criminalization of children and youth more likely through the emphasis of punitive consequences, student exclusion, and juvenile justice system involvement (Advancement Project, 2011).

The school-to-prison pipeline results from two primary forces: the influence of the most recent "tough on crime" approach to youthful offenders and school districts' increased utilization of zero tolerance policies (Stinchcomb, Bazemore, and Riestenberg, 2006). Zero tolerance policies prioritize disciplinary measures for disruptive youth behaviors in schools, including suspensions and expulsions, school-based arrests (for mostly misdemeanor offenses), disciplinary alternative schools, and referrals to the juvenile courts, though evidence increasingly indicates that these zero tolerance policy measures do not make schools safer or improve short-term or long-term student behaviors (Advancement Project, 2005; American Psychological Association, 2006).

Youth with learning disabilities and emotional problems are disproportionately represented within this pipeline. Youth with these difficulties are often disproportionately suspended or removed from schools, compared to their non-disabled peers, and referred to the juvenile courts, though the explanations for this phenomenon are as yet unclear (Federal Advisory Committee on Juvenile Justice, 2010; Fenning and Rose, 2007; Raffaele-Mendez, 2003). It is clear, though, that punitive school policies have an impact, as public school youth suspension rates doubled from 1974 to 2000, disproportionately affecting minority youth (Advancement Project, 2005) and also presumably disproportionately affecting youth with disabilities. Suspended youth are much more likely to be unsupervised during the day, to fail academically, and to drop out of school. These are all precipitating factors for juvenile court involvement (Wald and Losen, 2003).

Reducing the impact of the flow into the school-to-prison pipeline will require cutting back disciplinary actions and increasing preventative and non-exclusionary intervention strategies. These preventative interventions include positive behavioral support programs, peer mediation programs, conflict resolution programs, and other restorative justice models (Committee on School Health of the American Academy of Pediatrics, 2003; National Association of School Psychologists, 2008; U.S. Department of Justice, 2007). Research shows that restorative justice models have improved outcomes for youth with disabilities in numerous school jurisdictions, and, in particular, when cross-system stakeholders—schools, juvenile courts, law enforcement, and social service agencies—have coordinated efforts to reduce school arrests, minimizing juvenile court involvement (Advancement Project 2010; Cregor and Hewitt, 2011). In addition, if a school district utilizes police officers for security purposes, it is important that these officers be well trained in a broad array of non-disciplinary alternatives, or else it is likely that responses to youth behavioral problems may disproportionately be arrest and juvenile court referral (Kim and Geronimo, 2009).

The restorative justice model, as noted, initially an alternative to the disciplinary approach, has been increasingly piloted within schools and was first utilized in the later 1990s in some districts in Colorado, Minnesota, Arizona, and New York (Karp and Breslin, 2001). While not evaluated well enough to date to know if this program is more than just a promising alternative approach, many stakeholders are searching for non-punitive and non-disciplinary ways to handle youth behavioral problems (Morrison, 2001; Riestenberg, 2003). Within this model's restorative process, participants respond to conflict, offenses, or violations by bringing together the person who was harmed, the perpetrator of the harm, and other involved stakeholders (family, teachers, and students, among others). This process thus allows the perpetrator to acknowledge the harm, take responsibility, and promote acceptance by the involved parties. In order to avoid future reoccurrences, the focus is on changing the youth behavior and circumstances of the harm (Braithwaite, 2002; Van Ness and Strong, 2001). In three case studies of restorative justice programs in St. Paul, Minnesota, over the course of three academic years, in-school suspensions decreased by more than 30 percent, out-of-school suspensions decreased by over 60 percent, and behavioral problem referrals decreased by over 50 percent (Stinchcomb et al., 2006).

When a youth with a learning disability or emotional problem does become involved with the juvenile court, what happens during the intake process is crucial, as has been discussed. Early identification by juvenile court personnel of learning or emotional difficulties and consequent coordination with the school district are crucial for positive outcomes. To support these efforts, juvenile court personnel should be effectively trained in interviewing skills with youth and families, in how to request appropriate and necessary school records, in background knowledge of school educational services, and in how to coordinate the necessary activities (Mallett, 2011b).

Mental Health and Substance Abuse

Coordinating services and utilizing effective interventions for youth with mental health and substance abuse disorders are very challenging for stakeholders. Locally, juvenile courts cannot be expected to have the resources available within their budgets to effectively identify the problems under discussion here and to offer appropriate services. Given that between 25 and 80 percent of formally court-involved youthful offenders have at least one identified mental health or substance abuse problem, and upwards of 20 percent of these youth have a severe and debilitating impairment, including a significantly high rate of suicidal behaviors (Abram et al., 2003; Chassin, 2008; Douglas et al., 2006; Grisso, 2008; Hayes, 2004; Shufelt and Cocozza, 2006), problems such as these require a spectrum of services including primary care, specialty medical care, and social services, often within the home, school, and community environments.

As mentioned previously, coordinating the financing of these services can often become a complex and perplexing matter. Also, even after this sort of disability is identified and diagnosed, barriers are encountered both in arranging access to services and also in obtaining subsequent financial support for those services (Centers for Disease Control and Prevention, 2009). A number of resources finance these youth mental health services, including federal grants as well as federal and private insurance. Juvenile justice grants, offered by the Office of Juvenile Justice and Delinquency Prevention, include block and state juvenile justice formula grants that cover a limited percentage of necessary mental health services. Mental health grants, offered by the Comprehensive Community Mental Health Services for Children and Families (United States Department of Health and Human Services), are available to develop community-based systems of care. Medicaid and the Children's Health Insurance Program (CHIP) provide health insurance coverage for children and youth living in poor families, covering the largest number of at-risk children and youth. In most states Medicaid provides coverage for a variety of mental health services including rehabilitation, prescription drugs, school-based care, non-physician services, and case management programs (Mechanic, 2008). Private insurance, while covering the largest percentage, indeed a majority of all children and youth, generally provides fewer mental health services than Medicaid (Models for Change, 2011).

Most youth who are formally juvenile court involved or adjudicated delinquent reside in lower-income families and can use Medicaid or CHIP health insurance coverage for mental health services. Juvenile justice system personnel should become adept at screening for mental health problems, utilizing any number of standardized assessments that are available (Skowyra and Cocozza, 2007), determining Medicaid eligibility or financial service coverage for youth in the juvenile justice system, and then linking eligible youngsters to appropriate community-based services as soon as possible after intake. While there is a fairly long history of collaboration between the local juvenile justice and mental health systems, a majority of states have not attempted to coordinate the funding streams that support these mental health services, causing significant barriers in youth and family treatment (Cooper et al., 2008; Druss and Mauer, 2010; Models for Change, 2011).

Broader efforts have been taken in working with at-risk youth, in particular those with significant mental health problems, including the systems of care initiative. A system of care is a coordinated network of community-based, culturally competent services, along with individual and family supports offered in the least restrictive environment. The concept of systems of care has had a significant impact on shaping mental health policy and related services for this youth population (Stroul, Blau, and Friedman, 2010; Stroul, Blau, and Sondheimer, 2008). The systems of care initiative originally focused on youth with severe emotional disabilities, though over time and in some jurisdictions it has effectively incorporated the broader juvenile justice system population as well. Results in some areas have been positive, but significant barriers remain in optimizing this system. Improved organization and integration of services is often insufficient to affect youth outcomes, though it is an important starting point in breaking down coordination barriers sharing costs among systems. Financial "turf battles" across agencies and systems as to the financing of youth case plans and interventions are significant barriers to the system of care initiative, limiting its impact on youthful offenders (Bickman, 1996, 1999; Manntueffel et al., 2008).

Collaborative Efforts to Reform Juvenile Detention

Reform efforts to move away from detaining youthful offenders have been led by The Annie E. Casey Foundation's Juvenile Detention Alternatives Initiative (JDAI), an almost two-decade movement to assist juvenile courts in decreasing their use of detention and improving youth recidivism rates by focusing on youth risks and disabilities (Annie E. Casey Foundation, 2009). JDAI works to decrease the use of detention through collaboration across youth-caring systems, including child welfare, mental health, schools, social service agencies; builds community-based rehabilitative alternatives; and utilizes standardized assessment instruments and data collection within juvenile courts to direct decision-making.

Results, depending on length of implementation, have been positive in the over 150 jurisdictions in thirty-five states in which the JDAI has been involved. These results include the lowering of detention populations and youth reoffending rates, sometimes by over 40 percent, and state incarceration placements by more than 34 percent, thus often freeing up limited juvenile justice system resources to be used for more productive and cost-effective programming. For example, in Albuquerque, New Mexico, JDAI reduced the detention population by 44 percent through reorganization of the city's resources, thus expanding innovated, community-based treatment alternatives. Ultimately, juvenile court staff members in this jurisdiction were reassigned from the two closed secure detention facilities that were no longer needed to front-end delinquency diversion and treatment services, shifting emphasis to prevention (Annie E. Casey Foundation, 2009; Mendel, 2011).

Across jurisdictions that have reformed their detention placement usage a number of important factors have been identified, including strong judicial leadership, local collaboratives that include all stakeholders, the use of detention and disability data, and often the reformation of management information systems to guide decision making (Henry, 2011). Though these detention reform efforts require collaboration, the capacity to change the systems is a building process, not one that often occurs simply because of stakeholder agreements to work together, thus requiring a key leader. In addition, front-line staff and workers should be involved early and continually in the reformation process, while recognizing that what has worked in some jurisdictions may not work in others (Feely, 2011). While these are effective detention reform results, over 450 youth detention centers and hundreds of state incarceration facilities nationwide have still not moved significantly away from the punitive model (Holman and Ziedenberg, 2006).

In similar efforts at decreasing youthful offender incarceration, a number of states have shifted financial incentives to encourage local juvenile courts to utilize non-incarceration alternatives. This has occurred in Alabama, Illinois, Ohio, Pennsylvania, Texas, Wisconsin, and New York with effective results: finding between 25 and 63 percent reductions in state incarceration rates. Often, the funds are utilized for disability identification, treatment, and diversion. Through a different initiative, in California nonviolent youthful offender are no longer adjudicated and placed into any state-run residential facility, significantly decreasing this state's facilities population (Austin, Johnson, and Weitzer, 2005; Butts and Evans, 2011; Illinois Department of Human Services, 2008; Justice Policy Institute, 2009; Lowenkamp and Latessa, 2005; National Juvenile Justice Network, 2011; New York Juvenile Justice Coalition, 2009).

Minimizing the Link from these Risks to Incarceration

While efforts to improve collaboration and coordination within the juvenile justice system are important and may be imperative in obtaining better results for youth already involved with the juvenile courts, particularly for serious and chronic offenders, early identification and prevention efforts are most assuredly more efficient, effective, and fiscally responsible approaches. Without system and policy change, today's children with disabilities will continue to be disproportionately represented in the serious youthful offender population, and, in turn, will be on the pathway to juvenile and adult incarceration. As has been reviewed, stakeholders and policy makers can take steps to decrease the odds that children with trauma victimizations, mental health and substance abuse disorders, and learning disabilities will fall into the serious youthful offending pathway while improving their odds for successful young adult lives.

Earlier chapters have explained that the easiest way to impact child maltreatment is to prevent it from occurring. The most effective prevention methods appear to be home visiting programs, parent training and education, family/parent support groups, parent substance abuse treatment, sex abuse prevention, treatment foster care, and public education and information efforts. Stakeholders and policy makers could greatly decrease the risk of serious youthful offending by decreasing maltreatment victimizations of children and youth. When such victimizations occur, many potential problems may arise, including mental health disorders, substance abuse, school and learning difficulties, running away from home, and offending behaviors. Many interventions are available to work with victimized children and their families to minimize harmful effects and improve outcomes.

Mental health problems not only result from maltreatment victimization but may have significantly broader epidemiological origins. Identifying such problems, as well as intervening with effective treatments and programming as early as possible, is highly important to obtaining optimum outcomes. Many anxiety, behavior, and mood disorders do not improve on their own and often lead to other harmful symptoms. emerging as children and youth get older. If left unchecked, a proportion of these children will become severely impaired, while treating the symptoms and problems at a later time is both much more involved and costly with lower chances for full recovery. It bears repeated emphasis that youth with severe emotional disturbances comprise up to 20 percent of youth in state incarceration facilities, and are much more likely to continue these offending behaviors and recidivism as adults. Often these youth with serious mental health problems also have substance use and/or abuse problems. Treatment of youth substance abuse can be effective and often includes working with and treating the parents/caregivers, too; however, the services and links must be coordinated to access the necessary treatment.

Youth with special education disabilities, primarily learning disabilities and emotional problems, are also disproportionately represented in the juvenile courts, detention centers, and incarceration facilities. Although the explanations for this phenomenon are still being investigated, action can be taken and effective interventions can be put into place. Schools are responsible for accurate identification of these disabilities and can subsequently offer an array of education-based programming to support the child. These include in-classroom settings and teacher interactions, school-based interventions, and in-and outside-classroom classroom tutoring. When such youth enter the juvenile courts, intake professionals, probation officers, magistrates, and judges can pursue efforts at coordinating care and treatment of the youth with school district personnel and special education teams.

Delinquency Is Not Inevitable

It bears reinforcing that while the risks, disabilities, and deficits discussed throughout this book greatly increase the chances for youth delinquency and juvenile court involvement, these outcomes are not inevitable. Many children and youth experience early traumatic and maltreatment victimizations without significant long-term harm; the same is true for early mental health difficulties whereby many children and youth are less susceptible to these challenges. While learning disabilities are often long-term in nature, there are significant educational and interventive strategies to assist those afflicted in coping and functioning fully in their schools and communities.

Additionally, many children and youth have people, relationships, and supports in their lives that are able to protect them from the impact of many of these delinquency and disability risks (Collishaw et al., 2007; Fraser, 2004). There are also individual traits and strengths that often enable children and youth to avoid or minimize these risks and stay on pathways that lead to school and young adulthood success (Caspi et al., 2002; Masten et al., 1999; Werner and Smith, 2001). It is difficult to predict how an individual child or youth will respond to these various delinquency risk factors and experiences; some are more capable than others in avoiding the juvenile courts.

Conclusion

Not changing today's juvenile justice system handling of youth with mental health, substance abuse, trauma victimization, and learning problems will simply perpetuate this group's disproportionate—though not inevitable—representation in the detained and incarcerated youth population. These difficulties and disabilities, along with the detention and incarceration experience itself, leave little hope for these youth to successfully navigate into young adulthood. A society is judged not by the success of its most prominent or able-bodied but by how it treats its most disadvantaged. When looking at today's juvenile detention centers and punitively-focused incarceration facilities, it is difficult to draw any conclusion other than we have wholly failed many of these young people. We must do better.

Bibliography

Abram, K.M., Teplin, L.A., McClelland, G.M., and Dulcan, M.K. (2003). Comorbid psychiatric disorders in youth detention. *Archives of General Psychiatry*, 60, 1097-1108.

Acoca, L. (1998). Outside/inside: The violation of American girls at home, on the streets, and in the juvenile justice system. *Crime and Delinquency*, 44, 561-589.

Administration for Children and Families (2010). *Child maltreatment 2009*. U.S. Department of Health and Human Services, Washington D.C.

Administration for Children and Families (2011) National child abuse and neglect data system (NCANDS). U.S. Department of Health and Human Services, Washington D.C.

Advancement Project (2005). *Education on lockdown: The schoolhouse to jailhouse track*. Washington D.C.

Advancement Project (2010). *Test, punish, and pushout: How "zero tolerance" and high-stakes testing funnel youth into the "school-to-prison pipeline."* Advancement Project, Washington, D.C.

Advancement Project (2011). *Federal policy, ESEA reauthorization and the school-to-prison pipeline*. Advancement Project, Washington, D.C.

Alexander, J.F., Barton, C., Gordon, D., Grotpeter, J., Hansson, K., Harrison, R., Mears, S. Mihalic, S., Parsons, B., Pugh, C., Schulman, S., Waldron, H., and Sexton, T. (1998). *Blueprints for violence prevention, book three: Functional family therapy*. Center for the Study and Prevention of Violence, University of Colorado, Boulder, CO.

Alexander, J., Barton, C., Gordon, D., Grotpeter, J., Hansson, K., Harrison, R., Mears, S., Mihalic, S., Parsons, B., Pugh, C., Schulman, S., Waldron, H., and Sexton, T. (2007). *Functional family therapy: Blueprints for violence prevention, book three*. Blueprints for Violence Prevention Series (D.S. Elliott, Series Editor). Boulder, CO: Center for the Study and Prevention of Violence, Institute of Behavioral Science, University of Colorado.

Alexander, J.F., Pugh, C., Parsons, B., and Sexton, T. (2002). *Blueprints for violence prevention: Functional family therapy, volume book 3*. Center for the Study and Prevention of Violence, University of Colorado, Boulder, CO.

Almeida, M.C., Hawkins, R.P., Meadowcroft, P., and Luster, W.C. (1989). Evaluation of foster-family-based treatment in comparison with other programs: A preliminary analysis. In J. Hudson & B. Galaway (eds), *The state as parent* (299-314). Dordrecht, The Netherlands: Kluwer.

Almqvist, F., Puura, K., Kumpulainen, K. Tuompo-Johansson, E., Henttonen, I., Huikko, E., Linna, S., Ikaheimo, K. Aronen, E., Katainen, S., Piha, J.,

Moilanen, I., Rasanen, E., and Tamminen, T. (1999). Psychiatric disorders in 8-9-year-old children based on a diagnostic interview with the parents. *European Child and Adolescent Psychiatry*, 8(4), 17-28.

Altarac, M. and Saroha, E. (2007). Lifetime prevalence of learning disability among US children. *Pediatrics*, 119, 577-584.

Amaya-Jackson, L. and DeRosa, R.R. (2007). Treatment considerations for clinicians in applying evidence-based practice to complex presentations in child trauma. *Journal of Traumatic Stress*, 20, 379–390.

American Academy of Child and Adolescent Psychiatry (1997). Practice parameters for the assessment and treatment of children, adolescents, and adults with attention deficit/hyperactivity disorder. *Journal of the American Academy of Child and Adolescent Psychiatry*, 36 (Suppl.), 85S-121S.

American Correctional Association (2008). *Directory: Adult and juvenile correctional departments, institutions, agencies, and probation and parole authorities.* Alexandria, VA.

American Psychiatric Association (2000). *Diagnostic and statistical manual of mental disorders IV – TR*. American Psychiatric Association Press, Washington, D.C.

American Psychological Association (2006). *Are zero tolerance policies effective in the schools?* American Psychological Association Zero Tolerance Task Force, Washington, D.C.

Andreassen, T.H., Armelius, B., Egelund, T., and Ogden T. (2006). *Cognitive-behavioural treatment for antisocial behavior in youth in residential treatment (Protocol).* Cochrane Database of Systematic Reviews, Issue 1., Oslo, Norway.

Angold, A., Erkanli, A., Farmer, E.M., Fairbank, J.A., Burns, B.J., Keeler, G., and Costello, J. (2002). Psychiatric disorder, impairment, and service use in rural African American and white youth. *Archives of General Psychiatry*, 59, 893-901.

Anne E. Casey Foundation (2006). *Juvenile detention risk assessment: A practice guide to juvenile detention reform.* Baltimore, MD.

Annie E. Casey Foundation (2009). *Detention reform: An effective approach to reduce racial and ethnic disparities in juvenile justice.* Baltimore MD.

Aos, S. (2004). *Washington state's family integrated transitions program for juvenile offenders: Outcome evaluation and benefit-cost analysis.* Washington State Institute for Public Policy, Olympia, WA.

Aos, S., Lee, S., Drake, E., Pennucci, A., Klima, T., Miller, M., Anderson, L., Mayfield, J., and Burley, M. (2011). *Return on investment: Evidence-based options to improve statewide outcomes.* Washington State Institute for Public Policy, Olympia, WA.

Aos, S., Lieb, R. Mayfield, J., Miller, J. and Pennuchi, A. (2004). *Benefits and costs of prevention and early intervention programs for youth.* Washington State Institute for Public Policy, Olympia, WA.

Aos, S., Phipps, P., Barnoski, R., and Lieb, R. (1999). *The comparative costs and benefits of programs to reduce crime: A review of national research findings with implications for Washington state.* Washington State Institute for Public Policy, Olympia, WA.

Aos, S., Phipps, P., Barnoski, R., and Lieb, R. (2001). *The comparative costs and benefits of programs to reduce crime (version 4.0).* Washington State Institute for Public Policy, Olympia, WA.

Armeluis, B.A. and Andreassen, T.H. (2007). *Cognitive-behavioural treatment for antisocial behavior in youth in residential treatment.* The Campbell Collaboration, Oslo, Norway.

Armstrong, K.H., Dedrick, R.F., and Greenbaum, P.E. (2003). Factors associated with community adjustment of young adults with serious emotional disturbances: A longitudinal analysis. *Journal of Emotional and Behavioral Disorders*, 11, 66-76.

Aronwitz, B., Liebowitz, M.R., Hollander, E., Fazzini, E., Durlach-Misteli, C., Frenkel, M., Mosovich, S., Garfinkel, R., Saoud, J., and DelBene, D. (1994). Neuropsychiatric and neuropsychological findings in conduct disorder and attention-deficit hyperactivity disorder. *Journal of Neuropsychiatry and Clinical Neurosciences*, 6(3), 245-249.

Atkins, D.L., Andres, J., Pumariega, A.J., Rogers, K., Montgomery, L., Nybro, C., Jeffers, G., and Sease, F. (1999). Mental health and incarcerated youth: I. prevalence and nature of psychopathology. *Journal of Child and Family Studies*, 8, 183-204.

Austin, J., Johnson, K.D., and Weitzer, R. (2005). *Alternatives to the secure detention and confinement of juvenile offenders.* Office of Juvenile Justice and Delinquency Prevention, U.S. Department of Justice, Washington, D.C.

Austin A.M., MacGowan M.J., and Wagner E.F. (2005). Effective family-based intervention for adolescents with substance use problems: A systematic review. *Research on Social Work Practice*, 15(2), 67-83.

Baer, R.A. and Nietzel, M.T. (1991). Cognitive and behavioural treatment of impulsivity in children: A meta analytic review of the outcome literature. *Journal of Clinical Child Psychology*, 20, 400-412.

Bailey, K.A., Baker, A.L., Webster, R.A., and Lewin, T.J. (2004). Pilot randomized controlled trial of a brief alcohol intervention group for adolescents. *Drug and Alcohol Review*, 23, 157-66.

Baird, C. (1991). *Validating risk assessment instruments used in community corrections.* National Council on Crime and Delinquency, Madison, WI.

Baker, A.J., Wulczyn, F., and Dale, N. (2005). Covariates of length of stay in residential treatment. *Child Welfare*, 84, 363-386.

Balfanz, R. and Legters, N. (2004). *Locating the dropout crisis. Which high schools produce the nation's dropouts? Where are they located? Who attends them?* Center for Social Organization of Schools, Johns Hopkins University, Baltimore, MD.

Barkley, R.A. (1990). *Attention deficit hyperactivity disorder: A handbook for diagnosis and treatment.* New York: Guilford Press.

Barkley, R.A. (1996). Attention-deficit/hyperactivity disorder. In E. Mash & R. Barkley (eds), *Child psychopathology* (63-112). New York: Guilford Press.

Barkley, R.A. (2002). Major life activity and health outcomes associated with attention-deficit/hyperactivity disorder. *Journal of Clinical Psychiatry*, 63(112), 10-15.

Barkley, R.A., Edwards, G.H., and Robin, A.L. (1999). *Defiant teens: A clinician's annual for assessment and family interventions.* New York: Guilford Press.

Barkley, R.A., Fischer, M., Edelbrock, C.S., and Smallish, L. (1990). The adolescent outcome of hyperactive children diagnosed by research criteria:

An eight year prospective follow-up study. *Journal of the American Academy of Child and Adolescent Psychiatry*, 29, 546-557.

Barlow, J. and Parsons, J. (2002). Group-based parent-training programmes for improving emotional and behavioural adjustment in 0-3 year old children. The Cochrane Library (3), The Cochrane Collaboration.

Barnard, W.M. (2004). Parent involvement in elementary school and educational attainment. *Children and Youth Services Review,* 26(1), 39–62.

Barnofski, R. (2009). *Providing evidence-based programs with fidelity to Washington state juvenile courts: Cost analysis.* Washington State Institute for Public Policy, Olympia, WA.

Baron, S.W. (2003). Self control, social consequences, and criminal behavior: Street youth and the general theory of crime. *Journal of Research in Crime and* Delinquency, 40(4), 403-425.

Barrett, P.M. (1998). Evaluation of cognitive-behavioral group treatments for childhood anxiety disorders. *Journal of Clinical Child Psychology*, 27, 459-468.

Barrett, P.M., Dadds, M.R., and Rapee, R.M. (1996). Family treatment of childhood anxiety: A controlled trial. *Journal of Counseling and Clinical Psychology*, 64, 333-342.

Barth, R.B. (2009). Preventing child abuse and neglect with parent training: Evidence and opportunities. *The Future of Children*, 19(2), 95-118.

Barth, R.P., Blythe, B.J., Schinke, S.P., and Schilling, R.F. (1983). Self-control training with maltreating parents. *Child Welfare*, 62, 313-324.

Barth, R.P., Landsverk, J., Chamberlain, P., Reid, J.B., Rolls, J.A., Hurlburt, M.S., Farmer, E.M.Z., James, S., McCabe, K.M., and Kohl, P.L. (2005). Parent-training programs in child welfare services: Planning for a more evidence-based approach to serving biological parents. *Research on Social Work Practice*, 15, 353-371.

Battin-Pearson, S., Newcomb, M.D., Abbott, R.D., Hill, K.G., Catalano, R.F., and Hawkins, J.D. (2000). Predictors of early high school dropout: A test of five theories. *Journal of Educational Psychology*, 92(3), 568-582.

Baum, K. (2005). *Juvenile victimization and offending, 1993-2003.* Office of Juvenile Justice and Delinquency Prevention, Office of Justice Programs, U.S. Department of Justice, Washington D.C.

Bauman, K.E., Foshee, V.A., Ennett, S.T., Pemberton, M., Hicks, K.A., King, T.S., and Koch, G.G. (2001). The influence of a family program on adolescent tobacco and alcohol. *American Journal of Public Health* 91(4), 604–610.

Baumer, E. (1997). Levels and predictors of recidivism: The Malta experience. *Criminology*, 35, 601-628.

Bazelon Center for Mental Health Law (2003). *Teaming up: Using the IDEA and Medicaid to secure comprehensive mental health services for children and youth.* Washington, D.C.

Beard, K.Y. and Sugai, G. (2004). First step to success: An early intervention for elementary children at risk for antisocial behavior. *Behavioral Disorders*, 29(4), 396-409.

Beck, A.J. and Shipley, B. (1989). *Recidivism of prisoners released in 1983.* Bureau of Justice Statistics, U.S. Department of Justice, Washington D.C.

Becker, S.J. and Curry, J.F. (2008). Outpatient interventions for adolescent substance abuse: A quality of evidence review. *Journal of Consulting and Clinical Psychology*, 76(4), 531-543

Belenko, S.R. (2001). *Research on drug courts: A critical review, 2001 update.* National Center on Addiction and Substance Abuse, New York, NY.

Bellair, P.E. and Kowalski, B.R. (2011). Low-skill employment opportunity and African American-white difference in recidivism. *Journal of Research in Crime and Delinquency*, 48(2), 176-208.

Belsky, J. (1984). The determinants of parenting: A process model. *Child Development*, 55, 83-96.

Bender, K. (2009). Why do some maltreated youth become juvenile offenders? A call for further investigation and adaption of youth services. *Children Youth Services Review,* 32, 466-473.

Bernazzani, O. and Tremblay, R.E. (2006). Early parent training. In B.C. Welsh & D.P. Farrington (eds), *Preventing crime: What works for children, offenders, victims, and places* (2-21). Dordrecht, The Netherlands: Springer.

Berry, M., Charlson, R., and Dawson, K. (2003). Promising practices in understanding and treating child neglect. *Child and Family Social Work*, 8, 13-24.

Besinger, B.A., Garland, A.F., Litrownik, A.J., and Landsverk, J.A. (1999). Caregiver substance abuse among maltreated children placed in substitute care. *Child Welfare*, 78(2), 221-239.

Bettman, J.E. and Jasperson, R.A. (2009). Adolescents in residential and inpatient treatment: A review of the outcome literature. *Child Youth Care Forum*, 38, 161-183.

Bickman, L. (1996). A continuum of care: More is not always better. *American Psychologist*, 51, 689-701.

Bickman, L. (1999). Practice makes perfect and other myths about mental health services. *American Psychologist*, 54, 965-978.

Bilhulka, O., Hahn, R.A., Crosby, A., Fullilove, M.T., Liberman, A., Moscicki, E., Snyder, S., Tuma, F., Corso, P., Schofield, A., Briss, P.A., and Task Force on Community Preventative Services (2005). *American Journal of Preventative Medicine*, 28, 11-39.

Birmaher, B., Axelson, D.A., Monk, K., Kalas, C., Clark, D.B., Ehmann, M., Bridge, J., Heo, J., and Brent, D.A. (2003). Fluoxetine for the treatment of childhood anxiety disorders. *Journal of the American Academy of Child and Adolescent Psychiatry*, 42, 415-423.

Bishop, D.M. (2000). Juvenile offenders in the adult criminal justice system. *Crime and Justice*, 27, 81-167.

Bishop, D.M. (2006). The role of race and ethnicity in juvenile justice processing. In D.F. Hawkins & K. Kempf-Leonard (eds), *Our children, their children: Confronting racial and ethnic differences in American juvenile justice* (23-82). Chicago: University Press.

Blanz, B. and Schmidt, M.H. (2000). Preconditions and outcome of inpatient treatment in child and adolescent psychiatry. *Journal of Child Psychology and Psychiatry, and Allied Disciplines*, 41(6), 703-712.

Bolen, M. (2001). *Child sexual abuse: Its scope and out failure.* New York: Kluwer Academic/Plenum Publishers.

Botvin, G., Baker, E., Dusenbury, L., Botvin, E., and Diaz, T. (1995). Long-term follow-up results of a randomized drug-abuse prevention trial in a white middle class population. *Journal of the American Medical Association*, 273, 1106–1112.

Botvin, G., Griffin, K.W., Paul, E., and Macaulay, A.P. (2003). Preventing tobacco and alcohol use among elementary school students through life skills training. *Journal of Child and Adolescent Substance Abuse,* 12(4), 1–18.

Bradley, R.H. and Corwyn, R.F. (2002). Socioeconomic status and child development. *Annual Review of Psychology*, 53, 371-399.

Braithwaite, J. (2002). *Restorative justice and responsive regulation.* New York: Oxford University Press.

Breda, C.S. (1995). Delinquency and mental illness: The intersection of problems and systems. In C.J. Liberton, K. Kutash, & R.M. Friedman (eds), *8th annual conference proceedings: A system of care for children's mental health: Expanding the research base.* Research and Training Center for Children's Mental health, Florida Mental Health Institute, Tampa, FL.

Breda, C.S. (2003). Offender ethnicity and mental health service referrals from juvenile courts. *Criminal justice and Behavior*, 30(6), 644-667.

Brent, D.A and Poling, K. (1997). *Cognitive therapy treatment manual for depressed and suicidal youth.* University of Pittsburgh, Pittsburgh, PA.

Bridgeland, J.M., DiIulio, J.J., and Morison, K.B. (2006). *The silent epidemic: Perspectives of high school dropouts.* Civic Enterprises, LLC, Washington, D.C.

Brier, N. (1989). The relationship between learning disability and delinquency: A review and reappraisal. *Journal of Learning Disabilities*, 22, 546-553.

Brook, J.S., Whiteman, M., Finch, S., and Cohen, P. (1998). Mutual attachment, personality, and drug use: Pathways from childhood to young adulthood. *Genetic, Social, and General Psychology Monographs*, 124(4), 492–510.

Brooks-Gunn, J., Berlin, L.J., and Fuligni, A.S. (2000). Early childhood intervention programs: What about the family? In J.P. Shonkoff & S.J. Meisels (eds), *Handbook on early childhood intervention (2nd ed)* (549-588). New York: Cambridge University.

Brooks-Gunn, J. and Duncan, G.J. (1997). The effects of poverty on children. *The Future of Children: Children and Poverty*, 7, 55-71.

Brown, T.L., Borduin, C.M., and Henggeler, S.W. (2001). Treating juvenile offenders in community settings. In J. Ashford, B. Sales, & W. Reid (eds), *Treating adult and juvenile offenders with special needs* (445-464). American Psychological Association, Washington D.C.

Brown, R.T. and LaRosa, A. (2002). Recent developments in the pharmacotherapy of attention-deficit/hyperactivity disorder (ADHD). *Professional Psychology-Research and Practice*, 33(6), 591-595.

Brown, W.K., Miller, R.L., Jenkins, R., and Rhodes, W.A. (1989). The effect of early juvenile court adjudication on adult outcome. *International Journal of Offender Therapy and Comparative Criminology*, 33(3), 177-183.

Brunelle, N., Brochu, S., and Cousineau, M. (2000). Drug-crime relations among drug-consuming juvenile delinquents: A tripartite model. *Contemporary Drug Problems*, 27(4), 835-867.

Bruns, E.J., Walker, J.S., Adams, J., Miles, P., Osher, T., Rast, J., and VanDenBerg, J. (2004). *Ten principles of the wraparound process.* National Wraparound Initiative, Research and Training Center on Family Support and Children's Mental Health, Portland State University, Portland, OR.

Bryant, E.S., Rivard, J., and Cowan, T.M. (1994). Frequency and correlates of juvenile justice system involvement among children and adolescents with severe emotional disturbance. In C.J. Liberton, K. Kutash, & R.M. Friedman (eds), *7th annual conference proceedings: A system of care for children's mental health: Expanding the research base.* Research and Training Center for Children's Mental Health, Florida Mental Health Institute, Tampa, FL.

Buffington, K., Pierkhising, C.B., and Marsh, S. (2010). *Ten things every juvenile court judge should know about trauma and delinquency.* National Council of Juvenile and Family Court Judges, Reno, NV.

Burchard, J.D., Bruns, E.J., and Burchard, S.N. (2002). *The wraparound process. Community-based treatment for youth.* Oxford: Oxford University Press.

Bureau of Justice Assistance (2003). *Juvenile drug court: Strategies in practice.* Bureau of Justice Assistance, U.S. Department of Justice, Washington, D.C.

Burley, M. and Halpern, M. (2001). *Educational attainment of foster youth: Achievement and graduation outcomes for children in state care.* Washington State Institute for Public Policy, Olympia, WA.

Burns, B.J., Costello, E.J., Angold, A., Tween, D., Stangl, D., Farmer, E.M.Z., and Erkanli, A. (1995). Children's mental health service use across service sectors. *Health Affairs*, 14, 147-159.

Burrell, S. and Warboys, L. (2000). *Special education and the juvenile justice system.* Office of Juvenile Justice and Delinquency Prevention, Office of Justice Programs, U.S. Department of Justice, Washington, D.C.

Butts, J.A. and Evans, D.N. (2011). *Resolution, reinvestment, and realignment: Three strategies for changing juvenile justice.* Research and Evaluation Center, Jon Jay College of Criminal Justice, City University of New York.

Bynum, J.E., and Thompson, W.E. (1996). *Juvenile delinquency: A sociological approach (3rd ed).* Needham Heights, MA: Allyn & Bacon.

Caldwell, M.F., Vitacco, M., & Van Rybrock, G.J. (2006). Are violent delinquents worth treating? A cost benefit analysis. *Journal of Research in Crime and Delinquency*, 43, 148-168.

California Education Collaborative for Children in Foster Care (2008). *Ready to succeed: Changing systems to give California's foster children the opportunities they deserve to be ready for and succeed in school.* Center for the Future of Teaching and Learning, Santa Cruz, CA.

Campaign for Youth Justice (2011). *Youth justice system survey.* Washington, D.C.

Campbell, M.A. and Schmidt, F. (2000). Comparison of mental health and legal factors in the disposition outcome of young offenders. *Criminal Justice and Behavior*, 27, 688-715.

Carroll, K.M., Easton, C.J., Nich, C., Hunkele, K.A., Neavins, T.M., Sinha, R., Ford, H.L., Vitolo, S.A., Doebrick, C.A., and Rounsaville, B.J. (2006). The use of contingency management and motivational/skills-building therapy to treat young adults with marijuana dependence. *Journal of Consulting and Clinical Psychology*, 74(5), 955-66.

Casey Family Programs (1994). *Treatment foster care guidelines*. Casey Family Programs, Seattle, WA.

Casey Family Programs (2001). *Starting early, starting smart: Summary of early findings*. Casey Family Programs and the Substance Abuse and Mental Health Services Administration, U.S. Department of Health and Human Services, Washington, D.C.

Casey, P. and Keilitz, I. (1990). Estimating the prevalence of learning disabled and mentally retarded juvenile offenders: A meta-analysis. In P.E. Leone (ed), *Understanding troubled and troubling youth* (82-101). Newbury Park, CA: Sage Publications.

Caspi, A., McClay, J., Moffitt, T.E., Mill, J., Martin, J., Craig, I.W., Taylor, A., and Poulton, R. (2002). Role of genotype in the cycle of violence in maltreated children. *Science*, 297, 851-854.

Catalano, R.F., Berglund, M., Ryan, J., Lonczak, H., and Hawkins, D. (1999). Positive youth development in the U.S.: Research findings on evaluations of the positive youth development programs. Carnegie Corporation, New York, NY.

Catalano, R.F., Gainey, R.R., Fleming, C.B., Haggerty, K.P., and Johnson, N.O. (1999). An experimental intervention with families of substance abusers: One-year follow-up of the Focus on Families Project. *Addiction*, 94(2), 241–254.

Cauffman, E. (2004). A statewide assessment of mental health symptoms among juvenile offenders in detention. *Journal of the American Academy of Child & Adolescent Psychiatry*, 43, 430-439.

Centers for Disease Control and Prevention (2008a). *2007, US suicide injury deaths and rates per 100,000*. Atlanta, GA.

Centers for Disease Control and Prevention (2008b). *Reducing psychological harm from traumatic events: Cognitive behavior therapy for children and adolescents (individual & group), guide to community preventive services*. Atlanta, GA.

Centers for Disease Control and Prevention (2009). *Suicide prevention: Youth suicide*. National Center for Injury Prevention and Control, Division of Violence Prevention, Atlanta, GA.

Centers for Disease Control and Prevention (2010). *Child maltreatment: Facts at a glance*. National Center for Injury Prevention and Control, Altanta, GA.

Center for Juvenile Justice Reform (2011). *Crossover youth practice model*. Georgetown University, Washington, D.C.

Center for Juvenile Justice Reform (2011). *Practice model*. Center for Juvenile Justice Reform, Working Across Systems of Care. Georgetown University, Washington, D.C.

Chaffin, M., Kelleher, K., and Hollenberg, J. (1996). Onset of physical abuse and neglect: Psychiatric, substance abuse, and social risk factors from prospective community data. *Child Abuse and Neglect*, 20(3), 191-203.

Chamberlain, P. (1990). Comparative evaluation of specialized foster care for seriously delinquent youths: A first step. *Community Alternatives*, 2(2), 21-36.

Chamberlain, P. (1996). Community-based residential treatment for adolescents with conduct disorder. In T.H. Ollendick & R.J. Prinz (eds), *Advances in clinical child psychology, Volume 18* (63-89). New York: Plenum.

Chamberlain, P. (1998). *Treatment foster care*. Juvenile Justice Bulletin, Office of Juvenile Justice and Delinquency Prevention, U.S. Department of Justice, Washington, D.C.

Chamberlain, P. (2003). *Treating chronic juvenile offenders: Advances made through the Oregon multidimensional treatment foster care model.* American Psychological Association, Washington, D.C.

Chamberlain, P., Leve, L., and DeGarmo, D. (2007). Multidimensional treatment foster care for girls in the juvenile justice system: Two year follow-up of a randomized clinical trial. *Journal of Consulting and Clinical Psychology*, 75(1), 187-193.

Chambless, D.L. and Ollendick, T.H. (2001). Empirically supported psychological interventions: Controversies and evidence. *Annual Review of Psychology*, 52, 685–716.

Chapin, D.A. and Griffin, P.A. (2005). Juvenile diversion. In K. Heilbrun, N.E. Goldstein, and R.E. Redding, *Juvenile delinquency: Prevention, assessment, and intervention* (161-178). New York: Oxford University Press.

Chassin, L. (2008). Juvenile justice and substance abuse. *The Future of Children*, 18(2), 165-184.

Chesney-Lind, M. (1995). Girls, delinquency, and juvenile justice: Toward a feminist theory of young women's crime. In B.R. Price & N.J. Sokoloff (eds), *The criminal justice system and women* (2nd ed) (71-88). New York: McGraw-Hill.

Chesney-Lind, M. (2003). "Out of sight, out of mind": Girls in the juvenile justice system. In C.M. Renzetti and L. Goodstein, (eds), *Women, crime, and juvenile justice* (27-43). Los Angeles CA: Roxbury Publishing Company.

Chesney-Lind, M. and Irwin, K. (2008). *Beyond bad girls: Gender, violence and hype*. New York: Routledge.

Child Trends. (2010). *Teen homicide, suicide, and firearm deaths*. Washington D.C.

Child Welfare Information Gateway (2011). *Child maltreatment prevention: Past, present, and future*. Administration on Children, Youth, and Families Children's Bureau, Administration for Children and Families, U.S. Department of Health and Human Services, Washington, D.C.

Child Welfare League of America (2001). *National fact sheet*. Child Welfare League of America, Washington, D.C.

Children's Defense Fund (2009). *Cradle to prison pipeline: State fact sheets*. Washington D.C.

Children's Law Center (2003). *Education summit*. Symposium Report, May 16, 2003. Washington, D.C.

Children's Research Center (1998). *California structured decision making system, field test report*. National Council on Crime and Delinquency, Children's Research Center, Madison, WI.

Children's Research Center (1999). *A new approach to child protective services: Structured decision making*. National Council on Crime and Delinquency, Children's Research Center, Madison, WI.

Chou, C., Montgomery, S., Pentz, M., Rohrbach, L., Johnson, C., Flay, B., and Mackinnon, D. (1998). Effects of a community-based prevention program in decreasing drug use in high-risk adolescents. *American Journal of Public Health*, 88, 944–948.

Cicchetti, D., Rogosch, F.A., Lynch, M., and Holt, K.D. (1993). Resilience in maltreated children: Processes leading to adaptive outcomes. *Development and Psychopathology*, 5, 629-647.

Clark, G.N., Hornbrook, M., Lynch, F., Polen, M., Gale, J., Beardslee, W., O'Connor, E., and Seeley, J. (2001). A randomized trial of a group cognitive intervention for preventing depression in adolescent offspring of depressed parents. *Archives of General Psychiatry*, 58, 1127-1134.

Clark, H., Boyde, L., Redditt, C., Foster-Johnson, L., Hardy, D., Kuhns, J., Lee, G., and Stewart, E. (1993) An individualized system of care for foster children with behavioral and emotional disturbances: Preliminary findings. In K. Kutash, C. Liberton, A. Algarin, and R. Friedman, (eds), *5th annual research conference proceedings for a system of care for children's mental health* (365-370). University of South Florida, Florida Mental Health Institute, Research and Training Center for Children's Mental Health, Tampa FL.

Cloitre, M., Koenen, K.C., Cohen, L.R., and Han, H. (2002). Skills training in affective and interpersonal regulation followed by exposure: A phase-based treatment for PTSD related to childhood abuse. *Journal of Consulting and Clinical Psychology*, 70(5), 1067-1074.

Coalition for Juvenile Justice (1998). *A celebration or a wake: The juvenile court after 100 years*. Washington D.C.

Cocozza, J.J. and Shufelt, J.L. (2006). *Juvenile mental health courts: An emerging strategy*. National Center for Mental Health and Juvenile Justice, Delmar, NY.

Cocozza, J. and Skowyra, K. (2000). Youth with mental health disorders: Issues and emerging responses. *Juvenile Justice Journal*, 7(1), 3-13.

Code of Federal Regulations (2011). 34 C.F.R. § 300.8(c)(10)(1); 300.8(c)(10)(i-ii).

Cohen, J.A., Deblinger, E., Mannarino, A.P., and Streer, R. (2004). A multisite, randomized controlled trail for children with sexual abuse-related PTSD symptoms. *Journal of the American Academy of Child and Adolescent Psychiatry*, 43, 393-402.

Cohen, M.A. and Piquero, A.R. (2009). New evidence of the monetary value of saving a high risk youth. *Journal of Quantitative Criminology*, 25, 25-49.

Cohn, D.A. (1997). *An approach to preventing child abuse*. National Committee to Prevent Child Abuse, Chicago, IL.

Coleman, M.S. (2004). *Children left behind: The educational status and needs of youth living in foster care in Ohio*. National Center for Research and Data, The Child Welfare League of America, Washington, D.C.

Collishaw, S., Pickles, A., Messer, J., Rutter, M., Shearer, C., and Maughan, B. (2007). Resilience to adult psychopathology following childhood maltreatment: Evidence from a community sample. *Child Abuse and Neglect*, 31, 211-229.

Colson, D.B., Murphy, T., O'Malley, F., and Hyland, P.S. (1990). Assessing difficulties in the hospital treatment of children and adolescents. *Bulletin of the Menninger Clinic*, 54(1), 78-89.

Committee on School Health of the American Academy of Pediatrics (2003). Policy statement: Out-of-school suspension and expulsion. *Pediatrics*, 112, 1206-1209.

Conklin, J.E. (2003). *Why crime rates fell*. Boston: Allyn & Bacon.

Conger, D. and Rebeck, A. (2001). *How children's foster care experiences affect their education*. Vera Institute for Justice, New York, NY.

Conner, K.R. & Goldston, D.B. (2007). Rates of suicide among males increase steadily from age 11 to 21: Developmental framework and outline for prevention. *Aggression and Violent Behavior*, 12, 193-207.

Conners, C.K. (2002). Forty years of methylphenidate treatment in attention-deficit/hyperactivity disorder. *Journal of Attention Disorders*, 6(Supp 1), S-17-S-30,

Connor D.F. (2002). *Aggression and antisocial behaviour in children and adolescents: Research and treatment*. New York: The Guilford Press.

Connors, C.K., Epstein, J.N., March, J.S., Angold, A., Wells, K.C., and Klaric, J. (2001). Multimodal treatment of ADHD in the MTA: An alternative outcome analysis. *Journal of the American Academy of Child and Adolescent Psychiatry*, 40, 159-167.

Conrad, D., Dobson, C., Schick, S., Runyan, D., and Perry, B. (1998). *A successful public/private partnership in children's protective services: The children's crisis care center*. Unpublished paper presented at the Twelfth International Congress on Child Abuse and Neglect, Auckland, New Zealand.

Cooper, C.S. (2001). *Juvenile drug court programs*. Juvenile Accountability Incentive Block Grant Bulletin, Office of Juvenile Justice and Delinquency Prevention, U.S. Department of Justice, Washington, D.C.

Cooper, J.L., Aratani, Y., Knitzer, J., Doublas-Hall, A., Masi, R., Banghart, P., and Dababnah, S. (2008). *Unclaimed children revisited: The status of children's mental health policy in the United States*. The National Center for Children in Poverty, New York, NY.

Coordinating Council on Juvenile Justice and Delinquency Prevention (2008). *Report of activities and recommendations to Congress, 2001-2008*. Washington, D.C.

Cornwall, A. and Bawden, H.N. (1992). Reading disabilities and aggression: A critical review. *Journal of Learning Disabilities*, 25(5), 281-288.

Costello, J.E., Angold, A., Burns, B., Stangl, D., Tween, D.L., Erkanli, A., and Worthman, C.M. (1996). The great smoky mountains study of youth: Goals, design, methods, and the prevalence of DSM-III-R Disorders. *Archives of General Psychiatry*, 43(12), 1129-1136.

Costello, J.E.., Egger, H.L., and Angold, A. (2005a). 10-year research update review: The epidemiology of child and adolescent psychiatric disorders: I. methods and public health burden. *Journal of the American Academy of Child and Adolescent Psychiatry*, 44(10), 972-986.

Costello, J.E., Egger, H.L., and Angold, A. (2005b). The developmental epidemiology of anxiety disorders: Phenomenology, prevalence, and comorbidity. *Child and Adolescent Psychiatric Clinics of North America*, 14, 631−648.

Costello, J.E., Mustillo, S., Keeler, G., and Angold, A. (2004). Prevalence of psychiatric disorders in childhood and adolescence. In B.L. Levin, J.

Petrila, & K.D. Hennessy (eds), *Mental health services: A public health perspective second edition* (111-128). New York: Oxford University Press.

Costello, J.E., Pine, D.S., Hammen, C., March, J.S., Plotsky, P., Weissman, M.M., Biederman, J., Goldsmith, H.H., Kaufman, J., Lewinsohn, P.M., Heelander, M., Hoagwood, K., Koretz, D.S., Nelson, C.A., and Leckman, J.F. (2002). Development and natural history of mood disorders. *Biological Psychiatry*, 52, 529-42.

Coultin, C.J., Korbin, J.E., Su, M., and Chow, J. (1995). Community level factors and child maltreatment rates. *Child Development*, 66(5), 1262-1276.

Council for Learning Disabilities (2011). Comprehensive assessment and evaluation of students with learning disabilities. *Learning Disability Quarterly*, 34(1), 3-16.

Council of Juvenile Correctional Administrators (2009). *CJCA yearbook: A national perspective on juvenile corrections*. Braintree, MA.

Courtney, M.E., Roderick, M., Smithgall, C., Gladden, R.M., and Nagaoka, J. (2004). *The educational status of foster children*. Chicago, IL: Chapin Hall Center for Children.

Courtney, M.E., Terao, S., and Bost, N. (2004). *Midwest evaluation of the adult functioning of former foster youth: Conditions of youth preparing to leave state care*. Chapin Hall Center for Children, Chicago, IL.

Cregor, M. and Hewitt, D. (2011). Dismantling the school-to-prison pipeline: A survey from the field. *Poverty and Race*, 20(1), 5-8.

Crick, N.R. and Dodge, K.A. (1994). A review and reformulation of social information-processing mechanisms in children's social adjustment. *Psychological Bulletin*, 115, 74-101.

Croysdale, A., Drerup, A., Bewsey, K., and Hoffman, N. (2008). Correlates of victimization in a juvenile justice population. *Journal of Aggression, Maltreatment and Trauma, 17*(1), 103-117.

Cruise, K.R., Evans, L.J., and Pickens, I.B. (2010). Integrating mental health and special education needs into comprehensive service planning for juvenile offenders in long-term custody settings. *Learning and Individual Differences*, 21, 30-40.

Cuffee, S.P., Addy, C.L., Garrison, C.Z., Waller, J.L., Jackson, K.L., McKeown, R.E., and Chilappagari, S. (1998). Prevalence of PTSD in a community sample of older adolescents. *Journal of the American Academy of Child and Adolescent Psychiatry*, 37(2), 147-154.

Culhane, D.P., Byrne, T., Metraux, S., Moreno, M., Toros, H., and Stevens, M. (2011). *Young adult outcomes of youth exiting dependent or delinquent care in Los Angeles County*. Conrad N. Hilton Foundation, Los Angeles, CA.

Currie, J. and Tekin, E. (2006). *Does child abuse cause crime?* Andrew Young School of Policy Studies, Georgia State University.

Currie, J. and Tekin, E. (2006). *Does child abuse cause crime?* Andrew Young School of Public Policy, Research Paper Studies, Georgia State University.

Curry J.F. and Wells, K.C. (2005). Striving for effectiveness in the treatment of adolescent depression: Cognitive behavior therapy for multisite community intervention. *Cognitive and Behavioral Practice*, 12, 177-185.

Cusick, G.R., Goerge, R.M., and Bell, K.C. (2009). *From corrections to community: The juvenile reentry experience as characterized by multiple systems involvement.* Chapin Hall Center for Children at University of Chicago, Chicago, IL.

Daro, D. and Dodge, K.A., (2009). Creating community responsibility for child protection: Possibilities and challenges. *The Future of Children*, 29(2), 67-93.

Daro, D. and McCurdy, K. (2007). Interventions to prevent maltreatment. In L. Doll, S. Bonzo, D. Sleet, J. Mercy, and E.N. Haas (eds), *The handbook of injury and violence prevention* (137-155). New York: Springer.

Davis, A.B., Foster, P.H., and Whitworth, J.M. (1984). Medical foster family care: A cost effective solution to a community problem. *Child Welfare*, 63(4), 341-349.

Davis, A., Tsukida, C., Marchionna, S., and Krisberg, B. (2008). *The declining number of youth in custody in the juvenile justice system.* National Council on Crime and Delinquency, Oakland, CA.

deBettencourt, L. and Zigmond, N. (1990). The learning disabled secondary school dropout: What teachers should know. What teachers can do. *Teacher Education and Special Education*, 13, 17-20.

De Li, S. (1999). Legal sanctions and youths' status achievement: A longitudinal study. *Justice Quarterly*, 16, 377-401.

Debar, L.L., Clarke, G.N., O'Connor, E., and Nichols, G. (2001). Treated prevalence, incidence, and pharmacotherapy of child and adolescent mood disorders in an HMO. *Mental Health Services Research*, 3(2), 73-89.

Degue, S. and Widom, C.S. (2009). Does out-of-home placement mediate the relationship between child maltreatment and adult criminality? *Child Maltreatment*, 14(4), 344-355.

DeLisi, M. and Gatling, J.M. (2003). Who pays for a life of crime? An empirical assessment of the assorted victimization costs posed by career criminals. *Criminal Justice Studies: A Critical Journal of Crime, Law, and Society*, 16, 283-293.

DeMatteo, D. and Marczyk, G. (2005). Risk factors, protective factors, and the prevention of antisocial behavior among juveniles. In K. Heilbrun, N.E. Seven Goldstein, and R.E. Redding (eds), *Juvenile delinquency: Prevention, assessment, and intervention.* New York: Oxford University Press.

Dembo, R., Wareham, J., Poythress, N., Meyers, K., and Schmeidler, (2008). Psychosocial functioning problems over time among high-risk youth: A latent class transition analysis. *Crime and Delinquency*, 54(4), 644-670.

Dembo, R., Wothky, W., Shemwell, M., Pacheco, K., Seeberger, W, Rollie, M., Smeidler, J., and Livingston, S. (2000). A structural model of the influence of family problems and child abuse factors on serious delinquency among youths processed at a juvenile assessment center. *Journal of Child and Adolescent Substance Abuse*, 10, 17-31.

Dennis, M.L., Feeney, T., Stevens, L.H., and Bedoya, L. (2006). *Global appraisal of individual needs –short screener (GAIN-SS): Administration and scoring manual for the GAIN-SS version 2.0.1.* Bloomington, IL: Chestnut Health Systems.

Dennis, M.L., Godley, S.H., Diamond, G., Tims, F.M., Babor, T., Donaldson, J., Liddle, H., Titus, J.C., Kaminer, Y., Webb, C., Hamilton, N., and Funk, R. (2004). The cannabis youth treatment (CYT) study: Main findings from two randomized trials. *Journal of Substance Abuse Treatment*, 27, 197-213.

DePanfilis, D., Dubowitz, H., and Kunz, J. (2008). Assessing the cost-effectiveness of family connections. *Child Abuse & Neglect*, 32(3), 335-351.

Dhuey, E. and Lipscomb, S. (2010). Disabled or young? Relative age and special education diagnoses. *Economics of Education Review*, 29, 857-872.

Dishion, T.J., Capaldi, D.M., and Yoerger, K. (1999). Middle childhood antecedents to progression in male adolescent substance use: An ecological analysis of risk and protection. *Journal of Adolescent Research*, 14, 175-205.

Dishion, T.J., Kavanagh, K., Schneiger, A.K.J., Nelson, S., and Kaufman, N. (2002). Preventing early adolescent substance use: A family centered strategy for the public middle school. *Prevention Science*, 3(3), 191–202.

Dodge, K.A. (1993). Social-cognitive mechanisms in the development of conduct disorder and depression. *Annual Reviews of Psychology*, 44, 559-584.

Dodge, K.A., Dishion, T.J., & Landsford, J.E. (eds) (2006). *Deviant peer influences in programs for youth.* New York: Guilford Press.

Dodge, K.A. and Pettit, G.S. (2003). A biopsychosocial model of the development of chronic conduct problems in adolescence. *Developmental Psychology*, 39, 349-371.

Domalanta, D.D., Risser, W.L., Roberts, R.E., and Risser, J.M.H. (2003). Prevalence of depression and other psychiatric disorders among incarcerated youths. *Journal of the American Academy of Child and Adolescent Psychiatry*, 42, 477-484.

Dong, M., Anda, R.F., Felitti, V.J., Dube, S.R., Williamson, D.F., Thompson, T.J., Loo, C.M., and Giles, W.H. (2004). The interrelatedness of multiple forms of childhood abuse, neglect, and household dysfunction. *Child Abuse and Neglect*, 28(7), 771-784.

Door, M.M. and Lee, J.M. (1999). The role of parents training with abusive and neglectful parents. *Family Relations*, 48, 313-325.

Dore, M.M., Doris, J.M., and Wright, P. (1994). Identifying substance abuse in maltreating families: A child welfare challenge. *Child Abuse and Neglect*, 19, 541-543.

Doren, B., Bullis, M, and Benz, M.R. (1996). Predicting the arrest status of adolescents with disabilities in transition. *The Journal of Special Education*, 29(4), 363-380.

Douglas, K.S., Herbozo, S., Poythress, N.G., Belfrage, H., and Edens, J.F. (2006). Psychopathy and suicide: A multisample investigation. *Psychological Services*, 3(2), 97-116.

Drake, B., Johnson-Reid, M., and Sapokaite, L. (2006). Reporting of child maltreatment: Does participation in other public sector services moderate the likelihood of a second maltreatment report? *Child Abuse and Neglect*, 30(11), 1201-1226.

Dretzke, J., Frew, E., Davenport, C., Barlow, J., Stewart-Brown, S., Sandercock, J., Bayliss, S., Raftery, J., Hyde, C., and Taylor, R. (2004). *The effectiveness and cost effectiveness of parent-training/education programmes for the treatment of conduct disorder, including oppositional defiant disorder in children.* Wes Midlands Health Technology Assessment Collaboration, Department of Public health and Epidemiology, University of Birmingham, Birmingham.

Druss, B.J. and Mauer, B.J. (2010). Health care reform and care at the behavioral health-primary care interface. *Psychiatric Services*, 61(11), 1087-1092

DuBois, D.L., Holloway, B.E., Valentine, J.C., and Cooper, H.M. (2002). Effectiveness of mentoring programs for youth: A meta-analytic review. *American Journal of Community Psychology*, 30, 157-197.

DuBois, D.L. and Karcher, J.J. (2005). Youth mentoring: Theory, research, and practice. In D. L. DuBois and M. J. Karcher (eds), *Handbook of youth mentoring* (2-12). Thousand Oaks, CA: Sage.

DuPaul, G.J. and Eckert, T.L. (1997). The effects of school-based interventions for attention deficit hyperactivity disorder: A meta-analysis. *School Psychology Review*, 26(1), 5-28.

Dunn C., Deroo, L., and Rivara, F.P. (2001). The use of brief interventions adapted from motivational interviewing across behavioral domains: A systematic review. *Addiction*, 96, 1725-1742.

Dunst, C. (1995). *Key characteristics and features of community-based family support program.* The Family Resource Coalition, Chicago, IL.

Durlak, J.A., Furhman, T., and Lampman, C. (1991). Effectiveness of cognitive behavioural therapy for maladapting children: A meta-analysis. *Psychological Bulletin*, 110, 204-214.

Durlak, J.A. and Weissberg, R.P. (2007). *The impact of afterschool programs that promote personal and social skills.* Collaborative for Academic, Social, and Emotional Learning, Chicago, IL.

Dusenbury, L. (2000). Family-based drug abuse prevention programs: A review. *The Journal of Primary Prevention*, 20(4): 337-353.

Duwe, G. and Donnay, W. (2008). The impact of Megan's Law on sex offender recidivism: The Minnesota experience. *Criminology*, 46(2), 411-446.

Dykman, R., McPherson, B., Ackerman, P.T., Newton, J.E., Mooney, D.M., Wherry, J., and Chaffin, M. (1997). Internalizing and externalizing characteristics of sexually and/or physically abused children. *Integrative Physiological & Behavioral Science*, 32(1), 62-74.

Eggert, L.L., Thompson, E.A., Herting, J.R., and Randall, B.P. (2001). Reconnecting youth to prevent drug abuse, school dropout, and suicidal behaviors among high-risk youth. In E. Wagner and H.B. Waldron (eds), *Innovations in adolescent substance abuse intervention* (51-84). Oxford: Elsevier Science.

Elander, J., Siminoff, E., Pickles, A., Holmshaw, J., and Rutter, M. (2000). A longitudinal study of adolescent and adult conviction rates among children referred to child psychiatric services for behavioural or emotional problems. *Criminal Behaviour and Mental Health*, 10, 40-59.

Elbaum, B., Vaughn, S., Hughes, M.T., and Moody, S.W. (2000). How effective are one-to-one tutoring programs in reading for elementary students at risk for reading failure? A meta-analysis of the intervention research. *Journal of Educational Psychology*, 92(4), 605-619.

Elder, T.E. and Lubotsky, D.H. (2009). Kindergarten entrance age and children's achievement: Impacts of state policies, family background, and peers. *Journal of Human Resources*, 44(3), 641-683.

Elster, A., Jarosik, J., VanGeest, J., and Fleming, M. (2003). Racial and ethnic disparities in health care for adolescents: A systematic review of the literature. *Archives of Pediatric and Adolescent Medicine*, 157, 867-874.

Epstein, J.A. and Spirito, A. (2009). Risk factors for suicidality among a nationally representative sample of high school students. *Suicide and Life-Threatening Behavior*, 39(3), 241-251.

Esposito, C. and Clum, G. (1999). Specificity of depressive symptoms and suicidality in juvenile delinquent population. *Journal of Psychopathology and Behavioral Assessment, 21*, 171-182.

Evans, C.C. and Vander-Stoep, A. (1997). Risk factors for juvenile justice system referral among children in a public mental health system. *The Journal of Mental Health Administration*, 24, 443-455.

Evans, E., Hawton, K., and Rodham, K. (2004). Factors associated with suicidal phenomena in adolescents: A systematic review of population-based studies. *Clinical Psychology Review, 24*, 957-979.

Fabiano, G.A., Pelham, W.E., Ghangy, E.M., Coles, E.K., and Wheeler-Cox, T. (2000). *A meta-analysis of behavioral and combined treatments for ADHD*. American Psychological Association, Washington, D.C.

Fader, J.J., Harris, P.W., Jones, P.R., and Poulin, M.E. (2001). Factors involved in decisions on commitment to delinquency programs for first-time offenders. *Justice Quarterly*, 18, 323-341.

Fagan, J. (1995). Separating the men from the boys: The comparative advantage of juvenile versus criminal court sanctions on recidivism among adolescent felony offenders. In J.C. Howell, B. Krisberg, D. Hawkins, and J.J. Wilson (eds), *A sourcebook: Serious, violent, and chronic juvenile offenders* (238-257). Thousand Oaks CA: Sage Publications.

Fagan, J. (2008). Juvenile crime and criminal justice: Resolving border disputes. *The Future of Children*, 18, 81-118.

Falconer, M.K., Haskett, M.E., McDaniels, L., Dirkes, T., and Siegel, E.C. (2008). Evaluation of support groups for child abuse prevention: Outcomes of four state evaluations. *Social Work with Groups*, 31(2), 165-182.

Falkenbach, D.M., Poythress, N.G., and Heide, K.M. (2003). Psychopathic features in a juvenile diversion population: Reliability and predictive validity of two self-report measures. *Behavioral Sciences and the Law*, 21, 787-805.

Famularo, R., Kinscherff, R., and Fenton, T. (1992). Parental substance abuse and the nature of child maltreatment. *Child Abuse and Neglect*, 16(4), 475-483.

Farrington, D.P. (1997). Early prediction of violent and nonviolent youthful offending. *European Journal on Criminal Policy and Research*, 5, 51-66.

Farrington D.P. (2002). Developmental criminology and risk-focused prevention. In M. Maguire, R. Morgan, & R. Reiner (eds). *The Oxford Handbook of Criminology* (657-701). Oxford: Oxford University Press.

Farrington, D.P. and Welsh, B.C. (2003). Family-based prevention of offending: A meta-analysis. *Australian and New Zealand Journal of Criminology*, 36, 127-151.

Fashola, O.S. (2001). *Building effective afterschool programs*. Thousand Oaks, CA: Corwin Press.

Fazel, S., Doll., H., and Langstrom., N. (2008). Mental disorders among adolescents in juvenile detention and correctional facilities: A systematic review and metaregression analysis of 25 surveys. *Journal of the American Academy of Child and Adolescent Psychiatry*, 47(9), 1010-1019.

Federal Advisory Committee on Juvenile Justice (2010). *Annual report 2010.* Washington D.C.

Feely, K. (2011). *Pathways to juvenile detention reform: Collaboration and leadership in juvenile detention reform.* The Annie E. Casey Foundation, Baltimore, MD.

Feld, B. (1987). The juvenile court meets the principle of the offense: Legislative changes to juvenile waiver statutes. *Journal of Criminal Law and Criminology,* 78(3), 471-533.

Feld, B. (2009). Violent girls or relabeled status offenders?: An alternative interpretation of the data. *Crime & Delinquency,* 55(2), 241-165.

Felitta, V.J., Anda, R.F., Nordenberg, D., Williamson, D.F., Spitz, A.M., Edwards, V., Koss, M.P., and Marks, J.S. (2008). The relationships of adult health status to childhood abuse and household dysfunction. *American Journal of Preventive Medicine,* 14, 245-258.

Fendrich M. and Archer M. (1998). Long-term re-arrest rates in a sample of adjudicated delinquents: Evaluating the impact of alternative programs. *The Prison Journal,* 78(4), 360-389.

Fenning, P. and Rose, J. (2007). Overrepresentation of African American students in exclusionary discipline: The role of school policy. *Urban Education,* 42(6), 536-559.

Fergus, S. and Zimmerman, M.A. (2004). Adolescent resilience: A framework for understanding healthy development in the face of risk. *Annual Review of Public Health, 26,* 399-419.

Fergusson, D.M., Boden, J.M., and Horwood, L.J. (2008). Exposure to childhood sexual and physical abuse and adjustment in early adulthood. *Child Abuse and Neglect,* 32(6), 707-619.

Fergusson D.M. and Horwood, L. (2001). The Christchurch health and development study: Review of findings on child and adolescent mental health. *Australian and New Zealand Journal of Psychiatry,* 35, 287-296.

Ferrer-Wreder, L., Stattin, H., Lorente, C.C., Tubman, J., and Adamson, L. (2003). *Prevention and youth development programs: Across borders.* New York: Kluwer/Plenum Academic Publishers.

Finkelhor, D. (2008). *Childhood victimization: Violence, crime, and abuse in the lives of young people.* New York, NY: Oxford University Press.

Finkelhor, D. (2009). The prevention of childhood sexual abuse. *The Future of Children,* 19(2), 169-194.

Finkelhor, D., Asdigian, N., and Dziuba-Leatherman, J. (1995). The effectiveness of victimization prevention programs for children: A follow up. *American Journal of Public Health* 85(12), 1684-1689.

Finkelhor, D., Ormrod, R., Turner, H., and Hamby, S.L. (2005). The victimization of children and youth: A comprehensive, national survey. *Child Maltreatment,* 19(1), 5-25.

Finkelhor, D., Turner, H., Ormrod, R., and Hamby, S.L. (2009). Violence, abuse, and crime exposure in a national sample of children and youth. *Pediatrics,* 124(5) 1-13.

Finkelhor, D. and Wells, M. (2003). Improving national data systems about juvenile victimization. *Child Abuse and Neglect,* 27(1), 77-102.

Flisher, A., Kramer, R., Hoven, C., Kind, R., Bird, H., Davies, M, Gould, M.S., Greenwald, S., Lahey, B.B., Reigier, D., Schwab-Stone, M., and Shaffer, D. (2000). Risk behavior in a community sample of children and adolescents. *Journal of the American Academy of Child and Psychiatry, 39*, 881-887.

Florida Department of Juvenile Justice (2010). *2010 Legislative & General Budget Report*. Tallahassee, FL.

Foa, E.B. and Meadows, E.A. (1997). Psychosocial treatments for posttraumatic stress disorder: A critical review. *Annual Review of Psychology*, 48, 449-480.

Foltz, R. (2004). The efficacy of residential treatment: An overview of the evidence. *Residential Treatment for Children & Youth*, 22(2), 1-18.

Fombonne, E., Simmons, H., Ford, T., Meltzer, H., and Goodman, R. (2001). Prevalence of pervasive developmental disorders in the British nationwide survey of child mental health. *Journal of the American Academy of Child and Adolescent Psychiatry*, 40(7), 820-827.

Ford, J.D., Chapman, J.F, Hawke, J., and Albert, D. (2007). *Trauma among youth in the juvenile justice system: Critical issues and new directions*. Delmar, NY: National Center for Mental Health and Juvenile Justice.

Ford, J.D., Courtois, C., van der Hart, O., Nijenhuis, E., and Steele, K. (2005). Treatment of complex post-traumatic self-dysregulation. *Journal of Traumatic Stress*, 18, 476-477.

Forehand, R., Wierson, M., Frame, C., Kempton, T., and Armisted, L. (1991). Juvenile delinquency entry and persistence: Do attention problems contribute to conduct problems? *Journal of Behavioural Therapy and Experimental Psychiatry*, 22, 261-264.

Forness, S.R. and Kavale, K.A. (1996). Treating social skills deficits in children with learning disabilities: A meta-analysis of the research. *Learning Disability Quarterly*, 19, 2-13.

Foster Family-based Treatment Association (2004). *Program standards for treatment foster care*. Foster Family-based Treatment Association, Hackensack, NJ.

Fox, D.L. and Forbing, S.E. (1991). Overlapping symptoms of substance abuse and learning handicaps: Implications for educators. *Journal of Learning Disabilities*, 24(1), 24-31.

Fraser, M.W. (ed) (2004). *Risk and resilience in childhood: An ecological perspective, 2nd edition*. Washington DC: NASW Press.

Friedman R.M., Best, K.A., Armstrong M.I., Duchnowski A.J., Evans M.E., Hernandez M., Hodges, S., and Kutash, K.B. (2004). Child mental health policy. In: B.L. Levin, J. Petrila, and K. Hennessy (eds). *Mental health services: A public health perspective, 2nd Edition*. New York: Oxford University Press.

Freidman, R.M., Katz-Leavy, J.W., Mandersched, R., and Sondheimer, D. (1996). Prevalence of serious emotional disturbance in children and adolescents. In R. Mandersched and M. Sonnenschein (eds), *Mental health, United States: 1996* (71-89), U.S. Department of Health and Human Services, Washington, D.C.

Frick, P.J. (1998). *Conduct disorder and severe antisocial behavior*. New York: Plenum.

Frick, P.J. and Hare, R.D. (2001). *The anti-social screening device*. Toronto: Multi-Health Systems.

Frischer, M., Crome, I., Macleod, J., Bloor, R., and Hickman, M. (2007). Predictive factors for illicit drug use among young people: A literature review. *Home Office Online Report*, London.

Froehlick, J., Doepfner, M., and Lehmkuhl, G. (2002). Effects of combined cognitive behavioural treatment with parent management training in ADHD. *Behavioural and Cognitive Psychotherapy*, 30(1), 111-115.

Frontline (2005). *The new asylums*. Public Broadcasting Service. Arlington, VA.

Frothingham, T.E., Hobbs, C.J., Wynne, J.M., Yee, L., Goyal, A., and Wadsworth, D.J. (2000). Follow up study eight years after diagnosis of sexual abuse. *Archives of the Disabled Child*, 83, 132-134.

Funderburk, L., Schwartz, J., and Nye, C. (2007). *Social skills training for children with learning disabilities*. Campbell Collaboration, Nordic Campbell Center, Copenhagen, Denmark.

Gallagher, C. and Dobrin, A. (2005). The association between suicide screening practices and attempts requiring emergency care in juvenile justice facilities. *Journal of the American Academy of Child & Adolescent Psychiatry, 44*(5), 485-493.

Gallagher, C. and Dobrin, A. (2006). Facility-level characteristics associated with serious suicide attempts and deaths from suicide in juvenile justice residential facilities. *Suicide and Life Threatening Behavior, 36*(3), 363-375.

Gamm, S. (2008). *Disproportionality in special education: Identifying where and why overidentification of minority students occurs*. LRP, Bethesda, MD.

Garland, A.F., Hough, R.L., McCabe, K.M., Yeh, M., Wood, P.A., and Aarons, G. (2001). Prevalence of psychiatric disorders in youths across five sectors of care. *Journal of the American Academy of Child and Adolescent Psychiatry*, 49(4), 409-426.

Garrido, V. and Morales, L.A. (2007). *Serious (violent and chronic) juvenile offenders: A systematic review of treatment effectiveness in secure corrections*. The Campbell Collaboration Reviews of Intervention and Policy Evaluations (CT-RIPE), Campbell Collaboration, Philadelphia, PA.

Gendreau, P., Little, P., and Goggin, C. (1996). A meta-analysis of the predictors of adult offender recidivism: What works!. *Criminology*, 34, 575-607.

Gershater-Molko, R.M., Lutzker, J.R., and Welsch, D. (2003). Project safecare: Improving health, safety, and parenting skills in families reported for, and at risk for child maltreatment. *Journal of Family Violence*, 18, 377-386.

Giaconia, R.M., Reinherz, H.Z., Silverman, A.B., Pakiz, B., Frost, A.K., and Cohen, E. (1994). Ages of onset of psychiatric disorders in a community population of older adolescents. *Journal of the American Academy of Child and Adolescent Psychiatry*, 33(5), 706-717.

Glaze, L.E. (2010). *Correctional populations in the United States, 2009*. Bureau of Justice Statistics, Office of Justice Programs, U.S. Department of Justice, Washington, D.C.

Gleason, P. and Dynarski M. (2002). Do we know whom to serve? Issues in using risk factors to identify dropouts. *Journal of Education for Students Placed at Risk*, 7(1), 25-41.

Glick, B. (1996). Aggression replacement training in children and adolescents. *The Hatherleigh Guide to Child and Adolescent Therapy 5*, 191-226.

Glisson, C. (1996). Judicial and service decisions for children entering state custody: The limited role of mental health. *Social Service Review*, 70, 257-281.

Goerge, R.M., VanVoorhis, J., Grant, S., Casey, K., and Robinson, M. (1992). Special education experiences of foster children: An empirical study. *Child Welfare*, 71, 419-437.

Goldstein, N., Olubadewo, O., Redding, R., and Lexcen, F. (2005). Mental health disorders: The neglected risk factor in juvenile delinquency. In K. Heilbrum, (ed), *Juvenile delinquency: Prevention, assessment and intervention* (85-110). New York, NY: Oxford University Press.

Gomby, D.S., Culross, P.L., and Behrman, R.E. (1999). Home visiting: Recent program evaluations – analysis and recommendations. *The Future of Children*, 9(1), 4-26.

Gomez-Beneyto, M., Bonet, A., Catala, M.A., Puche, E., and Vila, V. (1994). Prevalence of mental disorders among children in Valencia, Spain. *Acta Psychiatry Scandanavia*, 89(5), 352-357.

Gordon, J.A., Moriarty, L.J., and Grant, P.H. (2000). The impact of a juvenile residential treatment center on minority offenders. *Journal of Contemporary Criminal Justice*, 16(2), 194-208.

Gordon, H. and Weldon, B. (2003). Impact of career and technical education programs on adult offenders: Learning behind bars. *Journal of Correctional Education*, 54(4), 200-209.

Gorman-Smith, D. and Tolan, P.H. (1998). The role of exposure to violence and developmental problems among inner-city youth. *Development and Psychopathology*, 10, 101-116.

Gottfredson, D.C., Cross, A., and Soule, D.A. (2007). Distinguishing characteristics of effective and ineffective afterschool programs to prevent delinquency and victimization. *Criminology and Public Policy*, 6(2), 289-318.

Gottfredson, G.D., Gottfredson, D.C., Czeh, E.R., Cantor, D., Crosse, S., and Hantman, I. (2000). *National study of delinquency prevention in schools*. Final report, Gottfredson Associates, Inc., Ellicott City, MD.

Gould, M.S., Greenberg, T., Velting, D.M., and Shaffer, D. (2003). Youth suicide risk and preventive interventions: A review of the past 10 years. *Journal of the American Academy of Child and Adolescent Psychiatry*, 42, 386-405.

Gould, N.G. and Richardson, J. (2006). Parent-training/education programmes in management of children with conduct disorders: Developing an integrated evidence-based perspective for health and social care. *Journal of Children's Services*, 1(4), 47-60.

Graham, T. and Corcoran, K. (2003). Mental health screening results for Native American and Euro-American youth in Oregon juvenile justice settings. *Psychological Reports,* 92(3), 1053-1061h.

Gray, D., Achilles, J., Keller, T., Tate, D., Haggard, L., Rolfs, R., Cazier, C,, Workman, J., and McMahon, W. (2002). Utah youth suicide study, phase 1: Government agency contact before death. *Journal of the American Academy of Child and Adolescent Psychiatry*, 41(4), 427-434.

Green, B. and Ritter, C. (2000). Marijuana use and depression. *Journal of Health and Social Behavior*, 41(1), 40-49.

Green, S.T. (2005). Prosecutorial waiver into adult criminal court: A conflict of interests violation amounting to the states' legislative abrogation of juveniles' due process rights. *Pennsylvania State Law Review*, 110, 233-357.

Greenberg, M.T. and Kusche, C.A. (1998). Promoting alternative thinking strategies. In *Blueprint for Violence Prevention (Book 10)*. Center for the Study of Prevention and Violence, Institute of Behavioral Sciences, University of Colorado, Boulder, CO.

Greenberg, M.T., Weissberg, R.P., O'Brien, M.U., Zins, J.E., Fredericks, L., Resnik, H., and Elias, M.J. (2003). Enhancing school-based prevention and youth development through coordinated social, emotional, and academic learning. *American Psychologist. Special issue: Prevention that Works for Children and Youth*, 58, 466-474.

Greenberg, M.T., Kusché, C. and Mihalic, S.F. (2006). *Promoting alternative thinking strategies (PATHS): Blueprints for violence prevention, book ten*. Blueprints for Violence Prevention Series (D.S. Elliott, Series Editor). Center for the Study and Prevention of Violence, Institute of Behavioral Science, University of Colorado, Boulder CO.

Greenberg, P. (2008). Prevention and intervention programs for juvenile offenders. *The Future of Children*, 18(2), 185-210.

Greenwood, P. and Turner, S. (2009). Overview of prevention and intervention programs for juvenile offenders. *Victims & Offenders*, 4(4), 365-374.

Griffin, P. (2003). *National overviews: State juvenile justice profiles*. National Center for Juvenile Justice, Pittsburgh, PA.

Griffin, P., Addie, S., Adams, B., and Firestine, K. (2011). *Trying juveniles as adults: An analysis of state transfer laws and reporting*. Office of Juvenile Justice and Delinquency Prevention, Office of Justice Programs, U.S. Department of Justice, Washington D.C.

Griffin, P. and Torbet, P. (eds) (2000). *Desktop guide to good juvenile probation practice*. Office of Juvenile Justice and Delinquency Prevention, National Center for Juvenile Justice, Washington, D.C.

Grisso, T. (2005). Why we need mental health screening and assessment in juvenile justice programs. In T. Grisso, G. Vincent, & D. Seagrave (eds), *Mental health screening and assessment in juvenile justice* (3-21). New York: Guilford Press.

Grisso, T. (2008). Adolescent offenders with mental disorders. *The Future of Children*, 18(2), 143-162.

Grisso, T. and Barnum, R. (2000). *Massachusetts Youth Screening Instrument-2: User's manual and technical report*. University of Massachusetts Medical School, Worchester, MA.

Grisso, T., Barnum, R., Fletcher, K., Cauffman, E., and Peuschold, D. (2001). Massachusetts youth screen instruments for mental health needs of juvenile justice youths. *Journal of the American Academy of Child and Adolescent Psychiatry*, 40, 541-548.

Grisso, T., Vincent, G., and Seagrave, D. (eds) (2005). *Mental health screening and assessment in juvenile justice*. New York: Guildford Press.

Guo, S., Barth, R.P., and Gibbons, C. (2006). Propensity score matching strategies for evaluating substance abuse services for child welfare clients. *Children and Youth Services Review*, 28(4), 357-383.

Guterman, N.B. (1997). Early prevention of physical child abuse and neglect: Existing evidence and future directions. *Child Maltreatment*, 2(1), 12-34.

Guterman, N.B. (2001). *Stopping child maltreatment before it starts: Emerging horizons in early home visitation services.* Thousand Oaks, CA: Sage Publications.

Hahn, R.A., Bilukha, O., Lowy, J., Crosby, A., and Fullilove, M.T. (2005). The effectiveness of therapeutic foster care for the prevention of violence: A systematic review. *American Journal of Preventative Medicine*, 28, 72-90.

Hahn, R.A., Lowy, J., Bilukha, O., Snyder, S., Briss, P., Crosby, A., Fullilove, M.T., Tuma, F., Moscici, E.K., Liberman, A., Schofield, A., and Corso, P.S. (2004). Therapeutic foster care for the prevention of violence. *Morbidity and Mortality Weekly Report*, 53(RR-10), 1-8.

Halemba, G.J., Siegel, G., Lord, R.D., and Zawacki, S. (2004). *Arizona dual jurisdiction study: Final Report.* National Center for Juvenile Justice, Pittsburgh, PA.

Hall, J.C. (2003). *Mentoring and young people: A literature review.* Glasgow, Scotland: The SCRE Centre, University of Glasgow.

Hamilton, C.E. and Browne, K.D. (1998). The repeat victimization of children: Should the concept be revised? *Aggression and Violent Behavior*, 3, 47-60.

Hamilton, C.E, Falshaw, L., and Browne, K.D. (2002). The link between recurrent maltreatment and offending behavior. *International Journal of Offender Therapy and Comparative Criminology*, 46, 75-94.

Hammond, C., Linton, D., Smink, J., and Drew, S. (2007). *Dropout risk factors and exemplary programs: A technical report.* National Dropout Prevention Center/Network, Clemson, SC.

Hamre, B.K. and Pianta, R.C. (2005). Can instructional and emotional support in the first-grade classroom make a difference for children at risk of school failure? *Child Development*, 76(5), 949-967.

Hanson, R.K., Gordon, A., Harris, A., Marques, J.K., Murphy, W., Quinsey, V.L., and Seto, M.C. (2002). First report of the collaborative outcome data project on the effectiveness of psychological treatment for sexual offenders. *Sexual Abuse: A Journal of Research and Treatment*, 14(2), 169-194.

Harding, K., Galano, J., Martin, J., Huntington, L., and Schellenbach, C. (2006). Healthy Families America effectiveness: A comprehensive review of outcomes. *Journal of Prevention and Intervention in the Community, 34(1/2)*, 149–179.

Harrison, A.G. (2005). Recommended best practices for the early identification and diagnosis of children with specific learning disabilities in Ontario. *Canadian Journal of School Psychology*, 20, 21-43.

Harvard Family Research Project (2010). *Family engagement as a systemic, sustained, and integrated strategy to promote student achievement.* Harvard Graduate School of Education, Cambridge, MA.

Hawkins, J.D., Arthur, M.W., and Catalano, R.F. (1995). Preventing substance abuse. In M. Tonry and D. Farrington (eds), Building a safer society: Strategic approaches to crime prevention, Crime and justice: A review of research (343-427). Chicago: University of Chicago Press.

Hawkins, J.D., Catalano, R.F., Kosterman, R., Abbott, R., and Hill, K.G. (1999). Preventing adolescent health-risk behaviors by strengthening protection during childhood. *Archives of Pediatric and Adolescent Medicine*, 153, 226–234.

Hawkins, J.D., Herrenkohl, T.I., Farrington D.P., Brewer, D., Catalano, R.F., Harachi, T.W., and Cothern, L. (2000). *Predictors of youth violence.* Office of Juvenile Justice and Delinquency Prevention, Office of Justice Programs, U.S. Department of Justice, Washington D.C.

Hawkins, J.D., Herrenkohl, T.L., Farrington, D.P., Brewer, D., Catalano, R.F., and Harachi, T.W. (1998). A review of predictors of youth violence. In R. Loeber & T.P. Farrington (eds), *Serious and violent juvenile offenders: Risk factors and successful interventions* (106-146). Thousand Oaks, CA: Sage Publications.

Hayes, L. (2004). *Juvenile suicide in confinement: A national survey (NCJ 213691).* National Center on Institutions and Alternatives. Baltimore, MD.

Hayes, L. (2009). Characteristics of juvenile suicide in confinement. Office of Juvenile Justice and Delinquency Prevention, Office of Justice Programs, U.S. Department of Justice, Washington, D.C.

Heilbrun, K. (1997). Prediction versus management models relevant to risk assessment: The importance of legal decision-making context. *Law and Human Behavior*, 21, 347-359.

Heilbrun, K., Brock, W., Waite, D., Lanier, A., Schmid, A., Witte, G., Keeney, M., Westendorf, M., Buinavert, L., and Shumate, M. (2000). Risk factors for juvenile criminal recidivism: The postrelease community adjustment of juvenile offenders. *Criminal Justice and Behavior*, 27, 275-291.

Heilbrun, K., Goldstein, N., and Redding, R. (2005). *Juvenile delinquency: Prevention, assessment, and intervention.* New York: Oxford University Press.

Heller, S.S., Larrieu, J.A., D'Imperio, R., and Boris, N.W. (1999). Research on resilience to child maltreatment: Empirical considerations. *Child Abuse and Neglect*, 23(4), 321-338.

Henggeler, S.W. (1989). *Causes of delinquency.* Newbury Park, CA.: Sage Publications.

Henggeler, S.W., Mihalic, S.F. Rone, L., Thomas, C., and Timmons–Mitchell, J. (2006). *Blueprints for violence prevention, book 6: Multisystemic therapy.* Center for the Study and Prevention of Violence, University of Colorado, Boulder, CO.

Henggeler, S.W., Schoenwald, S.K., Rowland, M.D., and Cunningham, P.B. (2002). Serious emotional disturbance in children and adolescents: Multisystemic therapy. New York: Guilford Press.

Hennessey, M., Ford, J.D., Mahoney, K., Ko, S.J., and Siegfried, C.B. (2004). *Trauma among girls in the juvenile justice system.* National Child Traumatic Stress Network, Los Angeles, CA.

Henry, B., Avshalon, C., Moffitt, T.E., and Silva, P.A. (1996). Temperamental and familial predictors of violent and non-violent convictions. *Developmental Psychology*, 32, 614-623.

Henry, D.A. (2011). *Pathways to juvenile detention reform: Reducing unnecessary delay, innovations in case processing.* The Annie E. Casey Foundation, Baltimore, MD.

Herr, C.M. and Forness, S.R. (2003). Learning disabilities and the law. In H.L. Swanson, K.R. Harris, and S. Graham (eds), *Handbook of learning disabilities* (57-75). New York: The Guilford Press.

Herrera, C., Grossman, J.B., Kauh, T.J., Feldman, A.F., McMaken, J., and Jucovy, L.Z. (2007). *Big brothers big sisters school-based mentoring impact study*. Public/Private Ventures, Philadelphia, PA.

Herz, D.C. and Ryan, J.P. (2008). *Exploring the characteristics and outcomes of 241.1 youths in Los Angeles County*. The Administrative Office of the Courts, California Courts, San Francisco, CA.

Heyman, I., Fombonne, E., Ford, T., Meltzer, H., and Goodman, R. (2001). Prevalence of obsessive-compulsive disorder in the British nationwide survey of child mental health. *British Journal of Psychiatry*, 179, 324-329.

Hill, N.E. and Tyson, D. (2009). Parental involvement in middle school: A meta-analytic assessment of the strategies that promote achievement. *Developmental Psychology*, 45(3), 740–763.

Hiller, M.L., Malluche, D., Bryan, V., DuPont, M.L., Martin, B., Abensur, R., Leukefeld, C., and Payne, C. (2010). A multisite description of juvenile drug courts: Program models and during-program outcomes. *International Journal of Offender Therapy and Comparative Criminology*, 54(2), 213–35.

Hirschfield, P.J. and Piquero, A.R. (2010). Normalization and legitimization: Modeling stigmatizing attitudes toward ex-offenders. *Criminology*, 48(1), 27-55.

Hockenberry, S., Sickmund, M., and Sladky, A. (2010). *Juvenile residential facility census, 2006: Selected findings*. Office of Juvenile Justice and Delinquency Prevention, Office of Justice Programs, U.S. Department of Justice, Washington D.C.

Hoge, R.D. (1999). An expanded role for psychological assessments in the juvenile justice system. *Criminal Justice and Behavior*, 26, 251-266.

Hoge, R.D. (2001). *The juvenile offender: Theory, research and applications*. Norwell, MA: Kluwer Plenum.

Hogue, A. and Liddle, H.S. (2009). Family-based treatment for adolescent substance abuse: Controlled trials and new horizons in services research. *Journal of Family Therapy*, 31, 126-154.

Holman, B. and Ziedenberg, J. (2006). *The dangers of detention: The impact of incarcerating youth in detention and other secure congregate facilities*. The Annie E. Casey Foundation, Baltimore MD.

Holsinger, K. and Holsinger, A. (2005). Differential pathways to violence and self-injurious behavior: African American and white girls in the juvenile justice system. *Journal of Research in Crime and Delinquency, 42*, 211-242.

Hooper, S.R., Murphy, J. Devaney, A., and Hultman, T. (2000). Ecological outcomes of adolescents in a psychoeducational residential treatment facility. *The American Journal of Orthopsychiatry*, 70(4), 491-500.

Horowitz, J.L. and Garber, J. (2006). The prevention of depressive symptoms in children and adolescents: A meta-analytic review. *Journal of Consulting and Clinical Psychology*, 24(3), 401-415.

Howard, K.S. and Brooks-Gunn, K. (2009). The role of home-visiting programs in preventing child abuse and neglect. *The Future of Children*, 19(2), 119-146.

Howe, D. (2009). ADHD and its comorbidity: An example of gene-environment interaction and its implications for child and family social work. *Child and Family Social Work*, 15, 265-275.

Howell, J.C. (ed) (1995). *Guide for implementing the comprehensive strategy for serious, violent, and chronic juvenile offenders*. Office of Juvenile Justice and Delinquency Prevention, Office of Justice Programs, U.S. Department of Justice, Washington, D.C.

Howell, J.C. (1996). Juvenile transfers to the criminal justice system: State-of-the-art. *Law and Policy*, 18(1/2), 17-60.

Howell, J.C. (2003). *Preventing & reducing juvenile delinquency: A comprehensive framework*. Thousand Oaks, CA: Sage Publications.

Huizinga, D., Loeber, R., Thornberry, T.P., and Cothern, L. (2000). *Co-occurrence of delinquency and other problem behaviors*. Juvenile Justice Bulletin, Office of Juvenile Justice and Delinquency Prevention, U.S. Department of Justice, Washington, D.C.

Hunter, J.A. (2009). *Juvenile sex offenders: A cognitive-behavioral treatment program*. New York: Oxford University Press.

Hyames, S. and de Hames, M.V. (2000). *Educational experiences and achievement of children and youth in the care of the department receiving services from Chicago public schools*. Children and Family Resource Center, University of Illinois, Urbana-Champaign, IL.

Ialongo, N., Poduska, J., Werthamer, L., and Kellam, S. (2001). The distal impact of two first-grade preventive interventions on conduct problems and disorder in early adolescence. *Journal of Emotional and Behavioral Disorders*, 9, 146-160.

Igelman, R., Taylor, N., Gilbert, A., Ryan, B., Steinberg, A., Wilson, C., and Mann, G. (2007). Creating more trauma-informed services for children using assessment-focused tools. *Child Welfare*, 86(5), 15-33.

Ihlanfeldt, K. and Sjoquist, D. (1998). The spatial mismatch hypothesis: A review of recent studies and their implications for welfare reform. *Housing Policy Debate*, 9, 849-892.

Illinois Department of Human Services (2008). *Redeploy Illinois annual report: Implementation and impact*. Chicago, IL.

Ingels, S.J., Curtin, T.R., Kaufman, P., Alt, M.N., and Chen, X. (2002). *Coming of age in the 1990s: The eighth-grade class of 1988 12 years later*. National Center for Education Statistics, U.S. Department of Education, Washington D.C.

Institute of Education Services (2009). *Intervention: Read 180*. What Works Clearinghouse, U.S. Department of Education, Washington, D.C.

Iowa Collaboration for Youth Development (2010). *2010 Annual Report*, Des Moines, IO.

Ireland, T.O., Smith, C.A., and Thornberry, T.P. (2002). Developmental issues in the impact of child maltreatment on later delinquency and drug use. *Criminology*, 40, 359-399.

Irvine, A. (2005). *Girls circle: Summary of outcomes for girls in the juvenile justice system*. Ceres Policy Research, Santa Cruz, CA.

Jainchill, N., Hawke, J., DeLeon, G., and Yagelka, J. (2000). Adolescents in therapeutic communities: One-year post treatment outcomes. *Journal of Psychiatric Drugs*, 32, 81-94.

Jekielek, S.M., Moore, K.A., Hair, E.C., and Scarupa, H.J. (2002). *Mentoring: A promising strategy for youth development (research brief)*. Child Trends, Washington, D.C.

Jenkins, J.R. and O'Connor, R.E. (2002). Early identification and intervention for young children with reading/learning disabilities. In R. Bradley, L. Danielson, and D.P. Hallahan (eds), *Identification of Learning Disabilities* (99-161), Mahwah, NJ: LEA Publishers.

Jensen, P.S., Hinshaw, S.P., Swanson, J.M., Greenhill, L.L., Conners, K.C., Arnold, E.L., Abikoff, H.B., Elliott, G., Hechtman, L., Hoza, B., March, J.S., Newcorn, J.G., Severe, J.B., Vitiello, B., Wells, K., and Wigal, T. (2001). Findings from the NIMH multimodal treatment study of ADHD (MTA): Implications and applications for primary care providers. *Journal of Developmental and Behavioral Pediatrics*, 22(1), 60-73.

Jeynes, W. (2007). The relationship between parental involvement and urban secondary school student academic achievement: A meta-analysis. *Urban Education*, 42(1), 82–110.

Johnston, L.D., O'Malley, P.M., and Bachman, J.G. (2002). *Monitoring the future national survey results on drug use, 1975–2002. Volume 1: Secondary School Students*. National Institute on Drug Abuse, Bethesda, MD.

Johnston, L.D., O'Malley, P.M., Bachman, J.G., and Schulenberg, J.E. (2011). *Monitoring the future national results on adolescent drug use: Overview of key findings, 2010*. Institute for Social Research, The University of Michigan, Ann Arbor, MI.

Johnson-Reid, M. and Barth, R.P. (2000). From maltreatment report to juvenile incarceration: The role of child welfare services. *Child Abuse and Neglect*, 24, 505-520.

Jolliffe, D. and Farrington, D.P. (2007). *A rapid evidence assessment of the impact of mentoring on re-offending: A summary*. Cambridge University Online Report.

Justice Policy Institute (2009). *The costs of confinement: Why good juvenile justice policies make good fiscal sense*. Washington D.C.

Kaminski, J.W., Valle, L.A., Filene, J.H., and Boyle, C.L. (2008). A meta-analysis review of components associated with parent training program effectiveness. *Journal of Abnormal Psychology*, 36, 567-589.

Kammer, J.J., Minor, K.I., and Wells, J.B. (1997). An outcome study of the diversion plus program for juvenile offenders. *Federal Probation*, 61, 51-56.

Kamphaus, R. and Reynolds, C. (2011). *Behavioral and emotional screening system (BESS)*. Circle Pines, MN: American Guidance Service.

Kamradt, B. (2000). Wraparound Milwaukee: Aiding youth with mental health needs. *Juvenile Justice Journal*, 7(1), 14–23.

Karp, D. and Bresliln, B. (2001). Restoative justice in school communities. *Youth and Society*, 33, 249-272.

Kashani, J.H., Jones, M.R., Bumby, K.M., and Thomas, L.A. (1999). Youth violence: Psychosocial risk factors, treatment, prevention, and recommendations. *Journal of Emotional and Behavioral Disorders*, 7, 200-210.

Kaslow, N.J. and Thompson, M.P. (1998). Applying the criteria for empirically supported treatments to studies of psychosocial interventions for child and adolescent depression. *Journal of Clinical Child Psychology*, 27, 146-156.

Katsiyannis, A. and Archwamety, T. (1997). Factors related to recidivism among delinquent youths in a state correctional facility. *Journal of Child and Family Studies*, 6(1), 43-55.

Kaufman, K.L. (2010). *The prevention of sexual violence: The practitioner's sourcebook*. Holyoke, MA: NEARI Press.

Kavale, K.A. and Forness, S.R. (1995). Social skills deficits and training: A meta-analysis of the research in learning disabilities. In T.E. Scruggs and M.A. Mastropieri (eds), *Advances in learning and behavior difficulties, volume 9* (119-160). St. Louis, MO: JAI Press, Inc.

Kavale, K.A. and Forness, S.R. (1996). Social skills deficits and learning disabilities: A meta-analysis. *Journal of Learning Disabilities*, 29(3), 226-237.

Kavale, K.A. and Mostert, M.P. (2004). Social skills interventions for individuals with learning disabilities. *Learning Disability Quarterly*, 27, 31-43.

Kazdin, A.E. and Weisz, J.R. (1998). Identifying and developing empirically supported child and adolescent treatments. *Journal of Consulting and Clinical Psychology*, 66, 19-36.

Keilitz, I., Zaremba, B.A., and Broder, P.K. (1979). The link between learning disabilities and juvenile delinquency: Some issues and answers. *Learning Disabilities Quarterly*, 2, 2-11.

Keith, J.M. and McCray, A.D. (2002). Juvenile offenders with special needs: Critical issues and bleak outcomes. *Qualitative Studies in Education*, 15(6), 691-710.

Keleher, T. (2000). *Racial disparities related to school zone tolerance policies*. Testimony to the U.S. Commission on Civil Rights, February 18, 2000. Applied Research Center, New York, NY.

Kelleher, K., Chaffin, M., Hollenberg, J., and Fisher, E. (1994). Alcohol and drug disorders among physical abuse and neglectful parents in a community-based sample. *Journal of Public Health*, 84, 1586-1590.

Kelley, T.M., Schulman, J.L., and Lynch, K. (1976). Decentralized intake and diversion: The juvenile court's link to the youth service bureau. *Juvenile Justice*, 27(1), 3-11.

Kelly, B.T., Thornberry, T.P., and Smith, C.A., (1997). *In the wake of childhood maltreatment*. Office of Juvenile Justice and Delinquency Prevention, U.S. Department of Justice, Washington D.C.

Kempf-Leonard, K. (2007). Minority youths and juvenile justice: Disproportionate minority contact after nearly 20 years of reform efforts. *Youth Violence and Juvenile Justice*, 5, 71-87.

Kempton, T. and Forehand, R. (1992). Suicide attempts among juvenile delinquents: The contribution of mental health factors. *Behaviour Research and Therapy*, 30(5), 537-541.

Kendall, P.C. and Suveg, C. (2006). Treating anxiety disorders in youth. In P.C. Kendall (ed), *Child and adolescent therapy: Cognitive-behavioral procedures (3rd ed.)*. New York: Guilford Press.

Kendrick, D., Elkan, R., Hewitt, M., Dewey, M., Blair, M., Robinson, J., Williams, D., and Brummell, K. (2000). Does home visiting improve parenting and the quality of the home environment? A systematic review and meta analysis. *Archives of Disease in Childhood*, 82(6), 443-451.

Kessler, R.C., Berglund, P., Demler, O., Jin, R., Merikangas, K.R., and Walters, E.E. (2005). Lifetime prevalence and age-of-onset distributions of DSM-IV Disorders in the national comorbidity survey replication. *Archives of General Psychiatry*, 62(6), 593-602.

Kilpatrick, D.G., Ruggiero, K.J., Acierno, R., Saunders, B.E., Resnick, H.S., and Best, C.L. (2003). Violence and risk of PTSD, major depression, substance abuse/dependence, and comorbidity: Results from the national survey of adolescents. *Journal of Consulting and Clinical Psychiatry*, 71, 692-700.

Kim, C.Y. & Geronimo, I.I. (2009). *Policing in schools: Developing a governance document for school resource officers in K-12 schools. An ACLU white paper*. American Civil Liberties Union, New York, NY.

Kinscherff, R. (2012). *A primer for mental health practitioners working with youth involved in the juvenile justice system*. Technical Assistance Partnership for Child and Family Mental Health, Washington, D.C.

Kirchner, R. and Kirchner, T. (2007). *Model program for multi-jurisdictional, rural settings. Technical report*. Administrative Office of the Courts for Nevada, Western Regional Drug Court, State of Nevada.

Klevans, J. and Whittaker, D.J. (2007). Primary prevention of child physical abuse and neglect: Gaps and promising directions. *Child Maltreatment*, 12(4), 364-377.

Knoll, C. and Sickmund, M. (2010). *Delinquency cases in juvenile court, 2007*. Office of Juvenile Justice and Delinquency Prevention, Office of Justice Programs, US Department of Justice, Washington D.C.

Koball, H., Dion, R., Gothro, A., Bardo, M., Dworsky, A., Lansing, J., Stagner, M., Korom-Djakovic, D., Herrera, C., and Manning, A.E. (2011). *Synthesis of research and resources to support at-risk youth*, OPRE Report #2011-22. Washington DC: Office of Planning, Research and Evaluation, Administration for children and Families, U.S. Department of Health and Human Services.

Korbin, J.E., Coultin, C.J., Chard, S., Platt-Houston, C., and Su, M. (1998). Impoverishment and child maltreatment in African American and European American neighborhoods. *Development and Psychopathology*, 10, 215-233.

Kosterman, R., Hawkins, J.D., Spoth, R., Haggerty, K.P., and Zhu, K. (1997). Effects of a preventive parent-training intervention on observed family interactions: Proximal outcomes from preparing for the drug free years. *Journal of Community Psychology*, 25(4), 337–352.

Kowalski, K., Lindstrom, M., Rasmussen, P.S., Filges, T., and Jorgensen, A.K. (2011). *Title registration for a review proposal: Functional family therapy (FFT) for young people in treatment for illicit non-opiad drug use*. The Campbell Collaboration, Oslo, Norway.

Kracke, D. and Hahn, H. (2008). The nature and extent of childhood exposure to violence: What we know, why we don't know more, and why it matters. *Journal of Emotional Abuse*, 8(1-2), 24-49.

Kress, J.S. and Elias, M.J. (1993). Substance abuse prevention in special education populations: Review and recommendations. *Journal of Special Education*, 27(1) 35-51.

Krisberg, B. (2005). *Juvenile justice: Redeeming our children*. Thousand Oaks, CA: Sage.

Kroes, M., Kalff, A.C., Kessels, A.G., Steyaert, J., Feron, F.J., van Someren, A.J., Hurks, P.P., Hendriksen, J.G., van Zeban, T.M., Rosendaal, N., Crolla, I.F., Troost, J., Jolles, J., and Vles, J.S. (2001). Child psychiatric diagnoses in a population of Dutch school children aged 6 to 8 years. *Journal of the American Academy of Child and Adolescent Psychiatry*, 40(12), 1401-1409.

Kumpfer, K.L. (1999). *Strengthening America's families: Exemplary parenting and family strategies for delinquency prevention*. Office of Juvenile Justice and Delinquency Prevention, Office of Justice Programs, U.S. Department of Justice, Washington, D.C.

Kumpfer, K.L. and Alvarado, R. (1995). Strengthening families to prevent drug use in multiethnic youth. In G. Botvin, S. Schinke, and M. Orlandi (eds), *Drug abuse prevention with multiethnic youth* (253-292). Newbury Park, CA: Sage.

Kumpfer, K.L., Alvarado, R., Smith, P., and Bellamy, N. (2002). Cultural sensitivity in universal family-based prevention interventions. *Prevention Science*, 3(3), 241-246.

Kumpfer, K.L., Alvarado, R., and Whiteside, H.O. (2003). Family-based interventions for substance abuse and prevention. *Substance Use & Misuse*, 38, 1759-1787.

Kumpfer, K.L., Whiteside, H.O., Greene, J.A., and Allen, K.C. (2010). Effectiveness outcomes of four age versions of the strengthening families program in statewide field sites. *Group Dynamics: Theory, Research, and Practice*, 14(3), 211-229.

Kurtz, P.D., Gaudin, J.M., Wodarski, J.S., and Howing, P.T. (1993). Maltreatment and the school-aged child: School performance consequences. *Child Abuse and Neglect*, 17(5), 581-589.

Kvartordt, C.L., Purcell, P., and Shannon, P. (2005). Youth with learning disabilities in the juvenile justice system: A training needs assessment of detention and court services personnel. *Child and Youth Care Forum*, 34(1), 27-42.

LaFond, J.Q. (2005). *Preventing sexual violence: How society should cope with sex offenders*. American Psychological Association Press, Washington, D.C.

Langan, P.A. and Levin, D.J. (2002). *Recidivism of prisoners released in 1994*. Bureau of Justice Statistics, U.S. Department of Justice, Washington D.C.

Lansford, J., Dodge, K.A., Pettit, G.S., Bates, J.E., Crozier, J., and Kaplow, J. (2002). Maltreatment on psychological, behavioral, and academic problems in adolescence. *Archives of Pediatric and Adolescent Medicine*, 156, 824-830.

Lanza-Kaduce, L., Lane., J., Bishop, D.M., and Frazier, C.E. (2005). Juvenile offenders and adult felony recidivism: The impact of transfer. *Journal of Crime and Justice*, 28, 59-77.

Larzelere, R.E., Dinges, K., Schmidt, M.D., Spellman, D.F., Criste, R.R., and Connell, P. (2001). Outcomes of residential treatment: A study of the adolescent clients of girls and boys town. *Child and Youth Care Forum*, 30(3), 175-185.

Latessa, E.J., Shaffer, D., and Lowenkamp, C. (2002). *Outcome evaluation of Ohio's drug court efforts. Technical report.* Center for Criminal Justice Research, University of Cincinnati.

Lauer, P., Akiba, A.M., Wilkerson, S.B., Apthorp, H.S., Snow, D., and Martin-Glenn, M.L. (2006). Out-of-school time programs: A meta-analysis of effects for at-risk students. *Review of Educational Research*, 76, 275-313.

Lawrence, R. and Hemmens, C. (2008). *Juvenile justice: A text/reader.* Thousand Oaks, CA: Sage.

Layzer, J. and Goodson, B. (2001). *National evaluation of family support programs.* Prepared for the Administration for Children and Families, U.S. Department of Health and Human Services, ABT Associates, Cambridge, MA.

LD Online (2009). *Problem signs: Is it LD?* LD Online, Arlington, VA.

Learning Disabilities Association of America (2011). *Learning disabilities: Signs, symptoms and strategies.* Learning Disabilities Association of America, Pittsburgh, PA.

Lederman, C.S., Dakol, G.A., Larrea, M.A., and Li, H. (2004). Characteristics of adolescent females in juvenile detention. *International Journal of Law and Psychiatry*, 27, 321-337.

Lehr, C.A., Johnson, D.R., Bremer, C.D., Cosio, S., and Thompson, M. (2004). *Essential tools. Increasing rates of school completion: Moving from policy and research to practice.* National Center on Secondary Education and Transition, College of Education and Human Development, University of Minnesota, Minneapolis, MN.

Leiber, M.J. and Fox, K.C. (2005). Race and the impact of detention on juvenile justice decision making. *Crime and Delinquency*, 51, 470-497.

Leichtman, M., Leichtman, M.L., Barber, C.C., and Neese, D.T. (2001). Effectiveness of intensive short-term residential treatment with severely disturbed adolescents. *American Journal of Orthopsychiatry*, 71(2), 227-235.

Leiter, J. (2007). School performance trajectories after the advent of reported maltreatment. *Children and Youth Services Review*, 29, 363-382.

Leiter, J. and Johnson, M. (1997). Child maltreatment and school performance declines: An event-history analysis. *American Educational Research Journal*, 34(3), 563-589.

Lemert, E.M. (1981). What hath been wrought. *Journal of Research in Crime and Delinquency*, 18(1), 34-36.

Lemmon, J.H. (2006). The effects of maltreatment recurrence and child welfare services on dimensions of delinquency. *Criminal Justice Review,* 31(1), 5-32.

Lemmon J.H. (2009). How child maltreatment affects dimensions of juvenile delinquency in a cohort of low-income urban males. *Justice Quarterly*, 16, 357-376.

Leone, P.E. and Weinberg, L. (2010). *Addressing the unmet educational needs of children and youth in the juvenile justice and child welfare systems.* Center for Juvenile Justice Reform, Georgetown University, Washington, D.C.

Leone, P.E., Zaremba, B.A, Chapin, M.S., and Iseli, C. (1995). Understanding the overrepresentation of youths with disabilities in juvenile detention. *District of Columbia Law Review*, 3(Fall), 389-401.

Lexcon, F. and Redding, R.E. (2000). Mental health needs of juvenile offenders. *Juvenile Correctional Mental Health Report*, 3(1), 1, 2, 8-16.

Leventhal, J.M. (2005). Getting prevention right: Maintaining the status quo is not an option. *Child Abuse and Neglect*, 29, 209-213.

Lewinsohn, P.M., Clarke, G.N., Hops, H., and Andrews, J. (1990). Cognitive-behavioral treatment for depressed adolescents. *Behavior Therapy*, 21, 385-401.

Lewinsohn, P.M., Rohde, P., and Seeley, J.R. (1998). Major depressive disorder in older adolescents: Prevalence, risk factors, and clinical implications. *Clinical Psychology Review*, 18(7), 765-794.

Lipsey, M.W. and Derzon, M.H. (1999). *Predictors of violent or serious delinquency in adolescence and early adulthood: A synthesis of longitudinal research*. Thousand Oaks, CA: Sage.

Lipsey, M.W. (2009). The primary factors that characterize effective interventions with juvenile offenders: A meta-analytic overview. *Victims and Offenders*, 4(4), 124-147.

Lipsey, M.W., Howell, J.C., Kelly, M.R., Chapman, G., and Carver, D. (2010). *Improving the effectiveness of juvenile justice programs*. Center for Juvenile Justice Reform, Georgetown University, Washington, D.C.

Lipsey, M.W. and Landenberger, N.A. (2006). *Cognitive-behavioural programs for juvenile and adult offenders: A meta-analysis of controlled intervention studies*. The Campbell Collaboration, Oslo, Norway.

Lipsey, M.W. and Wilson, D.B. (1998). Effective intervention for serious juvenile offenders: A synthesis of research. In R. Loeber and D. Farrington (eds), *Serious and violent juvenile offenders: Risk factors and successful interventions* (313-341). Thousand Oaks, CA: Sage.

Little, J.H., Popa, M., and Forsythe, B. (2005). *Multisystemic therapy for social, emotional, and behavioral problems in youth aged 10-17*. Campbell Systematic Reviews, The Campbell Collaboration, Oslo, Norway.

Little, J.H. and Tajima, E.A. (2000). A multilevel model of client participation in intensive family preservation services. *Social Service Review*, 74, 405-435.

Livsey, S., Sickmund, M., and Sladky, A. (2009). *Juvenile residential facility census, 2004: Selected findings*. Office of Juvenile Justice and Delinquency Prevention, U.S. Department of Justice, Washington, D.C.

Lochman, J.E. and Wells, K.C. (2002). The coping power program at the middle-school transition: Universal and indicated prevention effects. *Psychology of Addictive Behaviors*, 16(45), S40–S54.

Loeber, R. and Farrington, D.P. (eds) (1998). *Serious and violent juvenile offenders: Risk factors and successful interventions*. Thousand Oaks, CA: Sage.

Loeber, R. and Farrington, D.P. (2001). The significant concern of child delinquency. In R. Loeber and D.P. Farrington (eds). *Child delinquents: Development, intervention, and service needs* (1-22). Thousand Oaks, CA: Sage.

Loeber, R. and Hay, D.F. (1996). Key issues in the development of aggression and violence from childhood to early adulthood. *Annual Review of Psychology*, 48, 371-410.

Loeber, R. and Keenan, K. (1994). Interaction between conduct disorder and its comorbid conditions: Effects of age and gender. *Clinical Psychology Review*, 14(6), 497-523.

London Department of Health (2001). *Treatment choice in psychological therapies and counselling: Evidence-based clinical practice guideline.* Care Guideline. London: Department of Health.

Loughran, T., Mulvey, E., Schubert, C., Fagan, J., Pizuero, A., and Losoya, S. (2009). Estimating a dose-response relationship between length of stay and future recidivism in serious juvenile offenders. *Criminology*, 47(3), 699-740.

Loving, R., Singer, J.K., and Maguire, M. (2008). *Homelessness among registered sex offenders in California: The numbers, the risks, and the response* (1-44). California Sex Offender Management Board, California State University, Sacramento, CA.

Lowenkamp, C.T. and Latessa, E. (2005). *Evaluation of Ohio's RECLAIM funded programs, community correctional facilities, and DYS facilities: Cost benefit analysis supplemental report.* University of Cincinnati, Cincinnati, OH.

Lowenkamp, C.T., Makarios, M.D., Latessa, E.J., Lemke, R., & Smith, P. (2010). Community corrections facilities for juvenile offenders in Ohio. *Criminal Justice and Behavior*, 37(6), 695-708.

Lundahl, B.W., Nimer, J., and Parson, B. (2006). Preventing child abuse: A meta-analysis of parent training programs. *Research on Social Work Practice*, 16, 251-262.

Luthar, S.S. (2003). *Resilience and vulnerability: Adaption in the context of childhood adversities.* Cambridge, UK: Cambridge University Press.

Luthar, S.S. (ed) (2004). *Resilience and vulnerability: Adaptation in the context of childhood adversities.* New York, NY: Cambridge University Press.

Lynch, J.P. and Sabol, W.J. (2001). *Prisoner reentry in perspective.* Urban Institute, Washington, D.C.

Lyons, J., Baerger, D., Quigley, P., Erlich, J., and Griffin, E. (2001). Mental health service needs of juvenile offenders: A comparison of detention, incarceration, and treatment settings. *Children's Services: Social Policy, Research, and Practice*, 4, 69-85.

Lyons, J.S. and Schaefer, K. (2000). Mental health and dangerousness: Characteristics and outcomes of children and adolescents in residential placements. *Journal of Child and Family Studies*, 9(1), 67-73.

Lyons, J.S., Terry, P., Martinovich, Z., Peterson, J., and Bouska, B. (2001). Outcome trajectories for adolescents in residential treatment: A statewide evaluation. *Journal of Child and Family Studies*, 10(3), 333-345.

MacDonald, G.M. and Turner, W. (2007). Treatment foster care for improving outcomes in children and young people. *Campbell Systematic Reviews*, 9, 1-67.

MacKinnon-Lewis, C., Kaufman, M., and Frabutt, J. (2002). Juvenile justice and mental health: Youth and families in the middle. *Aggression and Violent Behavior*, 7(4), 353-363.

Magruder, J. and Shaw, T.V. (2008). Children ever in care: An examination of cumulative disproportionality. *Child Welfare*, 87(2), 169-188.

Maguin, E., Hawkins, J.D., Catalano, R.F., Hill, K., Abbott, R., and Herrenkohl, T. (1995). *Risk factors measured at three ages for violence at age 17-18.* Paper presented at the American Society of Criminology, Boston, MA.

Magura, S. and Laudet, A. (1996). Parental substance abuse and child maltreatment: Review and implications for intervention. *Children and Youth Services Review*, 18(3), 193-220.

Malmgren, K., Abbott, R., and Hawkins, D. (1999). Learning disability and delinquency: Rethinking the "link". *Journal of Learning Disabilities, 32*, 194-200.

Mallett. C. (2003). Socio-historical analysis of juvenile offenders on death row. *Criminal Law Bulletin*, 39(4), 455-468.

Mallett, C. (2006). Juvenile court probation supervised youth: At-risk in Cuyahoga County, Ohio. *Corrections Compendium, 31*(2), 1-33.

Mallett, C. (2007). Death is not different: The transfer of juvenile offenders to adult criminal courts. *Criminal Law Bulletin*, 43(4), 523-547.

Mallett, C. (2008). The disconnect between delinquent youths with mental health and special education disabilities and juvenile court outcomes. *Corrections Compendium*, 33(5), 1-23.

Mallett, C. (2009). Disparate juvenile court outcomes for disabled delinquent youth: A social work call to action. *Child and Adolescent Social Work Journal*, 26, 197-207.

Mallett, C. (2011a). "Homicide: Life on the street" and sentenced to life behind bars: Juveniles without the possibility of parole. *Criminal Law Bulletin*, 47(6), 929-947.

Mallett, C. (2011b). *Seven things juvenile courts should know about learning disabilities*. National Council of Juvenile and Family Court Judges, Reno, NV.

Mallett, C. (2012). The child maltreatment to juvenile delinquency pathway. In P. Clements & S. Seedat (eds), *Mental Health Issues of Child Maltreatment*. St. Louis, MO: STM Publications.

Mallett, C. and Julian, L. (2008). Alternatives for youth's advocacy program: Effectively reducing minority youth's detention and incarceration placements in Cleveland, Ohio. *Juvenile and Family Court Journal*, 59(3), 1-17.

Mallett, C. and Stoddard-Dare, P. (2009). Maltreated children who are adjudicated delinquent: An at-risk profile. *International Journal of Child and Family Welfare*, 2(4), 134-144.

Mallett, C. and Stoddard-Dare, P. (2010). Predicting secure detention placement for African-American juvenile offenders: Addressing the disproportionate minority confinement problem. *Journal of Ethnicity in Criminal Justice*, 8, 91-103.

Mallett, C., Stoddard-Dare, P., and Seck, M. (2009). Predicting juvenile delinquency: The nexus of child maltreatment, depression, and bipolar disorder. *Criminal Behaviour and Mental Health,* 19(4), 235-246.

Mallett, C., Williams, M., and Marsh, S. (2012). Specialized detention facilities. In O. Thienhaus and M. Piasecki (eds), *Correctional Psychiatry, Volume 2*, Kingston, NJ: Civic Research Institute Publishers.

Manly, J.T., Kim, J.E., Rogosch, F.E., and Cicchetti, D. (2001). Dimensions of child maltreatment and children's adjustment: Contributions of developmental timing and subtype. *Development and Psychopathology*, 13, 759-782.

Mann-Feder, V.R. (1996). Adolescents in therapeutic communities. *Adolescence*, 31, 17-28.

Manteuffel, B., Stephens, R.L., Brashears, F., Krivelyova, A., and Fisher, S.K. (2008). Evaluation results and systems of care: A review. In B.A. Stroul, and G.M. Blau (eds), *The system of care handbook: Transforming mental health services for children, youth, and families*. Baltimore, Maryland: Paul H. Brookes Publishing Company.

Mape, P.A., Turner, J.K., and Josephson, A.M. (2001). Parent management training. *Child and Adolescent Psychiatric Clinics of North America*, 10, 451-464.

March, J., Silva, S., Petrycki, S., Curry, J., Wells, K., Fairbank, J., Burns, B., Domino, M., McNulty, S., Vitiello, B., and Severe, J. (2004). Treatment for adolescents with depression study (TADS) team. Fluoxetin, cognitive-behavioral therapy, and their combination for adolescents with depression: Treatment for adolescents with depression study (TADS) randomized controlled trial. *Journal of the American Medical Association*, 292(7), 807-820.

Margolin, G. and Gordis, E.B. (2000). The effect of family and community violence on children. *Annual Review of Psychology*, 51, 445-479.

Marrus, E. and Rosenberg, M. (2005). After Roper v. Simmons: Keeping kids out of adult criminal court. *San Diego Law Review*, 42, 1151-1176.

Marsh, J., Ryan, J., Choi, S., and Testa, M. (2006). Integrated services for families with multiple problems: Obstacles to family reunification. *Children and Youth Services Review*, 28(9), 1074-1087.

Marshall, D.B. &andEnglish, D. (2000). Neural network modeling of risk assessment in child protective services. *Psychological Methods,* 5(1), 102–124.

Martin, G. (2005). *Juvenile justice: Process and systems*. Thousand Oaks, CA: Sage.

Martin, T.W. & Grubb, H.J. (1990). Race bias in diagnosis and treatment of juvenile offenders: Findings and suggestions. *Journal of Contemporary Psychotherapy*, 20, 259-272.

Maryland Budget and Tax Policy Center and Advocates for Youth (2008). *Juvenile services budget: Funding for current operations but not for significant reforms*. Baltimore, MD.

Mason, M.A. and Gibbs, J.R. (1992). Patterns of adolescent psychiatric hospitalization: Implications for social policy. *American Journal of Orthopsychiatry*, 62, 447-457.

Masten, A.S. (2001). Ordinary magic: Resilience processes in development. *American Psychologist*, 56, 227-238.

Masten, A.S., Best, K.M., and Garmezy, N. (1990). Resilience and development: Contributions from the study of children who overcome adversity. *Development and Psychopathology*, 2, 425-444.

Masten, A.S., Hubbard, J.J., Gest, S.D., Tellegen, A., Garmezy, N., and Ramirez, M. (1999). Competence in the context of adversity: Pathways to resilience and maladaptation from childhood to adolescence. *Development and Psychopathology*, 11, 143-169.

Matta-Oshima, K.M., Huang, J., Jonson-Reid, M., and Drake, B. (2010). Children with disabilities in poor households: Association with juvenile and adult offending. *Social Work Research*, 34(2), 102-113.

Mauer, M. and King, R.S. (2007). *Uneven justice: State rates of incarceration by race and ethnicity*. The Sentencing Project, Washington D.C.

Maughan, D.R., Christiansen, E., Jenson, W.R., Olympia, D., and Clark, E. (2005). Behavioral parent training as a treatment for externalizing behaviors and disruptive behavior disorders: A meta-analysis. *School Psychology Review*, 34(3), 267-286.

Maxfield, M.G., Weiler, B.L., and Widom, C.S. (2000). Comparing self-reports and official records of arrest. *Journal of Quantitative Criminology*, 16(1), 87-110.

McCurdy, B.L. and McIntyre, E.K. (2004). "And what about residential . . .?" Re-conceptualizing residential treatment as a stop-gap service for youth with emotional and behavioral disorders. *Behavioral Interventions*, 19, 137-158.

McGarrell, E.F. and Hipple, N.K. (2007). Family group conferencing and re-offending among first-time juvenile offenders: The Indianapolis experiment. *Justice Quarterly*, 24(2), 221-246.

McGee, R., Wolfe, D., and Olson, J. (2001). Multiple maltreatment, attribution of blame, and adjustment among adolescents. *Development and Psychopathology*, 13, 827-846.

McGill, D.E., Mihalic, S.F., and Grotpeter, J.K. (1998). *Big brothers big sisters of America: Blueprints for violence prevention, book two*. Blueprints for Violence Prevention Series (D.S. Elliott, Series Editor). Boulder, CO: Center for the Study and Prevention of Violence, Institute of Behavioral Science, University of Colorado.

McGloin, J.M. and Widom, C.S. (2001). Resilience among abused and neglected children grown up. *Development and Psychopathology*, 13(4), 1021-1038.

McGuire J. (2000). *Cognitive-behavioural approaches: An introduction to theory and research. Communication Directorate*. London: Home Office.

McNiel, D.E. and Binder, R.L. (2007). Effectiveness of a mental health court in reducing criminal recidivism and violence. *American Journal of Psychiatry,* 164 (9), 1395–1403.

McNichol, T. and Tash, C. (2001). Parental substance abuse and the development of children in family foster care. *Child Welfare*, 80(2), 239-256.

McReynolds, L.S., Wasserman, G.A., DeComo, R.E., John, R., Keating, J.M., and Nolen, S. (2008). Psychiatric disorder in a juvenile assessment center. *Crime and Delinquency*, 54(2), 313-334.

Mears, D.P. and Aron, L.Y. (2003). *Addressing the needs of youth with disabilities in the juvenile justice system: The current state of knowledge*. Urban Institute, Justice Policy Center, Washington D.C.

Mears, D.P. and Kelly, W.R. (1999). Assessments and intake processes in juvenile justice processing; Emerging policy considerations. *Crime and Delinquency*, 45, 508-529.

Mechanic, D. (2008*). Mental health and social policy: Beyond managed care (5th ed).* Boston, MA: Pearson/Allyn & Bacon.

Medaris, M.L., Campbell, E., and James, B. (1997). *Sharing information: A guide to the Family Educational Rights and Privacy Act and participation in juvenile justice programs.* Office of Juvenile Justice and Delinquency Prevention, U.S. Department of Justice, Washington, D.C.

Melton, G.B. and Pagliocca, P.M. (1992). Treatment in the juvenile justice system: Directions for policy and practice. In J.J. Cocozza (ed.), *Responding to the mental health needs of youth in the juvenile justice system* (107-139). The National Coalition for the Mentally Ill in the Criminal Justice System, Seattle WA.

Meltzer, H., Gatward, R., and Goodman, R. (1999). *The mental health of children and adolescents in Great Britain.* Office of National Statistics, London.

Memory, J. (1989). Juvenile suicides in secure detention facilities: Correction of published rates. *Death Studies, 13,* 455-463.

Mendel, R. (2003). *Less hype, more help: Reducing juvenile crime, what works—and what doesn't.* American Youth Policy Forum, Washington, D.C.

Mendel, R. (2011). *No place for kids: The case for reducing juvenile incarceration.* The Annie E. Casey Foundation, Baltimore, MD.

Merikangas, K.R. (2005). Vulnerability factors for anxiety disorders in children and adolescents. *Child and Adolescent Psychiatric Clinics of North America,* 14, 649−679.

Michigan Family Independence Agency (1996). *CPS policy and procedures manual,* Family Independence Agency, Lansing, MI.

Mikton, C. and Butchart, A. (2009). Child maltreatment prevention: A systematic review of reviews. *Bulletin of the World Health Organization,* 87, 353-361.

Miley, K.K., O'Melia, M., and DuBois, B. (2006). *Generalist social work practice: An empowering approach, Fifth Edition.* New York: Allyn & Bacon.

Miller, F. and Lazowski, L. (2001). *The adolescent substance abuse subtle screening inventory – A2 (SASSI-A2).* SASSI Institute, Springville, IN.

Miller, W.R. and Rollnick, S. (2002). *Motivational interviewing: Preparing people for change. 2nd ed.* New York, NY: Guilford.

Miller, L.S., Wasserman, G.A., Neugebauer, R., Gorman-Smith, D., and Kamboukos, D. (1999). Witnessed community violence and antisocial behavior in high-risk, urban boys. *Journal of Clinical Child Psychology,* 28, 2-11.

Minton, T. (2010). *Prison and jail inmates at midyear.* Office of Justice Programs, Bureau of Justice Statistics, U.S. Department of Justice, Washington, D.C.

Minton, T. (2011). *Jail inmates at midyear 2010 – Statistical tables.* Bureau of Justice Statistics, Office of Justice Programs, U.S. Department of Justice, Washington, D.C.

Mock, R., Zempolich, K.A., Titus, J.C., Fisherman, M., Godley, M.D., and Schwebel, R. (2001). An overview of the effectiveness of adolescent substance abuse treatment models. *Youth and Society,* 33, 143-168.

Models for Change (2011). *Does mental health screening fulfill its promise?* Models for Change: Systems Reform in Juvenile Justice, The John D. and Catherine T. MacArthur Foundation, Chicago, IL.

Moffitt, T.E. (1993). Adolescence-limited and life-course-persistent antisocial behavior: A developmental taxonomy. *Psychology Review*, 100, 674-701.

Moffitt, T.E., Caspi, A., Rutter, M., and Silva, P.A. (2001). *Sex differences in antisocial behavior: Conduct disorder, delinquency, and violence in the Dundedin longitudinal study*. New York: Cambridge University Press.

Moffitt, T.E. and Scott, S. (2008). Conduct disorders of childhood & adolescence, in M. Rutter (ed), *Child Psychiatry* (Chapter 35). London: Wiley-Blackwell Publishers.

Molgaard, V.K., Spoth, R.L. and Redmond, C. (2000). *Competency training, the Strengthening Families Program: For parents and youth 10–14*. Office of Juvenile Justice and Delinquency Prevention, Juvenile Justice Bulletin, U.S. Department of Justice, Washington, D.C.

Monahan, J., Steadman, H.J., Silver, E., Appelbaum, P.S., Robbins, P.C., Mulvey, E.P., Roth, L., and Silver E. (2001). *Rethinking risk assessment: The MacArthur study of mental disorder and violence*. New York: Oxford University Press.

Moore, K. and Redd, Z. (2002). *Children in poverty: Trends, consequences and policy options*. Child Trends Research Brief. Child Trends, Washington D.C.

Moran, P., Ghate, D., and van der Merwe, A. (2004). *What works in parenting support: A review of the international evidence*. Policy Research Bureau, Department for Education and Skills, London, UK.

Morral, A., McCaffrey, D., and Ridgeway, G. (2004). Effectiveness of community-based treatment for substance-abusing dependents: 12-month outcomes of youths entering Phoenix Academy or alternative probation dispositions. *Psychology of Addictive Behaviors*, 18, 257-268.

Morris, K.A. and Morris, R.J. (2006). Disability and juvenile delinquency: Issues and trends. *Disability & Society*, 21(6), 613-627.

Morrison, B. (2001). The school system: Developing its capacity in the regulation of a civilized society. In J. Braithwaite & H. Strang (eds), *Restorative justice and civil society* (195-224). Cambridge, UK: Cambridge University Press.

MTA Cooperative Group (1999). A 14-month randomized clinical trial of treatment strategies for attention-deficit hyperactivity disorder. *Archives of General Psychiatry*, 56, 1073-1086.

Mulvey, E.P. (2011). *Highlights from pathways to desistance: A longitudinal study of serious adolescent offenders (Juvenile Justice Fact Sheet)*. Office of Juvenile Justice and Delinquency Prevention, Office of Justice Programs, U.S. Department of Justice, Washington D.C.

Mulvey, E.P. and Iselin, A. (2008). Improving professional judgments of risk and amenability in juvenile justice. *The Future of Children*, 18(2), 35-57.

Muris, P. and Broeren, S. (2009). Twenty-five years of research on childhood anxiety disorders: Publication trends between 1982 and 2006 and a selective review of the literature. *Journal of Child and Families Studies*, 18, 388-395.

Myers, W.C., Burton, P.R., Sanders, P.D., Donat, K.M., Cheney, J., Fitzpatrick, T., and Monaco, L. (2000). Project back-on-track at 1 year: A delinquency treatment program for early-career juvenile offenders. *Journal of American Child and Adolescent Psychiatry*, 39(9), 1127-1134.

Myner, J., Santman, J., Cappelletty, G., and Perlmutter, B. (1998). Variables related to recidivism among juvenile offenders. *International Journal of Offender Therapy and Comparative Criminology*, 42, 65-80.

Narrow, W.E., Regier, D.A., Goodman, S.H., Rae, D.S., Roper, M.T., Bourdon, K.H., Hoven, C., and Moore, R. (1998). A comparison of federal definitions of severe mental illness among children and adolescents in four communities. *Psychiatry Services*, 49(12), 1601-1608.

National Association of School Psychologists (2008). *Zero tolerance and alternative strategies: A fact sheet for educators and policymakers.* National Association of School Psychologists, Bethesda, MD.

National Center for Child Traumatic Stress (2009). *Child sexual abuse: Coping with the emotional stress of the legal system.* UCLA, Los Angeles, CA.

National Center for Children in Poverty (2000). *Promoting resilience: Helping young children and parents affected by substance abuse, domestic violence, and depression in the context of welfare reform.* New York, NY.

National Center for Learning Disabilities (2011). *LD basics.* New York, NY.

National Center for Mental Health and Juvenile Justice (2007). *Mental health screening within juvenile justice: The next frontier.* National Center for Mental Health and Juvenile Justice, Delmar, NY.

National Center on Addiction and Substance Abuse (2000). *Substance abuse and learning disabilities: Peas in a pod or apples and oranges?* The National Center on Addiction and Substance Abuse at Columbia University, New York, NY.

National Center on Education, Disability, and Juvenile Justice (2001). *Juvenile correctional education programs.* National Center on Education, Disability and Juvenile Justice, College Park, MD.

National Child Abuse and Neglect Data System (NCANDS) (2010). Administration for Children and Families, U.S. Department of Health and Human Services, Washington D.C.

National Child Traumatic Stress Network (NCTSN) (2008). *Child welfare trauma training tool kit: Comprehensive guide (2nd ed.).* National Center for Child Traumatic Stress, Los Angeles, CA.

National Council on Crime and Delinquency (2007). *And justice for some: Differential treatment of youth of color in the justice system.* Oakland, CA.

National Institute of Child Health and Human Development (2003). Social functioning in first grade: Prediction from home, child care and concurrent school experience. *Child Development*, 74, 1639-1662.

National Institute of Justice (2003). *2000 arrestee drug abuse monitoring: Annual report.* U.S. Department of Justice, Washington, D.C.

National Institute of Mental Health (2008). *Attention deficit hyperactivity disorder (ADHD).* National Institutes of Health, U.S. Department of Health and Human Services, Washington, D.C.

National Institute of Mental Health (2011). *Suicide: A major, preventable mental health problem.* National Institutes of Health, U.S. Department of Health and Human Services, Washington, D.C.

National Institute on Alcohol Abuse and Alcoholism (2011). *Alcohol screening and brief intervention for youth.* National Institutes of Health, Washington, D.C.

National Institute on Drug Abuse (2003). *Preventing drug use among children and adolescents: A research-based guide for parents, educators, and community leaders , second edition*. National Institutes of Health, U.S. Department of Health and Human Services, Washington, D.C.

National Juvenile Justice Network (2005). *Polling on public attitudes on the treatment of young offenders*. Washington, D.C.

National Juvenile Justice Network (2011). *Bringing youth home: A national movement to increase public safety, rehabilitate youth, and save money*. Washington D.C.

National Wraparound Initiative Advisory Group (2003). *History of the wraparound process*. Focal Point Bulletin. National Wraparound Initiative, Research and Training Center on Family Support and Children's Mental Health, Portland State University, Portland, OR.

Neelum, A. (2011). *State trends: Legislative changes from 2005 to 2010 removing youth from the adult criminal justice system*. Campaign for Youth Justice, Washington D.C.

Neighbors, B., Kempton, T., and Forehand, R. (1992). Co-occurrence of substance abuse with conduct, anxiety, and depression disorders in juvenile delinquents. *Addictive Behaviours*, 17, 379-386.

New Freedom Commission on Mental Health (2003). *Achieving the promise: Transforming mental health care in America, Final Report*. U.S. Department of Health and Human Services, Washington, D.C.

New York Juvenile Justice Coalition (2009). *RE-DIRECT NEW YORK: Reinvesting detention resources in community treatment*. New York, NY.

Nock, M.K., Kazdin, A.E., Hiripi, E., and Kessler, R.C. (2007). Lifetime prevalence, correlates, and persistence of oppositional defiant disorder: Results from the national comorbidity survey replication. *Journal of Child Psychology and Psychiatry*, 48(7), 703-713.

Novotney, L.C., Mertinko, J.L., and Baker, T.K. (2000). *Juvenile mentoring program: A progress review*. Juvenile Justice Bulletin, Office of Juvenile Justice and Delinquency Prevention, U.S. Department of Justice, Washington, D.C.

O'Donnell, J., Hawkins, J.D., Catalano, R.F., Abbott, R.D., and Day, L.E. (1995). .Preventing school failure, drug use, and delinquency among low-income children: Long-term interventions in elementary school. *American Journal of Orthopsychiatry*, 65, 87-100.

Office of Juvenile Justice and Delinquency Prevention (1998). *Juvenile mentoring program 1998: Report to Congress*. Office of Juvenile Justice and Delinquency Prevention, Office of Justice Programs, U.S. Department of Justice, Washington, D.C.

Office of Juvenile Justice and Delinquency Prevention (2011). *OJJDP model program guide*. Office of Justice Programs, U.S. Department of Justice, Washington, D.C.

Office of State Courts Administrator (2003). *Florida juvenile delinquency court assessment*. Office of Court Improvements, Tallahassee, FL.

Ohio Department of Youth Services (2010). *Annual report fiscal year 2010*. Ohio Department of Youth Services, Columbus, Ohio.

Ohio Department of Youth Services (2011). *Annual report fiscal year 2011*. Ohio Department of Youth Services, Columbus, Ohio.

Oldehinkel, A.J., Wittchen, H.U., and Schuster, P. (1999). Prevalence, 2-month incidence and outcome of unipolar depressive disorders in a community sample of adolescents. *Psychological Medicine*, 29(3), 655-668.

Olds, D.L. (2007). Preventing crime with prenatal and infancy support of parents: The nurse-family partnership. *Victims and Offenders*, 2, 205-225.

Olds, D.L., Eckenrode, J., Henderson, C.R., Kitzman, H., Powers, J., Cole, R., Sidora, K., Morris, P., Pettitt, L.M., and Luckey, D. (1997). Long-term effects of home visitation on maternal life course and child abuse and neglect: Fifteen-year follow-up of a randomized trial. *Journal of the American Medical Association*, 278, 637-643.

Olds, D.L., Henderson, C.R., Chamberlin, R., & Tatelbaum, R. (1986). Preventing child abuse and neglect: A randomized trial of nurse home visitation. *Pediatrics*, 78, 65-78.

Olfson, M., Kessler, R.C., Berglund, P.A., and Lin, E. (1998). Psychiatric disorder onset and first treatment contact in the United States and Ontario. *American Journal of Psychiatry*, 155, 1415-1422.

Orlando M., Chan K.S., and Morral A.R. (2003). Retention of court-referred youths in residential treatment programs: Client characteristics and treatment process effects. *American Journal of Drug and Alcohol* Abuse, 29(2), 337-357.

Pager, D. (2003). The mark of a criminal record. *American Journal of Sociology*, 108, 937-975.

Pandina, R.J., Johnson, V., and Labouvie, E.W. (1992). Affectivity: A central mechanism in the development of drug dependence. In M. Glants & R. Pickens (eds), *Vulnerability to drug abuse* (179-209). American Psychological Association, Washington, D.C.

Pasko, L. and Chesney-Lind, M. (2010). Under lock and key: Trauma, marginalization, and girls' juvenile justice involvement. *Justice Research and Policy*, 12(2), 25-49.

Pastor, P.N. and Reuben, C.A. (2008). *Diagnosed attention deficit hyperactivity disorder and learning disability: United States, 2004-2006*. National Center for Health Statistics, Centers for Disease Control and Prevention, Atlanta, GA.

Patterson, G.R., DeBarysche, B.D. and Ramsey, E. (1989). A developmental perspective on antisocial behavior. *American Psychologist*, 44, 329-335.

Pearl, R. and Bryan, T. (1994). Getting caught in misconduct: Conceptions of adolescents with and without learning disabilities. *Journal of Learning Disabilities*, 27(3), 193-197.

Pelham, W.E., Wheeler, T., and Chronis, A. (1998). Empirically supported psychosocial treatments for attention deficit hyperactivity disorder. *Journal of Clinical and Child Psychology*, 27(2), 190-205.

Penn, J., Esposito, C., Schaeffer, L, Fritz, G., and Spirito, A. (2003). Suicide attempts and self-multivariate behavior in a juvenile correctional facility. *Journal of the American Academy of Child and Adolescent Psychiatry*, 42(7), 121-135.

Pentz, M.A. (1998). Costs, benefits, and cost-effectiveness of comprehensive drug abuse prevention. In W.J. Bukoski and R.I. Evans (eds), *Cost-benefit/cost-effectiveness research of drug abuse prevention: Implications for programming and policy* (111-129). NIDA Research Monograph No. 176, U.S. Government Printing Office, Washington, D.C.

Pentz, M.A., Mihalic, S.F., and Grotpeter, J.K. (2006). *The midwestern prevention project: Blueprints for violence prevention, book two*. Blueprints for Violence Prevention Series (D.S. Elliott, Series Editor).

Center for the Study and Prevention of Violence, Institute of Behavioral Science, University of Colorado, Boulder, CO.

Perez, C. and Widom, C.S. (1994). Childhood victimization and long term intellectual and academic outcomes. *Child Abuse and Neglect*, 18, 617-633.

Perkeronigg, A., Kessler, R.C., Storz, S., and Wittchen, H.U. (2000). Traumatic events and post-traumatic stress disorder in the community: Prevalence, risk factors and comorbidity. *Acta Psychiatrica Scandinavica*, 101(1), 46-59.

Petro, J. (2007). *Juvenile justice and child welfare agencies: Collaborating to serve dual jurisdiction youth survey report.* Child Welfare League of America, Washington, D.C.

Petro, J. (2008). *Increasing collaboration and coordination of the child welfare and juvenile justice systems to better serve dual jurisdiction youth: A literature review.* Child Welfare League of America, Washington, D.C.

Petrosino, A., Turpin-Petrosino, C., and Guckenberg, S. (2010). *Formal system processing of juveniles: Effects on delinquency.* The Campbell Collaboration, Oslo, Norway.

Petteruti, A. and Walsh, N. (2008). *Jailing communities: The impact of jail expansion and effective public safety strategies.* Justice Policy Institute, Washington D.C.

Pew Center on the States (2011a). *One in 31: the long reach of American corrections.* The Pew Charitable Trusts, Washington D.C.

Pew Center on the States (2011b). *State of recidivism: The revolving door of America's prisons.* The Pew Charitable Trusts, Washington D.C.

Pianta, R.C., LaParo, K.M., Payne, C., Cox, M.J., and Bradley, R. (2002). The relation of kindergarten classroom environment to teacher, family, and school characteristics and child outcomes. *Elementary School Journal*, 201, 225-238.

Piquero, A.R. (2008). Disproportionate minority contact. *The Future of Children*, 18(2), 59-79.

Piquero, A.R., Farrington, D.P., Welsh, B.C., Tremblay, R., and Jennings, W.G. (2008). *Effects of early family/parent training programs on antisocial behavior & delinquency.* Campbell Systematic Reviews, The Campbell Collaboration, Oslo, Norway.

Pliszka, S., Sherman, J., Barrow, M., and Irick, S. (2000). Affective disorder in juvenile offenders: A preliminary study. *American Journal of Psychiatry*, 157, 130-132.

Podell, J.L. and Kendall, P.C. (2011). Mothers and fathers in family cognitive-behavioral therapy for anxious youth. *Journal of Child and Family Studies*, 20, 182-195.

Polinsky, M.L., Pion-Berlin, L., Williams, S., Long, T., and Wolf, A.M. (2010). Preventing child abuse and neglect: A national evaluation of parents anonymous groups. *Child Welfare*, 89(6), 43-62.

Prescott J.J. and Rockoff, J.E. (2008). *Do sex offender registration and notification laws affect criminal behavior?* National Bureau of Economic Research, Columbia University, Cambridge MA.

Prochaska, J.O. and DiClemente, C.C. (1984). *The transtheoretical approach: Crossing the traditional boundaries of therapy.* Malabar, FL: Krieger.

Putnins, A.L. (2005). Correlates and predictors of self-reported suicide attempts among incarcerated youths. *International Journal of Offender Therapy and Comparative Criminology*, 49, 143-157.

Puzzanchera, C. (2009). *Juvenile Arrests 2008*. Office of Juvenile Justice and Delinquency Prevention, Office of Justice Programs, U.S. Department of Justice, Washington D.C.

Puzzanchera, C., Adams, B., & Snyder, H. (2008). An interpretation of the national DMC relative rate indices for juvenile justice system processing in 2005. *National Disproportionate Minority Contact Databook*. Prepared by the National Center for Juvenile Justice for the Office of Juvenile Justice and Delinquency Prevention, U.S. Department of Justice, Washington D.C.

Puzzanchera, C. and Kang, W. (2008). *Juvenile court statistics databook*. Office of Juvenile Justice and Delinquency Prevention, Office of Justice Program, U.S. Department of Justice, Washington D.C.

Quinn, M.M., Rutherford, R.B., Leone, P.E., Osher, D.M., and Poirier, J.M. (2005). Youth with disabilities in juvenile corrections: A national survey. *Exceptional Children*, 71(3), 339-345

Raffaele-Mendez, L.M. (2003). Predictors of suspensions and negative school outcomes: A longitudinal investigation. *New Directions for Youth Development*, 99, 17-33.

Rapaport, J.L., Inoff-Germain, G., Weissman, M.M., Greenwald, S., Narrow, W.E., Jensen, P.S., Lahey, B.B., and Ganino, G. (2000). Childhood obsessive-compulsive disorder in the NIMH MECA study: Parent versus child identification of cases. Methods for the epidemiology of child and adolescent mental disorders. *Journal of Anxiety Disorders*, 14(6), 535-548.

Rapp, L. and Wodarski, J. (1997). The comorbodity of conduct disorder and depression in adolescents: A comprehensive interpersonal treatment technology. *Family Therapy*, 24(2), 81-100.

Rapp-Palicchi, L. and Roberts, A.R. (2004). Mental illness and juvenile offending. In A.R. Roberts (ed), *Juvenile justice sourcebook: Past, present, and future* (289-308). New York: Oxford University Press.

Redding, R. (2010). *Juvenile transfer laws: An effective deterrent to delinquency?* Office of Juvenile Justice and Delinquency Prevention, Office of Justice Programs, U.S. Department of Justice, Washington D.C.

Reddy, L.A. (2001). Serious emotional disturbance in children and adolescents: Current status and future directions. *Behavior Therapy*, 32, 667-691.

Reddy, L.A., DeThomas, C.A., Newman, E., and Chun, V. (2008). School-based prevention and intervention programs for children with emotional disturbance: A review of treatment components and methodology. *Psychology in the Schools*, 46(2), 132-153.

Reddy, L.A., Newman, E., De Thomas, C.A., and Chun, V. (2008). Effectiveness of school-based prevention and intervention programs for children and adolescents with emotional disturbance: A meta-analysis. *Journal of School Psychology*, 47, 77-99.

Reddy, L.A. and Pfeifer, S.I. (1997). Effectiveness of treatment foster care with children and adolescents: A review of outcome studies. *Journal of the American Academy of Child and Adolescent Psychiatry*, 36(5), 581-588.

Reddy, L.A. and Richardson, L. (2006). School-based prevention and intervention programs for children with emotional disturbance. *Education and Treatment of Children*, 29, 1-26.

Reinecke, M.A., Ryan, N.E., and DuBois, D.L. (1998). Cognitive-behavioral therapy of depression and depressive symptoms during adolescence: A review and meta-analysis. *Journal of the American Academy of Child and Adolescent Psychiatry*, 37, 26-34.

Reschly, D.J. (2002). Minority overrepresentation: The silent contributor to LD prevalence and diagnostic confusions. In R. Bradley, L. Danielson, and D.P. Hallahan (eds), *Identification of learning disabilities: Research to practice* (361-367), Mahwah, NJ: LEA Publishers.

Reynolds, W. (1988). *Manual for the suicidal ideation questionnaire.* Psychological Assessment Resources, Odessa, FL.

Riestenberg, N. (2003). *Zero and no: Some definitions.* Minnesota Department of Education, Roseville, MN.

Rhodes, J.E. (2002). *Stand by me: The risks and rewards of mentoring today's youth.* Cambridge, MA: Harvard University Press.

Rhodes, J.E., Bogat, G.A., Roffman, J., Edelman, P., and Galasso, L. (2002). Youth mentoring in perspective: Introduction to special issue. *American Journal of Community Psychology, 30*, 149-155.

Richardson, J. and Joughin, C. (2002). *Parent-training programmes for the management of young children with conduct disorders: Findings from research.* London: Gaskell.

Richters, J.E. and Martinez, P.E. (1993). Violent communities, family choices, and children's changes: An algorithm for improving the odds. *Development and Psychopathology*, 5, 609-627.

Rittner, B. and Davenport-Dozier, C. (2000). Effects of court-ordered substance abuse treatment in child protective services cases. *Social Work*, 45(2), 131-140.

Ritter, G., Denny, G., Albin, G., Barnett, and Blankship, V. (2007). *The effectiveness of volunteer tutoring programs: A systematic review.* Campbell Systematic Reviews, Oslo, Norway

Robins, L.N. (1978). Sturdy childhood predictors of adult antisocial behaviour: Replications from longitudinal studies. *Psychological Medicine*, 8, 611-622.

Robinson, K.E. and Rapport, L.J. (2002). Outcomes of a school-based mental health program for youth with serious emotional disorders. *Psychology in the Schools*, 39(6), 661-675.

Rogers, K.M., Powell, E., and Strock, M. (1998). The characteristics of youth referred for mental health evaluation in the juvenile justice system. In J. Willis, C. Liberton, K. Kutash, and R. Friedman (eds), *The 10th annual research conference proceedings, a system of care for children's mental health: Expanding the research based* (329-334). University of South Florida, Tampa. FL.

Romano, E., Tremblay, R.E., Vitaro, F., Zoccolillo, M., and Pagani, L. (2001). Prevalence of psychiatric diagnoses and the role of perceived impairment: Findings from an adolescent community sample. *Journal of Child Psychology and Psychiatry*, 42(4), 451-461.

Rosado, L.M. (2005). Training mental health and juvenile justice professionals in juvenile forensic assessment. In K. Heilbrun, M.E. Sevin-Goldstein, and R.E. Redding (eds), *Juvenile delinquency: Prevention, assessment, and intervention* (310-322). New York: Oxford University Press.

Rosenblatt, J.A., Rosenblatt, A.R., and Biggs, E.E. (2000). Criminal behavior and emotional disorder: Comparing youth served by the mental health and juvenile justice systems. *The Journal of Behavioral Health Services and Research,* 27(2), 227-237.

Rousch, D.W. (1996). *Desktop guide to good juvenile detention practice.* Office of Juvenile Justice and Delinquency Prevention, U.S. Department of Justice, Washington, D.C.

Rowe, C.I. and Liddle, H.A. (2006). Treating adolescent substance abuse: State of the science. In H.A. Liddle and C.L. Rowe (eds), *Adolescent substance abuse – research and clinical advances* (1-21). New York: Cambridge University Press.

Rozalski, M., Deignan, M., and Engel, S. (2008). The world of juvenile justice according to the numbers. *Reading and Writing Quarterly: Overcoming Learning difficulties,* 24, 143-147.

Rumberger, R.W. (2004). Why students drop out of school. In G. Orfield (ed), *Dropouts in America: Confronting the graduation rate crisis.* Cambridge, MA: Harvard Education Press.

RUPP Anxiety Study Group (2001). Fluvoxamine for the treatment of anxiety disorders in children and adolescents. *The New England Journal of Medicine,* 344, 1279-1285.

Rutherford, R.B., Nelson, C.M., and Wolford, B.I. (1985). Special education in the most restrictive environment: Correctional/special education. *Journal of Special Education,* 19, 59-71.

Rutter, M. (2006). The promotion of resilience in the face of adversity. In S.S. Luther (ed), *Resilience and vulnerability: Adaption in the context of childhood adversities* (489-509). Cambridge, UK: Cambridge University Press.

Rutter, M. (2007). Psychopathological development across adolescence. *Journal of Youth and Adolescence, 36,* 101-110.

Ryan, E.P. and Redding, R.E. (2004). Mood disorders in juvenile offenders. *Psychiatric Services,* 55, 1397-1407.

Ryan, J.P., Herz, D., Hernandez, P., and Marshall, J. (2007). Maltreatment and delinquency: Investigating child welfare bias in juvenile justice processing. *Children and Youth Services Review,* 29, 1035-1050.

Salloum, A., Sulkowski, M.L., Sirrine, E., and Storch, E.A. (2009). Overcoming barriers to using empirically supported therapies to treat childhood anxiety disorders in social work practice. *Child and Adolescent Social Work Journal,* 26, 259-273.

Sampson, R.J. and Laub, J.H. (1993). *Crime in the making: Pathways and turning points through life.* Cambridge: Harvard University Press.

Sanders, M.R., Cann, W., and Markie-Dadds, C. (2003a). Why a universal population-level approach to the prevention of child abuse is essential. *Child Abuse Review,* 12(3), 145-154.

Sanders, M.R., Cann, W., and Markie-Dadds, C. (2003b). The triple p-positive programme: A universal population-level approach to the prevention of child abuse. *Child Abuse Review,* 12(3), 155-171.

Sawyer, M.G., Amey, F.M., Baghurst, P.A., Clark, J.J., Graetz, B.W., Kosky, R.J., Nurcombe, B., Patton, G.C., Prior, M.R., Raphael, B., Rey, J.M., Whaites, L.C, and Zubrick, S.R. (2001). The mental health of young people in Australia: Key findings from the child and adolescent component of the national survey of mental health and well-being. *Australia and New Zealand Journal of Psychiatry*, 35(6), 806-814.

Scarborough, A. and McCrae, J. (2009). School-age special education outcomes of infants and toddlers investigated for maltreatment. *Children and Youth Services Review*, 32(1), 80-88.

Schargel, F.P. (2004). Who drops out and why. In J. Smink, and F.P. Schargel, F.P. (eds.), *Helping students graduate: A strategic approach to dropout prevention*. Larchmont, NY: Eye on Education.

Scheier, L., Botvin, G., Diaz, T., and Griffin, K. (1999). Social skills, competence, and drug refusal efficacy as predictors of adolescent alcohol use. *Journal of Drug Education*, 29(3), 251–278.

Schmidt, F., Hoge, R., and Gomes, L. (2005). Reliability and validity analysis of the youth level of service/case management inventory. *Criminal Justice and Behavior*, 32(3), 329-344.

Schochet, P., Burghardt, J., and McConnell, S. (2006). *National job corps study and longer-term follow-up study: Impact and benefit-cost findings using survey and summary earnings records data final report*. Mathematica Policy Research, Princeton, NJ.

Schochet, P., Burghardt, J., and McConnell, S. (2008). Does job corps work? Impact findings from the national job corps study. *American Economic Review*, 98(5), 1864–1886.

Schram, P.J. and Gaines, L.K. (2005). Examining delinquent nongang members and delinquent gang members: A comparison of juvenile probationers at intake and outcomes. *Youth Violence and Juvenile Justice*, 3(2), 99-115.

Schumacher, M. and Kurz, G. (2000). *The 8% solution: Preventing serious, repeat juvenile crime*. Thousand Oaks, CA: Sage.

Schur, E. (1973). *Radical nonintervention: Rethinking the delinquency problem*. Englewood Cliffs, NJ: Prentice-Hall.

Schwalbe, C.S. (2008). A meta-analysis of juvenile justice risk assessment instruments: Predictive validity by gender. *Criminal Justice and Behavior*, 35(11), 1367-1381.

Schwalbe, C.S., Smith-Hatcher, S., and Maschi, T. (2009). The effects of treatment needs and prior social services use on juvenile court decision making. *Social Work Research*, 33(1), 31-40.

Schwartz, D. and Gorman, A. (2003). Community violence exposure and children's academic performance. *Journal of Educational Psychology*, 95, 163-173.

Scott, E.S. and Steinberg, L. (2008). Adolescent development and the regulation of youth crime. *The Future of Children*, 18(2), 18-33.

Scott, M., Snowden, L., and Libby, A.M. (2002). From mental health to juvenile justice: What factors predict this transition? *Journal of Child and Family Studies*, 11(3), 299-311.

Sebring, P.B., Allensworth, E., Bryk, A.S., Easton, J.Q., and Luppescu, S. (2006). *The essential supports for school improvement*. Consortium on Chicago School Research, Chicago, IL.

Sedlak, A. and Broadhurst, D. (1996). *Executive summary of the third national incidence study of child abuse and neglect*. National Center on Child Abuse and Neglect, Administration for Children, Youth, and Families, Administration for Children and Families, U.S. Department of Health and Human Services, Washington, D.C.

Sedlak, A.J. and McPherson, K. (2010). *Survey of youth in residential placement: Youth's needs and services.* Westat Corporation, Washington D.C.

Sedlak, A. and Schulz, D. (2005). Racial differences in child protective services investigations of abused and neglected children. In D.M. Derezoes, J. Poertner, and M.F. Testa (eds), *Race matters in child welfare: The overrepresentation of African American children in the system* (97-124). Child Welfare League of America, Washington, D.C.

Selzer, M.L. (1971). The Michigan alcoholism screening test: The quest for a new diagnostic instrument. *American Journal of Psychiatry*, 127 (12), 89-94.

Semidei, J., Radel, L.F., and Nolan, C. (2001). Substance abuse and child welfare: Clear linkages and promising responses. *Child Welfare*, 78, 109-128.

Semrud-Clikeman, M. and Schafer, V. (2000). Social and emotional competence in children with ADHD and/or learning disabilities. *Journal of Psychotherapy in Independent Practice*, 1(4), 3-19.

Serketich, W.J. and Dumas, J.E. (1996). The effectiveness of behavioural parent-training to modify anti-social behavior in children: A meta-analysis. *Behaviour Therapy*, 27, 171-186.

Sexton, T. and Alexander, J. (2000). *Functional family therapy.* Juvenile Justice Bulletin, Office of Juvenile Justice and Delinquency Prevention, U.S. Department of Justice, Washington, D.C.

Shaffer, D., Gould, M.S., Fisher, L.A., Trautman, P., Moreau, D., Kleinman, M., and Flory, M. (1996). Psychiatric diagnosis in child and adolescent suicide. *Archives of General Psychiatry*, 53, 339-348.

Shaffer, D., Lucas, C., and Fisher, P. (2011). *Diagnostic interview schedule for children version four.* DISC Development Group, New York, NY.

Shaywitz, S.E., Fletcher, J.M., Holahan, J.M., Schneider, A.E., Marchone, K.E., Stuebing, K.K., Francis, D.J., Pugh, K.R., and Shaywitz, B.A. (1999). Persistence of dyslexia: The Connecticut longitudinal study at adolescence. *Pediatrics*, 104(6), 1351-1359.

Sheldon, R.G. (1999). *Detention diversion advocacy: An evaluation.* Office of Juvenile Justice and Delinquency Prevention, Office of Justice Programs, U.S. Department of Justice, Washington D.C.

Shelton, D. (2004). Experiences of detained young offenders in need of mental health care. *Journal of Nursing Scholarship*, 36, 129-133.

Shufelt, J.L. and Cocozza, J.J. (2006). *Youth with mental health disorders in the juvenile justice system: Results from a multi-state prevalence study.* National Center for Mental Health and Juvenile Justice, Delmar, NY.

Shure, M.B. and Spivack, G. (1982). Interpersonal problem-solving in young children: A cognitive approach to prevention. *American Journal of Community Psychology*, 10, 341-356.

Sickmund, M. (2008). *Census of juveniles in residential placement databook.* Office of Juvenile Justice and Delinquency Prevention, Office of Justice Program, U.S. Department of Justice, Washington D.C.

Sickmund, M. (2009). *Juveniles in residential placement, 1997-2008.* Office of Juvenile Justice and Delinquency Prevention, Office of Justice Programs, U.S. Department of Justice, Washington D.C.

Sickmund, M, Sladky, and A, Kang, W. (2010). *Easy access to juvenile court statistics: 1985-2007*. Pittsburgh, PA: National Center for Juvenile Justice.

Siegel, G.L. and Loman, T. (2006). *Extended follow-up study of Minnesota's family assessment response: Final report*. Institute of Applied Research, St. Louis, MO.

Simonoff, E., Pickles, A., Meyer, J.M., Silberg, J.L., Maes, H.H., Loeber, R., Rutter, M., Hewitt, J.K., and Eaves, L.J. (1997). The Virginia twin study of adolescent behavioral development. Influences of age, sex, and impairment on rates of disorder. *Archives of General Psychiatry*, 54(9), 801-808.

Simpson, G.A., Bloom, B., Cohen, R.A., and Blumberg, S. (2005). *U.S. children with emotional and behavioral difficulties: Data from the 2001, 2002, and 2003 National Health Interview Surveys*. National Center for Health Studies, Hyattsville, MD.

Singer, S. (1996). *Recriminalizing delinquency: Violent juvenile crime and juvenile justice reform*. Melbrourne: Cambridge University Press.

Skowyra, K.R. and Cocozza, J.J. (2007). *Mental health screening within juvenile justice: The next frontier*. National Center for Mental Health and Juvenile Justice, Delmar, NY.

Slade, E.P. and Wissow, L.S. (2007). The influence of childhood maltreatment on adolescents' academic performance. *Economics of Education Review*, 26, 604-614.

Sloan, J. and Smykla, J.O. (2003). Juvenile drug courts: Understanding the importance of dimensional variability. *Criminal Justice Policy Review*, 14(3), 339-360.

Smith, B.D., Duffee, D.E., Steinke, C.M., Huang, Y., and Larkin, H. (2008). Outcomes in residential treatment for youth: The role of early engagement. *Children and Youth Services Review*, 30, 1425-1436.

Smith, B.D. and Testa, M.F. (2002). The risk of subsequent maltreatment allegations in families with substance-exposed infants. *Child Abuse and Neglect*, 26(1), 97-114.

Smith, C.A., Ireland, T.O., and Thornberry, T.P. (2005). Adolescent maltreatment and adolescent involvement in delinquency. *Child Abuse and Neglect*, 29, 1099-1119.

Smith, C.A. and Thornberry, T.O. (1995). The relationship between childhood maltreatment and adolescent involvement in delinquency. *Criminology*, 33(4), 451-481.

Smithgall, C., Gladden, R.M., Howard, E., Goerge, R., and Courtney, M.E. (2004). *Education experiences of children in out-of-home care*. Chicago, IL: Chapin Hall Center for Children.

Snyder, H.N. (1998). Serious, violent, and chronic juvenile offenders: An assessment of the extent of and trends in officially recognized serious criminal behavior in a delinquent population. In R. Loeber and D.P. Farrington (eds), *Serious and violent juvenile offenders: Risk factors and successful interventions* (440-472). Thousand Oaks, CA: Sage.

Snyder, H.N. (2000). *Sexual assault of young children as reported to law enforcement: Victim, incident, and offender characteristics*. Bureau of Justice Statistics, U.S., Department of Justice, Washington, D.C.

Snyder, H.N. (2004). An empirical portrait of the youth reentry population. *Youth Violence and Juvenile Justice*, 2(1), 39-55.

Soler, M., Shoenberg, D., and Schindler, M. (2009). Juvenile justice: Lessons for a new era. *Georgetown Journal on Poverty Law & Policy*, Volume XVI, Symposium Issue.

Solomon, A.L., Visher, C., LaVigne, N.G., and Osborne, J. (2006). *Understanding the challenges of prisoner reentry: Research findings from the Urban Institutes prisoner reentry portfolio*. Urban Institute, Washington, D.C.

Sontheimer H. and Goodstein, L. (1993). Evaluation of juvenile intensive aftercare. *Justice Quarterly*, 10, 197-227.

Spain, A. and Waugh, R. (2005). *Transition to and from facilities: Records transfer and maintenance*. National Evaluation and Technical Assistance Center for the Education of Children who are Neglected, Delinquent, or At Risk, Washington, D.C.

Spelman, W. (2000). The limited important of prison expansion. In A. Blumstein and J. Wallman (eds), *The crime drop in America* (125-153). New York: Cambridge University Press.

Spooner, C. (1999). Causes and correlates of adolescent drug abuse and implication for treatment. *Drug and Alcohol Review*, 18, 453-475.

Spooner, C., Noffs, W., and Mattick, R.P. (2001). Outcomes of a comprehensive treatment program for adolescents with a substance use disorder. *Journal of Substance Abuse Treatment*, 20, 205-213.

Spoth, R.L., Redmond, C., and Shin, C. (2001). Randomized trial of brief family interventions for general populations: Adolescent substance use outcomes four years following baseline. *Journal of Consulting and Clinical Psychology*. 69(4), 627–642.

Spoth, R.L., Redmond, D., Trudeau, L., and Shin, C. (2002). Longitudinal substance initiation outcomes for a universal preventive intervention combining family and school programs. *Psychology of Addictive Behaviors*, 16(2), 129–134.

SRI International, Center for Education and Human Services (1997). *The national longitudinal transition study: A summary of findings*. Office of Special Education Programs, U.S. Department of Education, Washington, D.C.

Stage, W.A. and Quiroz, D.R. (1997). A meta-analysis of interventions to decrease disruptive classroom behavior in public education settings. *School Psychology Review*, 26, 333-368.

Stagner, M.W. and Lansing, J. (2009). Progress toward a prevention perspective. *The Future of Children*, 29(2), 19-38.

Steen, S., Bond, C., Bridges, G., and Kubrin, C. (2005). Explaining assessments of future risk: Race and attributes of juvenile offenders in presentencing reports. In D.F. Hawkins and K. Kempf-Leonard (eds), *Our children, their children: Confronting racial and ethnic differences in American juvenile justice* (245-269), The MacArthur Foundation, Chicago, IL.

Steingard, R., Biederman, J., Spencer, T., Wilens, T., and Gonzalez, A. (1993). Comparison of clonidine response in the treatment of attention deficit hyperactivity disorder with and without comorbid tic disorders. *Journal of the American Academy of Child and Adolescent Psychiatry*, 32, 350-353.

Stephan, J.J. and Karberg, J.C. (2003). *Census of state and federal correctional facilities, 2000*. Bureau of Justice Statistics, Office of Justice Programs, U.S. Department of Justice, Washington, D.C.

Stewart, A., Livingston, M., and Dennison, S. (2008). Transitions and turning points: Examining the links between child maltreatment and juvenile offending. *Child Abuse and Neglect*, 32, 51-66.

Stinchcomb, J.B., Bazemore, G., and Riestenberg, N. (2006). Beyond zero tolerance: Restoring justice in secondary schools. *Youth Violence and Juvenile Justice*, 4(2), 123-147.

Stolzenberg L. and D'Alessio, S.J. (1997). "Three strikes and you're out": The impact of California's new mandatory sentencing law on serious crime rates. *Crime and Delinquency*, 43(4), 457-469.

Stone, S., D'Andrade, A., and Austin, M. (2007). Educational services for children in foster care: Common and contrasting perspectives of child welfare and education stakeholders. *Journal of Public Child Welfare*, 1(2), 53-70.

Stroul, B.A., Blau, G.M., and Friedman, R.B. (2010). *Updating the system of care concept and philosophy*. Georgetown University Center for Child and Human Development, Washington, D.C.

Stroul, B.A., Blau, G.M, and Sondheimer, D. (2008). Systems of care: A strategy to transform children's mental health care. In B. Stroul and G. Blau (eds), *The system of care handbook: Transforming mental health services for children, youth and families* (3- 24). Baltimore: Paul H. Brookes Publishing.

Stouthamer-Loeber, M., Wei, E.H., Homish, D.L., and Loeber, R. (2002). Which family and demographic factors are related to both maltreatment and persistent serious juvenile delinquency? *Children's Services: Social Policy, Research, and Practice*, 5(4), 261-272.

Streiner, D. (2003). Diagnosing tests: Using and misusing diagnostic and screen tests. *Journal of Personality Assessment*, 81, 209-219.

Substance Abuse and Mental Health Services Administration (2008a). *Trends in substance use, dependence or abuse, and treatment among adolescents: 2002-2007*. Office of Applied Studies, U.S. Department of Health and Human Services, Washington, D.C.

Substance Abuse and Mental Health Services Administration (2008b). *Mental health, United States, 2008*. Center for Mental Health Services, U.S. Department of Health and Human Services, Washington D.C.

Substance Abuse and Mental Health Services Administration (2009). *Addressing suicidal thoughts and behaviors in substance abuse treatment*. Center for Mental Health Services, U.S. Department of Health and Human Services, Washington D.C.

Substance Abuse and Mental Health Services Administration (2010a). *Results from the 2009 National Survey on Drug Use and Health: Mental health findings*. Office of Applied Studies, U.S. Department of Health and Human Services, Washington, D.C.

Substance Abuse and Mental Health Services Administration (2010b). *The dawn report: Emergency department visits for drug-related suicide attempts by adolescents: 2008*. Office of Applied Studies, U.S. Department of Health and Human Services, Washington D.C.

Substance Abuse and Mental Health Services Administration (2010c). *National survey on drug use and health: Summary of national findings*. Office of Applied Studies, U.S. Department of Health and Human Services, Washington, D.C.

Substance Abuse and Mental Health Services Administration (2011). *Best practices registry for suicide prevention*. National Registry of Evidence-Based Practices and Programs, U.S. Department of Health and Human Services, Washington, D.C.

Substance Abuse Subtle Screening Instrument Institute (2001). *Estimates of the reliability and criterion validity of the adolescent SASSI-2*. Substance Abuse Subtle Screening Instrument Institute, Springville, IN.

Sum, A., Khatiwada, I., McLaughlin, J., and Palma, S. (2009). *The consequences of dropping out of high school: Joblessness and jailing for high school dropouts and the high cost to taxpayers*. Center for Labor Market Studies, Northeastern University, Boston, MA.

Sun, A.P., Shillington, A.M., Hohman, M., and Jones, L. (2001). Caregiver AOD use, case substantiation, and AOD treatment: Studies based on two southwestern counties. *Child Welfare*, 80(2), 151-177.

Sussman, S., Dent, C.W., and Stacy, A.W. (2002). Project toward no drug abuse: A review of the findings and future directions. *American Journal of Health Behavior*, 26(5), 354–365.

Sussman, S., Rohrbach, L., and Mihalic, S. (2004). *Project towards no drug abuse: Blueprints for violence prevention, book twelve*. Blueprints for Violence Prevention Series (D.S. Elliott, Series Editor). Boulder, CO: Center for the Study and Prevention of Violence, Institute of Behavioral Science, University of Colorado.

Suveg, C., Kendall, P.C., Comer, J.S., and Robin, J. (2006). Emotion-focused cognitive-behavioral therapy for anxious youth: A multiple baseline evaluation. *Journal of Contemporary Psychotherapy*, 36, 77-85.

Sweet, M.A. and Applebaum, M.I. (2004). Is home visiting an effective strategy? A meta-analysis of home visiting programs for families with young children. *Child Development*, 75, 1435-1456.

Szapocznik, J. (1997). *Cultural competence and family program implementation*. Plenary Session Presented at the Office of Juvenile Justice and Delinquency Prevention–University of Utah Third National Training Conference on Strengthening America's Families, March 23–25, Washington, DC.

Tanenhaus, D.S. and Drizin, S.A. (2002). Owing to the extreme youth of the accused: The changing legal response to juvenile homicide. *Criminal Law and Criminology*, 92(3/4), 641-706.

Teplin, L., Abram, K., McClelland, G., Dulcan, M., and Mericle, A., (2002). Psychiatric disorders in youth in juvenile detention. *Archives of General Psychiatry*, 59, 1133-1143.

Teplin, L., Abram, K., McClelland, G., Mericle, A., Dulcan, M., and Washburn, D. (2006). *Psychiatric disorders of youth in detention*. Office of Justice Programs, Office of Juvenile Justice and Delinquency Prevention, U.S. Department of Justice, Washington D.C.

Testa, M.F. and Smith, B (2009). Prevention and drug treatment. *The Future of Children*, 19(2), 147-168.

Theodore, LA., Bray, M.A., and Kehle, T.J. (2004). A comparative study of group contingencies and randomized reinforcers to reduce disruptive classroom behavior. *School Psychology Quarterly*, 18, 253-271.

Thomas, D., Leicht, C., Hughes, C., Madigan, A., and Dowell, K. (2003). *Emerging practices in the prevention of child abuse and neglect.* U.S. Department of Health and Human Services, Washington, D.C.

Thomas, R. and Zimmer-Gembeck, M.J. (2011). Accumulating evidence for parent-child interaction therapy in the prevention of child maltreatment. *Child Development*, 82(1), 177-192.

Thompson, M., Ho, C., and Kingree, J. (2007). Prospective associations between delinquency and suicidal behaviors in a nationally representative sample. *Journal of Adolescent Health, 40*, 232-237.

Thompson, S. (1996). *Nonverbal learning disorders.* LD Online, Arlington, VA.

Thornberry, T.P., Ireland, T.O., and Smith, C.A. (2002). The importance of timing: The varying impact of childhood and adolescent maltreatment on multiple problem outcomes. *Developmental Psychopathology*, 13(4), 957-979.

Timmer, S.G., Urquiza, A.J., Zebell, N.M., and McGrath, J.M. (2005). Parent-child interaction therapy: Application to maltreating parent-child dyads. *Child Abuse and Neglect*, 29, 825-842.

Tolan, P.H. and Gorman-Smith, D. (1998). Development of serious and violent offending careers. In R. Loeber and D.P. Farrington (eds), *Serious and violent juvenile offenders: Risk factors and successful interventions* (68-85). Thousand Oaks, CA: Sage.

Tolan, P., Henry, D., Schoeny, M., and Bass, A. (2008). *Mentoring interventions to affect juvenile delinquency and associated problems.* Campbell Systematic Reviews, The Campbell Collaboration, Oslo, Norway.

Tolou-Shams, M., Brown, L., Gordon, G., and Fernandez, I. (2007). Arrest history as an indicator of adolescent/young adult substance use and HIV risk. *Drug and Alcohol Dependence, 88*, 87-90.

Torres, C. and Ooyen, Marcel, V. (2002). *Briefing paper*, Committee on Youth Services, New York, NY.

Tracy, E.M. (1994). Maternal substance abuse: Protecting the child, preserving the family. *Social Work*, 39, 534-540.

Tracy, P.E. and Kempf-Leonard, K. (1996). *Continuity and discontinuity in criminal careers.* New York: Plenum.

Tracy, P.E., Kempf-Leonard, K., and Abramoske-James, S. (2009). Gender differences in delinquency and juvenile justice processing: Evidence from national data. *Crime and Delinquency*, 55(2), 171-215.

Tremblay, R.E. and LeMarquand, D. (2001). Individual risk and protective factors. In R. Loeber and D.P. Farrington *(eds), Child delinquents: Development, intervention, and service needs (137-164),* Thousand Oaks, CA: Sage.

Tripodi, S.J. (2009). A comprehensive review: Methodological rigor of studies on residential treatment centers for substance-abusing adolescents. *Journal of Evidence-Based Social Work*, 6, 288-299.

Trulson, C.R., Haerle, D.R., DeLisi, M., and Marquart, J.W. (2011). Blended sentencing, early release, and recidivism of violent institutionalized delinquents. *The Prison Journal*, 91(3), 255-278.

Tuell, J. (2002). *Child maltreatment and juvenile delinquency: Raising the level of awareness.* Child Welfare League of America, Washington D.C.

Tuell, J. (2008). *Child welfare & juvenile justice systems integration initiative: A promising progress report*. Juvenile Justice Division, Child Welfare League of America, Washington, D.C.

Turner, S. and Fain, T. (2006). Validation of the risk and resiliency assessment tool for juveniles in the Los Angeles county probation system. *Federal Probation*, 70(2), 49-57.

Turner, H.A., Finkelhor, D., and Ormrod, R. (2006). The effect of lifetime victimization on the mental health of children and adolescents. *Social Science and Medicine,* 62, 13-27.

Turner, W., MacDonald, G.M., and Dennis J.A. (2007). *Cognitive-behavioural training interventions for assisting foster carers in the management of difficult behaviour*. Cochrane Database of Systematic Reviews, Issue 1.

Uggen, C. (2000). Work as a turning point in the life course of criminals: A duration model of age, employment, and recidivism. *American Sociological Review*, 65, 529-546.

U.S. Department of Education (2001a). *21st annual report to Congress on the implementation of the Individuals with Disabilities Education Act*. Office of Special Education and Rehabilitative Services, Office of Special Education Programs, Washington D.C.

U.S. Department of Education (2001b). *Safe, disciplined, and drug-free schools programs*. Office of Special Education Research and Improvement, Office of Reform Assistance and Dissemination, Washington, D.C.

U.S. Department of Education (2009). *28th annual report to Congress on the implementation of the Individuals with Disabilities Education Act, 2006*. Office of Special Education and Rehabilitative Services, Office of Special Education Programs, Washington, D.C.

U.S. Department of Education (2010*). 29th annual report to Congress on the implementation of the Individuals with Disabilities Education Act, 2007 (table 1-9)*. Office of Special Education and Rehabilitative Services, Office of Special Education Programs, Washington D.C.

U.S. Department of Education (2010). *Digest of education statistics, 2009*. National Center for Education Statistics, Washington D.C

U.S. Department of Health and Human Services (2001). *Youth violence: A report of the surgeon general*. Rockville, MD.

U.S. Department of Health and Human Services (2010). *Child maltreatment 2008*. U.S. Government Printing Office, Washington, D.C.

U.S. Department of Health and Human Servcies (2012). *Home visiting evidence of effectiveness*. Washington, D.C.

U.S. Department of Justice (2007). *Restorative justice*. National Institute for Justice, U.S. Department of Justice, Washington, D.C.

U.S. Department of Justice (2010). *Juvenile correctional facilities settlements and court decisions*. Civil Rights Division, U.S. Department of Justice, Washington, D.C.

U.S. Department of Labor (2009a). *Common sense, uncommon commitment: A progress report on the shared youth vision partnership*. U.S. Department of Labor, Washington, D.C.

U.S. Department of Labor (2009b). *Vision for youth: Advanced technical assistance forum participating states*. U.S. Department of Labor, Washington, D.C.

U.S. General Accounting Office (renamed U.S. General Accountability Office) (1998). *Foster care: Agencies face challenges securing stable homes for children of substance abusers.* U.S. General Accounting Office, Washington, D.C.

U.S. Surgeon General (2001). *Report on the surgeon general's conference on children's mental health.* U.S. Department of Health and Human Services, Washington, D.C.

Vacca, J.S. (2004). Education prisoners are less likely to return to prison. *The Journal of Correctional Education,* 55, 297-305.

Van Ness, D. and Strong, K.H. (2001). *Restorative justice (2ⁿᵈ ed).* Cincinnati, OH: Anderson.

Vander-Stoep, A., Evans, C., and Taub, J. (1997). Risk of juvenile justice system referral among children in a public mental health system. *Journal of Mental Health Administration,* 24, 428-421.

Vaughn, M.G. and Howard, M.O. (2004). Adolescent substance abuse treatment: A synthesis of controlled evaluation. *Research on Social Work Practice,* 14, 325-335.

Vaughn, M.G., Wallace, J.M, Davis, L.E., Fernandes, G.T. and Howard, M.O. (2008). Variations in mental health problems, substance use, and delinquency between African American and Caucasian juvenile offenders: Implications for reentry services. *International Journal of Offender Therapy and Comparative Criminology,* 53, 311-329.

Vazquez, B.E., Maddan, S., and Walker, J.T. (2008). The influence of sex offender registration and notification laws in the United States. *Crime and Delinquency,* 54(2), 175-192.

Velazquez, T. (2008). *The pursuit of safety: Sex offender policy in the United States.* New York: Vera Institute of Justice.

Veltman, M.W. and Browne, K.D. (2001). Three decades of child maltreatment research: Implications for the school years. *Trauma, Violence, and Abuse,* 2(3), 215-239.

Verhulst, F.C., van der Ende, J., Ferdinand, R.F., and Kasius, M.C. (1997). The prevalence of DSM-III-R diagnoses in a national sample of Dutch adolescents. *Archives of General Psychiatry,* 54(4), 329-336.

Verrecchia, P.J., Fetzer, M.D., Lemmon, J.H., and Austin, T.L. (2010). An examination of direct and indirect effects of maltreatment dimensions and other ecological risk on persistent youth offending. *Criminal Justice Review,* 35(2), 220-243.

Vincent, G.M. (2011). *Screening and assessment in juvenile justice settings: Identifying mental health needs and risk of reoffending.* Technical Assistance Partnership for Child and Family Mental Health, Washington, D.C.

Wade, W.A., Treat, T.A., and Stuart, G.L. (1998). Transporting an empirically supported treatment for panic disorder to a service clinic setting: A benchmarking strategy. *Journal of Consulting and Clinical Psychology,* 66, 231–239.

Wagner, D. and Bell, P. (1998). *The use of risk assessment to evaluate the impact of intensive protective service intervention I: A practice setting.* National Council on Crime and Delinquency, Children's Research Center, Madison, WI.

Wald, J. and Losen, D. (2003). Defining and re-directing a school-to-prison pipeline. *New Directions for Youth Development*, 99, 9-15.

Wald, M. &andMartinez, T. (2003). *Connected by 25: Improving the life chances of the country's most vulnerable 14-24 year-olds.* William and Flora Hewlett Foundation Working Paper. Menlo Park, CA.

Waldron, H.B. and Turner, C.W. (2008). Evidence-based psychosocial treatments for adolescent substance abuse. *Journal of Clinical Child and Adolescent Psychology*, 37(1), 238-261.

Walkup, J., Albano, A.M., Piacentini, J., Birmaher, B., Compton, S., Sherrill, J., Ginsburg, G., Rynn, M., McCracken, J., Waslick, B., Iyengar, S., March, J., and Kendall, P. (2008). Cognitive behavioral therapy, sertralie, or a combination in childhood anxiety. *New England Journal of Medicine*, 359, 2753-2766.

Wang, X., Blomberg, T.G., and Li, S.D. (2005). Comparison of the educational deficiencies of delinquent and nondelinquent students. *Evaluation Review A Journal of Applied Social Research*, 29(4), 291-312.

Washburn, J., Teplin, L., Voxx, L., Simon, C., Abram, K., and McClelland, G. (2008). Psychiatric disorders among detained youths: A comparison of youths processed in juvenile court and adult criminal court. *Psychiatric Services*, 59(9), 965-973.

Wasik, B. and Slavin, R. (1990). *One-to-one tutoring produces early reading success; large gains justify cost.* Center for Research on Effective Schooling for Disadvantaged Students, Baltimore, MD.

Washington State Institute for Public Policy (1998). *Watching the bottom line: Cost-effective interventions for reducing crime in Washington.* Evergreen State College, Olympia, WA.

Wasserman, G.A., Keenan, K., Tremblay, R.E., Cole, J.D., Herrenkohl, T.I., Loeber, R., and Petechuk, D. (2003). *Risk and protective factors of child delinquency.* Office of Juvenile Justice and Delinquency Prevention, U.S. Department of Justice, Washington, D.C.

Wasserman, G.A., McReynolds, L.S., Lucas, C.P., Fisher, P., and Santos, L. (2002). The voice DISC-IV with incarcerated male youths: Prevalence of disorder. *Journal of the American Academy of Child and Adolescent Psychiatry,* 41, 314-321.

Wasserman, G.A., McReynolds, L.S., Ko, S., Katz, L., and Carpenter, J. (2005). Gender differences in psychiatric disorders at juvenile probation intake. *American Journal of Public Health*, 95, 131-137.

Wasserman, G.A., McReynolds, L.S., Musabegovic, H., Whited, A.L., Keating, J.M., and Huo, Y. (2009). Evaluating project connect: Improving juvenile probationers' mental health and substance use services. *Administration and Policy in Mental Health*, 36, 393-405.

Watts, D. and Wright, L. (1990). The relationships of alcohol, tobacco, marijuana, and other illegal drug use to delinquency among Mexican-American, black, and white adolescent males. *Adolescence*, 25(97), 171-181.

Weatherburn, D. and Lind, B. (1997). *Social and economic stress, child neglect and juvenile delinquency.* New South Wales Bureau of Crime Statistics and Research, Sydney, Australia.

Webb, D.B. (1998). Specialized foster care as an alternative therapeutic out-of-home placement model. *Journal of Clinical Child Psychology*, 17(1), 34-43.

Webster, C.D., Hucker, S.J., and Bloom, H. (2002). Transcending the actuarial versus clinical polemic in assessing risk for violence. *Criminal Justice and Behavior*, 29(5), 659-665.

Webster, C.D., Muller-Isberner, R., and Fransson, G. (2002). Violence risk assessment: Using structured clinical guides professionally. *International Journal of Forensic Mental Health*, 1(2), 185-193.

Weeks, R. and Widom, C.S. (1998). *Early childhood victimization among incarcerated adult male felons.* National Institute of Justice, U.S. Department of Justice, Washington, D.C.

Weinberg, L., Zetlin, A.G., and Shea, N. (2001). *A review of literature on the educational needs of children involved in family and juvenile court proceedings.* Judicial Council of California, Center for Children, Families and the Court, San Francisco, CA.

Weinberg, L., Zetlin, A.G., and Shea, N. (2009). Removing barriers to educating children in foster care through interagency collaboration. *Child Welfare*, 88(4), 77-111.

Weinberg, N.Z. and Glantz, M.D. (1999). Child psychopathology risk factors for drug abuse: Overview. *Journal of Clinical Child Psychology*, 28(3), 290-297.

Weisz, J.R., Jensen-Doss, A., and Hawley, K.M. (2006). Evidence-based youth psychotherapies versus usual clinical care. *American Psychologist*, 61(7), 671-689.

Welsh, B.C., Loeber, R., Stevens, B., Stouthamer-Loeber, M., Cohen, M.A., and Farrington, D.P. (2008). Costs of juvenile crime in urban areas: A longitudinal perspective. *Youth Violence and Juvenile Justice*, 6(1), 3-27.

Werner, E.E. and Smith, R.S. (2001). *Journeys from childhood to midlife: Risk, resilience and recovery.* Ithaca, NY: Cornell University Press.

Westendorp F., Brink K.L., Roberson M.K., and Ortiz I.E. (1986). Variables which differentiate placement of adolescents in juvenile justice or mental health systems. *Adolescence*, 21, 23-37.

Western, B., Kling, J., and Weiman, D. (2001). The labor market consequences of incarceration. *Crime and Delinquency*, 47(3), 410-427.

White, N.A. and Loeber, R. (2008). Bullying and special education as predictors of serious delinquency. *Journal of Research in Crime and Delinquency*, 45(4), 380-397.

Widom, C.S. (1989). Child abuse, neglect, and violent criminal behavior. *Criminology*, 27(2), 251-271.

Widom, C.S. (2003). Understanding child maltreatment and juvenile delinquency: The research. In J. Wiig, C.S. Widom, and J.A. Tuell (eds), *Understanding child maltreatment & juvenile delinquency* (1-10), Child Welfare League of America Press, Washington D.C.

Widom, C.S. and Maxfield, M. (2001). *An Update on the 'Cycle of Violence'.* National Institute of Justice, U.S. Department of Justice, Washington D.C.

Widom, C.S. and White, H.R. (1997). Problem behaviours in abused and neglected children grown up: Prevalence and co-occurrence of substance abuse, crime, and violence. *Criminal Behaviour and Mental Health*, 7(4), 287-310.

Wiebush, R., Baird, C., Krisberg, B., and Onek, D. (1995). Risk assessment and classification for serious, violent, and chronic juvenile offenders. In J.C. Howell, B. Krisberg, and J.D. Hawkins (eds), *A sourcebook: Serious, violent, and chronic juvenile offenders* (171-202), Thousand Oaks, CA: Sage.

Wiebush, R., Freitag, R., and Baird, C. (2001). *Preventing delinquency through improved child protection services*. Office of Juvenile Justice and Delinquency Prevention, Office of Justice Programs, U.S. Department of Justice, Washington D.C.

Wierson, M., Forehand, R.L., and Frame, C.L. (1992). Epidemiology and treatment of mental health problems in juvenile delinquents. *Advanced Behavioral Research and Therapy*, 14, 93-120.

Wiggins, C., Fenichel, E., and Mann, T. (2007). *Developmental problems of maltreated children and early intervention options for maltreated children*. U.S. Department of Health and Human Services, Child Protective Services Project, Washington, D.C.

Wiig, J., Spatz-Widom, C., and Tuell, J.A. (2003). *Understanding child maltreatment & delinquency: From research to effective program, practice, and systematic solutions*. Child Welfare League of America, Washington D.C.

Williams, S.T. (2008). *Mental health screening and assessment tools for children: A literature review*. The Northern California Training Academy, Center for Human Services, University of California Davis Extension.

Willison, J.B., Brooks, L., Salas, M., Dank, M., Denver, M., Gitlow, E., Roman, J.K., and Butts, J.A. (2010). *Reforming juvenile justice systems: Beyond treatment*. Reclaiming Futures, Portland State University.

Wilkes, T.C.R., Belsher, G., Rush, A.J., and Frank, E. (1994). *Cognitive therapy for depression adolescents*. New York: Guilford Press.

Wilson, D.B., Gottfredson, D.C., and Najaka, S.S. (2001). School-based prevention of problem behaviors: A meta-analysis. *Journal of Quantitative Criminology*, 17, 247-272.

Wilson, J., Kelly, M., and Howell, J.C. (2012). *Juvenile justice system in Delware 2012: The little engine that could*. Comprehensive Strategy Group, Dover, DE.

Wilson, S.J. and Lipsey, M.W. (2006a). *The effects of school-based social information processing interventions on aggressive behavior, Part I: Universal programs*. Campbell Systematic Reviews, The Campbell Collaboration, Oslo, Norway.

Wilson, S.J. and Lipsey, M.W. (2006b). *The effects of school-based social information processing interventions on aggressive behavior, Part II: Selected/indicated pull-out programs*. Campbell Systematic Reviews, The Campbell Collaboration, Oslo, Norway.

Wilson, S.J., Lipsey, M.W., and Derzon, J.H. (2003). The effects of school-based intervention programs on aggressive behavior: A meta-analysis. *Journal of Consulting and Clinical Psychology*, 71(1), 136-149.

Winner, L., Lanza-Kaduce, L., Bishop, D.M., and Frazier, C.E. (1997). The transfer of juveniles to criminal court: Reexamining recidivism over the long term. *Crime and Delinquency*, 43, 548-563.

Winokur, K.P., Smith, A., Bontrager, S.R., and Blankenship, J.L. (2008). Juvenile recidivism and length of stay. *Journal of Criminal Justice*, 36, 126-137.

Winters, K.C., Stinchfield, R.D., Opland, E., Weller, C., and Latimer, W.W. (2000). The effectiveness of the Minnesota model approach in the treatment of adolescent drug abusers. *Addiction*, 95, 601-612.

Witt, W.P., Kasper, J.D., and Riley, A.W. (2003). Mental health services use among school-aged children with disabilities: The role of sociodemographics, functional limitations, family burdens, and care coordination. *Health Services Research*, 38, 1441-1466.

Wolff, N., Blitz, C., Shi, J., Siegel, J., and Bachman, R. (2007). Physical violence inside prisons: Rates of victimization. *Criminal Justice and Behavior*, 34, 588-599.

Wormer, J. and Lutze, F.E. (2010). *Managing and sustaining your juvenile drug court*. National Council of Juvenile and Family Court Judges, Reno, NV.

Wu, B. (1997). The effect of race and juvenile justice processing. *Juvenile & Family Court Judges*, 48, 43-51.

Wulczyn, F., Webb, M., and Haskins, R. (eds) (2007). *Child protection: Using research to improve policy and practice*. Washington, D.C.: Brookings Institution Press.

Youth Law Center (2009). *S.H. v. Strickrath*. Youth Law Center, San Francisco, CA.

Yun, I., Ball, J.D., and Lim, H. (2011). Disentangling the relationship between child maltreatment and violent delinquency: Using a nationally representative sample. *Journal of Interpersonal Violence*, 26(1), 88-110.

Zahn, M.A., Agnew, R., Fishbein, D., Miller, S., Winn, D., Dakoff, G., Kruttschnitt, C., Giordano, P., Gottfredson, D.C., Payne, A.A., Feld, B.C., and Chesney-Lind, M. (2010). *Girls study group: Causes and correlates of girls' delinquency*. Office of Juvenile Justice and Delinquency Prevention, Office of Justice Programs, U.S. Department of Justice, Washington D.C.

Zahn, M.A., Hawkins, S.R., Chiancone, J., and Whitworth, A. (2008). *The girls study group. Charting the way to delinquency prevention for girls*. Office of Juvenile Justice and Delinquency Prevention, Office of Justice Programs, U.S. Department of Justice, Washington D.C.

Zastrow, C. and Kirst-Ashman, K. (2006). *Understanding human behavior and the social environment, seventh edition*. Belmont, CA: Wadsworth/Thompson.

Zief, S.G., Lauver, S., and Maynard, R.A. (2006). *Impacts of after-school programs on student outcomes*. Campbell Systematic Reviews, The Campbell Collaboration, Oslo, Norway.

Zigmond, N. (1990). Rethinking secondary school programs for students with learning disabilities. *Focus on Exceptional Children*, 23, 1-24.

Zimmerman, J., Rich, W., Keilitz, I., and Broder, P. (1978). *Some observations on the link between learning disabilities and juvenile delinquency*. Office of Juvenile Justice and Delinquency Prevention, U.S. Department of Justice, Washington D.C.

Zingraff, M.T., Leiter, J., Johnsen, M.C., and Myers, K.A. (1993). The mediating effect of good school performance on the maltreatment-delinquency relationship. *Journal of Research on Crime and Delinquency*, 31, 62-91.

Zolotor, A., Kotch, J., Dufort, V., Winsor, J., Catellier, C. and Bou-Saada, I. (1999). School performance in a longitudinal cohort of children at risk of maltreatment. *Maternal and Child Health Journal*, 3(1), 19-27.

Zwi, K.J. (2007). School-based education programs for the prevention of child sexual abuse. *Cochrane Database for Systematic Reviews* 2, 1-44.

Index

About the Book

Christopher Mallett explores developmental pathways to juvenile delinquency, disentangling key risk factors for offending—and not least, showing how contact with the justice system may only compound the problem.

Tracing a child's life from the earliest years through adolescence, Mallett investigates the processes by which mental health disorders, learning disabilities, experiences of abuse, and combinations of these factors may increase the likelihood of delinquency. He also finds unexpected lessons in resilience. Throughout, he draws on these insights to suggest valuable new ways of responding to issues in vulnerable populations.

Christopher A. Mallett is associate professor of social work at Cleveland State University.